landing
on the
wrong
note

landing on the wrong note

Jazz, Dissonance, and Critical Practice

A J A Y   H E B L E

Routledge | New York and London

Published in 2000 by
Routledge
29 West 35th Street
New York, NY 10001

Published in Great Britain by
Routledge
11 New Fetter Lane
London EC4P 4EE

Routledge is an imprint of the Taylor & Francis Group.

Printed in the United States of America on acid-free paper.

10 9 8 7 6 5 4 3 2 1

Library of Congress Cataloging-in-Publishing Data

Heble, Ajay, 1961–
Landing on the wrong note : jazz, dissonance, and critical practice / Ajay Heble.
p. cm.
Includes bibliographical references and index.
ISBN 0-415-92348-4 — ISBN 0-415-92349-2 (pbk.)
1. Jazz—History and criticism. 2. Jazz—Social aspects. 3. Dissonance (Music) I. Title.

ML3506 .H42 2000
781.65—dc21 00-029117

For Sheila, Maya, and Kiran

Contents

Preface ix

Acknowledgments xi

Introduction 1

1. **The Poetics of Jazz: From Symbolic to Semiotic** 29

2. **The Rehistoricizing of Jazz: Chicago's "Urban Bushmen" and the Problem of Representation** 63

3. **Performing Identity: Jazz Autobiography and the Politics of Literary Improvisation** 89

4. **"Space Is the Place": Jazz, Voice, and Resistance** 117

5. **Nice Work If You Can Get It: Women in Jazz** 141
(with Gillian Siddall)

6. **Capitulating to Barbarism: Jazz and/as Popular Culture** 167

7. **Up for Grabs: The Ethicopolitical Authority of Jazz** 199

Conclusion: Alternative Public Spheres 229

Works Cited 239

Sound and Video Recordings Consulted 251

Index 253

Preface

G♯ is a note mistake; Armstrong meant to play G♮.

Gunther Schuller, *The Swing Era*, 163

There were no wrong notes on his pi-a-no had no wrong notes, oh no.

Chris Raschka, *Mysterious Thelonious*

The critical space traversed by these statements fascinates me. True, they are concerned with different historical periods in the music, and true, they are aimed at different readerships. By juxtaposing them here, I want to open up the admittedly giant question of how and what wrong notes mean (and have meant) in jazz—and, by extension, how and what they might mean for critical practice today and in the future. How is it—as in the case of Thelonious Monk's glorious dissonances, Ornette Coleman's angular melodies,

Cecil Taylor's spirited piano clusters—that outlawed musical gestures can be, well, so spot-on? In what follows, I'll argue that our capacity for such questioning has been invigorated by new methodologies in contemporary cultural theory, enlivened by key debates around issues of power, identity, representation, history, ethics, and social change. This is a book, then, about jazz as seen (and heard) in the context of these broader cultural concerns. As well, though, this is a book about dissonance: dissonance in the music, yes, but also the dissonance that results when our critical practice might in some ways be said to be "out of tune" with the musics and lives we seek to describe and interpret.

The musical examples I draw on in this book are by no means meant to be neutral or inclusive; indeed, for the most part they reflect my interests (as listener, cultural critic, and artistic director for a local music festival) in a particular kind of jazz and creative improvised music. Call it what you will—dissonant, innovative, free, "out," or avant-garde (indeed, many of its practitioners are explicit in insisting on the inadequacy of these and other terms)—this is music with a rich and varied history, music with an extraordinary critical edge. I've written this book in an attempt to elucidate and discover what gives the music that edge, and to spark further discussion and debate about why its out-of-tuneness must command our attention.

Acknowledgments

One of the arguments I make in the following pages is that jazz is about building purposeful communities of interest and involvement, about reinvigorating public life with the magic of dialogue and collaboration. The writing of this book could only have been accomplished with the gift of a similar kind of magic. I have benefited enormously from the advice and support of friends and colleagues who, over the course of the last several years, have given generously of their time in reading or discussing various parts of this manuscript. In particular, I'd like to thank Dug Al-Maini, Bill Ashcroft, Diana Brydon, Ron Cooley, Gregor Campbell, Robert Campbell, Charmaine Eddy, Terence Hawkes, Maryanne Kaay, Alan Kennedy, Bruce King, Ric Knowles, Rosemary Jolly, Danny O'Quinn, Tom Orman, Julian Patrick, and Howard Spring. Among the many scholars whose insights, guidance, and reflections have sustained my thinking throughout this project, I owe a special debt to three of my former teachers: Patricia Parker, for her encouragement at early stages of this project, Edward Said, for gifting me with his example of unwavering political commitment, and Linda Hutcheon, for her wisdom, her generosity, and her genuinely inspirational intellectual energy.

Thanks to my editor at Routledge, William Germano, for responding quickly and enthusiastically to my proposal, and for the skill and expertise with which he saw the book to press. Thanks too to the staff at Routledge, especially Jennifer Hirshlag, Julien Devereux, and Amy Reading. I'm grateful to my anonymous readers (both for the press and for the publications in which earlier versions of some of these chapters have appeared). They offered perspicacious comments and valuable criticisms from which I have benefited.

I am also greatly indebted to my remarkable research assistant, Emily Sanford, whose extraordinary initiative, sound judgment, and expert editorial help played a hugely important role in enabling me to turn several pages of disparate notes into a coherent manuscript. For additional help in tracking down research materials and sound recordings, thanks to Howard Mandel, Peter Hinds (at *Sun Ra Research*), Catherine Pickar, Patti O'Toole, Chip Calahan, Joanne Grodzinski, and Robert Pennee (at Carden Street Music Shop), Bob Rusch (and the crew at *Cadence*), and my wonderful community of colleagues at The Guelph Jazz Festival: Julie Hastings, Ross Butler, Bill Carter, Craig Storey, Judith Drost, and Julien Winter.

Warm thanks to all the performing artists who have graced The Guelph Jazz Festival with their remarkable artistry, and to all the speakers, panelists, and musicians who have participated in The Guelph Jazz Festival Colloquium.

In addition to the Guelph colloquia, several conferences and academic invitations over the course of the last decade have provided a valuable forum for energetic debate and discussion with an evolving community of jazz scholars and creative practitioners. I'm grateful both to have been invited into this community and to have had the opportunity to discuss my work at these venues. Chapter 2 grew out of a paper I presented for a session on "Black Artists and Chicago: Texts, Contexts, and Issues of Representation" at the Modern Languages Association conference in Chicago in December 1990. A version of chapter 3 was presented in April 1999 at "Improvising Across Borders: An Interdisciplinary Symposium on Improvised Music," sponsored by the Critical Studies and Experimental Practices Program, Department of Music, University of California, San Diego. Chapter 4 grew out of a paper I gave at "Race, Ethnicity, and 'Otherness' in America," the 1994 Canadian Association of American Studies Conference at Carleton University, Ottawa. Versions of chapter 5 were presented in April 1997 at the North Eastern Modern Language Association Conference in Philadelphia, and at "A Visionary Tradition: Canadian Literature and Culture at the Turn of the Century," University of Guelph, in November 1999. Chapter 7 grew out of talks I gave in March 1998 for the departments of English and Jazz Studies at St. Francis Xavier University, Antigonish, Nova Scotia, and the department of English and School of Music and Fine Arts at the University of New Brunswick in Fredericton. Thanks to Valerie Smith, Mark Reid, George Lewis, Dana Reason, Michael Dessen, Priscilla Walton, Katherine Boutry, John Ball, Maureen Moynagh, and Skip Beckwith. Extra special thanks to Mary and David Coyle.

An earlier version of chapter 1 appeared in *Textual Practice,* Vol. 2, No. 1 (1988). I am grateful to Routledge Journals, 11 New Fetter Lane, London, EC4P 4EE, UK, for permission to reprint that material here. Chapter 6 grew out of a piece published in *Pop Can: Popular Culture in Canada*. Thanks to the book's editors, Lynne Van Luven and Priscilla Walton, and to Prentice Hall Canada for permission to use that material in this book.

For intellectual solidarity and enthusiastic engagement with my project, I am especially grateful to Christine Bold, Melisa Brittain, Jesse Stewart, Tim Struthers, and Scott Thomson. All read parts of this manuscript and were extremely generous in offering advice when I most needed it. Daniel Fischlin—whose extraordinary ability to juggle scholarship, family life, music making, and community commitments continues to be a source of wonder to me—read the entire manuscript, offering thorough criticisms and helpful guidance. Daniel pushed me to think more rigorously about my arguments and methodology, and the resulting book is, without doubt, much better than it would have been without his indispensable input. Winston Smith, jazz broadcaster, bookseller *extraordinaire*, and a formidable expert on both jazz *and* cultural studies, provided invaluable assistance and criticisms at various stages of this project. His Toronto bookshop, Writers and Company, was, until its recent closing, an exciting example of an alternative public sphere, a community-powered space where many of us doing cultural work received our *real* education. It will be sorely missed.

My dear friend Jill Siddall deserves special mention not only for allowing me to include our coauthored essay on women in jazz as part of this book, but, more important, for being a constant source of strength and encouragement. Jill worked closely with me at every stage of this manuscript, and I deeply appreciate her brilliant critical insights, her moral support, and the warmth and generosity of her friendship.

Finally, I wish to thank my amazing family. The love I've received from my parents, Madhav and Sushila, and my sister, Sucheta, continues to sustain me in all my endeavors. My wife, Sheila O'Reilly, and my children, Maya and Kiran, are my closest companions and the loves of my life. They've been astonishingly patient in putting up with my passion for wrong notes, and, in the process, they've grown fond of listening to some of the most dissonant music on the planet. Their energy, commitment, good humor, wisdom, friendship, and encouragement are the inspiration that holds these pages together, and it is to them that I dedicate this book with my love.

Introduction

Jazz as Critical Practice

> **We must learn to judge a society more by its sounds, by its art, and by its festivals, than by its statistics.**
>
> **Jacques Attali, *Noise: The Political Economy of Music,* 3**

While I was writing my book on Canadian short story writer Alice Munro, friends and colleagues would frequently ask me whether I had ever met Munro. Did I, they wanted to know, have an opportunity to interview her as part of my research? Trained to be suspicious of what an author might have to say about his or her own writing—especially, in Munro's case, an author who herself was known to be coyly suspicious of academic models of inquiry—I would invent various excuses to justify my lack of interest in interviewing Munro. Perhaps I wasn't prepared for the resistance that

Munro, by her own admission an "old-fashioned writer," would likely have offered to my attempt to read her texts in the context of current debates in postmodern theory, but, whatever the case, I was convinced that the methodology of that project left no room for real-life interviews—this despite the fact that my book was, as I saw it then, very much caught up in an attempt to negotiate between textuality and, yes, real life. Now, as I write and revise the introduction to this very different book (though perhaps not so different: this too, after all, is a book about what Nathaniel Mackey, in explaining the title for his marvelous study *Discrepant Engagement*, calls "the rickety, imperfect fit between word and world" [19]), I must confess to some regret for not having had the foresight to consider conducting interviews as part of the methodology of my current project. For, as the founder and artistic director of The Guelph Jazz Festival, I have, for the past several years, been in the company of some remarkable musicians. Over the past years, for example, Randy Weston, perhaps one of the greatest living piano players in jazz and himself a magnificent *raconteur*, and Pauline Oliveros, considered by many to be the single most important composer for accordion music in the world and certainly one of the most significant women composers of our generation, have performed in Guelph as part of our festival. Both spent several days here, and both seemed more than happy to talk about their life and music. Surely firsthand accounts from these artists, I'm now thinking, would only have enriched my project, would only have broadened our understanding of the social and historical relevance of the arguments I'll be presenting in the chapters that follow.

Why is it that I am now inclined to change my opinion about interviews? Is there something about the nature of this current project on jazz that compels me to resist the kinds of academic assumptions that shaped the writing of my book on Alice Munro? Have I, perhaps, been swayed by Ingrid Monson's compelling claim "that the only ethical point of departure for work in jazz studies . . . remains the documentation and interpretation of vernacular perspectives, contemporary or historical, no matter how much we must rethink the claims we make for them in light of post-structural discussions of representation and the politics of knowing and being" (*Saying Something,* 6–7)? Or do I worry about having to count myself among those critics who, according to Paul Berliner's indictment, "are sometimes inclined to treat their own personal tastes as the measure of the value of jazz, without understanding artists' goals and values" (769)? And am I now wanting to invite from artists the very suspicion of and resistance to academic models of thinking that I tried to ward off when I said I didn't want to interview Munro? Jim Merod, an academic who has written some of the finest work on jazz in the context of contemporary critical theory, puts it thus: "My sense is that the jazz archive . . . eludes any inclusive theory of its achievement. . . . One merely thinks of the suspicion of so many magnificent jazz musicians who find the rational neatness and intellectual sweep of large interpretive frameworks about jazz to have no organic relationship to their lives' experiences, to the rhythm of creation and travel and invention that, against all odds, characterizes their work" ("Jazz as a Cultural Archive," 6). I suppose what I'm beginning to understand is that Randy Weston, Pauline Oliveros, and the many other artists who have performed at The Guelph Jazz Festival, had I taken the time to speak with them for this book, could have helped to inject some sense of that "rhythm of creation and travel and invention" into my academic frameworks for reading jazz. Now, I don't, by citing Merod's eloquent comments on the jazz archive, mean in any way to suggest that this is not an academic book, for it is; nor do I want to convey any misgivings about its academic moorings: even a quick glance at the table of contents should make this clear. More precisely, though, this is a book that emerges from my ongoing attempts, in both my teaching and research, to address another "rickety, imperfect fit," this one between the academy and the public sphere.

Much work in cultural studies and postcolonial theory is concerned with this very "fit," but its most magnificent and compelling handling can, I think, be found in the work of Edward Said.

Said's oeuvre, indeed, strikes me as being exemplary in this regard for he has, in various complex and sometimes unsuspected ways, demonstrated the urgency with which we need to take stock of the social processes and institutional practices that frame (and are shaping) the production of knowledge both inside *and* outside the academy. When, as a former student of Said's some ten or twelve years ago, I took the opportunity to talk to him about his interest in and work on music (would that it had been an interview!), he made very clear that he had little interest in jazz; Merod is, I think, right to call Said a "stubborn refuser of the great jazz tradition" ("Resistance," 193). But Merod is also right when he suggests that jazz criticism can be profoundly guided by Said's insights. In terms of the arguments I'll present about the social instrumentality of cultural practices that are "out of tune" with institutionalized models of knowledge production, it's interesting to note, too, that Said concludes his recently published autobiography with an explicit recognition of the value of dissonance. "With so many dissonances in my life," he writes, "I have learned actually to prefer being not quite right and out of place" (*Out of Place,* 295).

I'll come back to dissonance in a moment. But for now I want to suggest, by way of Said, that academic work needs to be more fundamentally connected with the world outside the academy. In this book, I turn to jazz not only to make the case that there is an opening for the kind of academic and theoretical writing on jazz that exists for literary studies, but also, especially in chapters 6 and 7, to draw on my (mostly) nonacademic work organizing and programming a community-based music festival. I say "mostly" because The Guelph Jazz Festival itself, from its very inception, has sought to overcome the split between "town" and "gown" that other local arts initiatives have often been accused of fostering, to turn that split, in effect, into a "fit," even if it is, to borrow Mackey's words once again, just a rickety and imperfect one. Indeed, our festival can attribute its success partly to its ongoing efforts to reconfigure the constituency traditionally defined as a jazz audience. We've done this, for example, by mounting as a regular part of the festival's schedule of events a colloquium, aimed at both academics and a general public, and featuring panel discussions, keynote talks, workshops, and, of course, musical performances. By bringing together musicians, academics, popular journalists, creative writers, filmmakers, and jazz fans, the colloquium has cut across a range of social and institutional locations, traversed various communities of interest and involvement, and provided a forum for appreciating some of the complex ways in which academic cultural analysts, jazz fans, and musicians can be seen to engage one another in purposeful debate.

Like the festival's colloquium, this book represents an attempt to bring together my academic work with my involvement in broader community-facing activities: a tricky feat, this, but one that strikes me as becoming increasingly urgent in the context of our current cultural and institutional moment. As higher education gets hijacked and privatized to serve the needs of a corporate elite, as our students get reconfigured as "consumers" both in government rhetoric and, consequently, in educational practice, it behooves us, as teachers and writers, to clarify our sense of intellectual purpose, to ensure that academic work achieve public legitimacy, that it address itself to pressing issues of public concern. For me, one of the things that's at issue in defining that sense of "purpose" is the attempt to mobilize academic work in ways that contest the kinds of objectifications, misrepresentations, and institutional disparagements that impede struggles for human agency.

So, why jazz? Surely if I had wanted to find ways to connect my own critical practice with socially responsible forms of community involvement, I ought to have more directly concerned myself with human rights, with struggles for social justice—to name only two of the many pressing social concerns that immediately leap to mind. I don't want to suggest that jazz should automatically or unproblematically be seen as some kind of substitute for these monumentally important global concerns. What I *do* want to argue, though, is that jazz has served and will continue to serve important cultural and political ends (desegregation, decolonization, civil rights, and struggles for equality, for access to self-representation, for control over modes of production, and so forth), and that a study of its history of theory and practice can reinvigorate our understanding of the social function of art, of culture's role in the process of unsettling historically and institutionally determined models of knowledge production. While the argument of this book, then, is predicated on an understanding of the political nature and orientation of jazz, I should perhaps point here to the obvious: jazz is clearly not all political in the same way. The complexities of jazz's entanglement in political debates and issues will likely become most evident in chapter 7, where I explore some of the highly fraught ethical questions opened up by the life and work of free jazz saxophonist Charles Gayle. There is, however, a more celebrated example attesting to the fact that not all jazz is oppositional in the ways I'm suggesting the work that emerges from our academies needs to be: the neoconservatism of Wynton Marsalis. Marsalis's call for a return to "traditional values," his sensational success in the mainstream media, and his attempt to reclaim the conventions of mainstream jazz have indeed become the subject of much recent controversy and debate. I'll not enter into that debate in this book, except perhaps—as I do here—in a passing way, to suggest a parallel between Marsalis's music and the forms of political and institutional retrenchment that, at least here in the West, are increasingly defining our current moment in history.

Conservative forms of resistance to the oppositional valences of jazz's politics have also been felt by those of us involved in organizing The Guelph Jazz Festival. Indeed, I'm now beginning to recognize the extent to which many of the festival's defining moments have, in effect, been nonmusical. Chapter 6, cowritten with my academic colleague and coconspirator in jazz, Gillian Siddall—also a founding organizer of the festival, and, until just recently, president of our board of directors—focuses on some of those moments by considering the problems that arose when we decided to program the 1997 season under the auspices of a theme celebrating the accomplishments of "women in jazz." While a backlash against the theme was something we had anticipated, perhaps, from a handful of unsolicited male artists or from greedy agents who'd want to try to inveigle us into engaging their (again, male) musicians, it's not something we had expected from our own community: from past supporters suddenly reluctant to advertise in our program, from one of our major sponsors, now putting unprecedented pressure on us to marginalize the already underrepresented women's community groups whose participation at information booths we had actively welcomed for some of our high-traffic area performances. It's interesting to note that the previous year, when our theme was "Jazz and the Worlds of Percussion," nobody bothered to give us any such feedback. Nonpercussionists did not come a-calling in an attempt to persuade us to change our theme in order to accommodate their interests, their repertoire, or their particular grouping of instruments and personnel. But when the theme became avowedly political, political, that is, in ways that made unmistakably apparent the festival's commitment to working in partnership with various women's rights activists in the community, political in ways that tried to encourage our audiences to see filaments of continuity between the historical struggle of women in jazz and the immediate social experiences of women in our own community, there were many who clearly wanted to resist a set of ideas that festival organizers had taken for granted: the idea that jazz is, and ought to be seen as, a political activity, that the activities of the festival could play some modest role in helping to foster alternatives to oppressive systems of knowledge production.

So, why jazz? I want to suggest that jazz is an innovative form of cultural practice, one that has enabled me to think with rigor about the forces and assumptions that have shaped and determined my interpretive and critical habits. Jazz has provided me with the opportunity to test and develop my own understanding of the rickety fit between theory and practice, between academic and public worlds, and between word and world. Like Ingrid Monson, I too believe that "academia *must* engage with the knowledges in circulation and the human beings outside of its walls in order to humanize, invigorate, and deepen its thinking, as well as to bring new people in" (*Saying Something,* 213). By writing this book, I want, then, to make the case that the volunteer hours I've put into organizing a community-based festival *are* of direct relevance to my critical work as a scholar and teacher in the humanities, and to argue, more generally, for an institutional valuing of our broader community-based activities. Indeed, one of the driving assumptions of recent scholarship and pedagogy in cultural studies is precisely its insistence that we find ways to legitimize, institutionalize, and value models of learning, research, and scholarship that encourage participation in public discourse. And, of course, vice versa: that is, the "drive" also goes in the reciprocal direction, so that the discourses of the (alternative) academy and of alternative public spheres are engaged in trying to reshape each other.

Jazz, moreover, as I hope to show in the pages that follow, offers a highly purposeful point of entry into some of the key—and most hotly contested—cultural debates and arguments of our era: debates, for example, about the political efficacy of an avant-garde aesthetic, the complex relationship between aesthetics and ethics, the public function of art, the politics of representation, the authority of history, the possibilities for resistance to embodied systems of culture and knowledge, and the relationship between language and reality. "The principal practices that define jazz music," writes George Lipsitz in his recent book *Dangerous Crossroads*, have "offered cultural, moral, and intellectual guidance to people all over the world" (178). They have done so, he suggests, "by privileging relentless innovation over static tradition" (178), not, as Marsalis would have it, through a wholesale reclamation of traditional jazz values. John Gennari, similarly, argues that one of the defining features of jazz has been "its role as a progenitor of new forms, an inventor of new languages, a creator of new ways to express meaning. The blue notes, microtones, polyrhythms, and extended harmonies of jazz constitute a musical vocabulary and grammar that cannot be accurately represented by the standard notational systems of Western music" (449). If from its very inception jazz has been about inventiveness, about the process of change, then, as I'll suggest in the chapters that follow, one of the ways in which that sense of change and inventiveness is most powerfully registered is in cultural forms that accent dissonance and contingency, in music making that explores the sonic possibilities of traditionally outlawed models of practice. I'm interested in thinking about how dissonance—by which I mean sounds (and, more generally, cultural practices) that are "out of tune" with orthodox habits of coherence and judgment—occasions a disturbance to naturalized orders of knowledge production. What changing roles, I want to ask, has dissonant jazz played for subordinated social groups struggling to achieve control over the ways in which their identities have been constructed, framed, and interpreted? At issue here are the interpretive frameworks for conceptualizing the production and the reception of jazz, and how they too have undergone significant changes of their own. This book attempts to account for those shifts in the way we understand jazz (and its dissonances) not in terms of the standard evolutionary narrative of the music that seems to have achieved something of an authoritative status in the field of jazz studies; instead, I'm interested in reading jazz in the context of parallel shifts and patterns of salience in the neighboring discipline(s) of literary and cultural theory, as well as in its complex presence as community discourse.

Guess Who's Coming to Dinner?

> **Once I played . . . for a conference of the American Architects' Association—it was for a discussion entitled "Beauty and Ugliness." . . . They told me that I represented ugliness.**
>
> **Ornette Coleman, quoted in Alfred Willener, *The Action-Image of Society,* 251**

"Once upon a short time ago," begins a 1956 article on jazz in *Good Housekeeping,* "if you liked jazz you were expected to dress like a freak, to speak in juggling phrases that started with the word 'Man!', to call something 'cool' when you meant 'good,' 'square' if you meant 'bad,' and generally to behave like a runaway idiot" (Mareck, 120). But now, we are told, "jazz has become respectable. Jazz used to be the boy with dirty hands whom you wouldn't let come into your house. Jazz was born in the gin mills; the dubious night spots; the after-hour clubs of New Orleans, Chicago, and Kansas City.... And now, with clean hands, it is to be found in the concert halls, the music conservatories, and by way of respectable and carefully produced LP records, in the nicest living rooms" (120). The evolutionary narrative that is presented here seems very much in keeping with the quasi-official history of jazz that scholars such as Scott DeVeaux have so rightly critiqued. "To judge from textbooks aimed at the college market," writes DeVeaux, "something like an official history of jazz has taken hold in recent years. On these pages, for all its chaotic diversity of style and expression and for all the complexity of its social origins, jazz is presented as a coherent whole, and its history as a skillfully contrived and easily comprehended narrative" ("Constructing," 525). Ronald Radano makes a similar point when, in the introduction to his book on saxophonist Anthony Braxton, he looks at the ways in which some critics have sought to elevate the social status of jazz by drawing comparisons between the history of jazz and the legacy of European concert music: "Employing a recycled version of the doctrine of progress, they constructed an evolutionary account of jazz history in which simple folk strains grew inexorably into complex patterns of greatness" (*New Musical Figurations,* 12). *Good Housekeeping*'s evolutionary narrative, I want to suggest, provides an evocative example of the ways in which jazz gets taken up by social actors in specific historical and institutional situations. If, as Radano points out, the 1956 article "alludes to the red-scare image of 'dirty hands,' linking blackness and bop with communism" (*New Musical Figurations,* 16), then jazz's newfound respectability, it would appear, can be won only at the expense of its own history and cultural origins: "respectable jazz," in other words, is jazz with its blackness, its racial history, removed, jazz turned into a domestic product for easy consumption in one's living room, jazz with no "wrong" notes. What does it mean, we need to ask, when "the music of a formerly enslaved people is designated a 'rare and valuable national American treasure' by the Congress, and beamed overseas as a weapon of the Cold War" (DeVeaux, "Constructing," 526)? Institutionalized not only in such publicly oriented organs of knowledge production as *Good Housekeeping*, but also in academic scholarship and pedagogy, evolutionary narratives of jazz history need to be interrogated for the ways in which they in fact elide the music's history of involvement in the construction of social identities and their attendant forms of privation and struggle.

Notes from the Academic Underground: Jazz Identities and Critical Theory

> **Music . . . is not the source of its own meaning. People acting in their collectivities are.**
>
> **John Shepherd, "Value and Power in Music," 197**

In "Welcome to the Jungle: Identity and Diversity in Postmodern Politics," Kobena Mercer suggests that "identity only becomes an issue when it is in crisis, when something assumed to be fixed, coherent and stable is displaced by the experience of doubt and uncertainty" (259). "In the realm of culture," writes another critic, Patrick Brantlinger, such "crisis occurs when an established system of representation is challenged by increasing numbers of people as *not* representing or as *mis*representing significant aspects of social experience" (128). In this book I'm interested in reading jazz and its texts—recordings, performances, festival programming and promotion—and also writings *about* jazz as cultural phenomena that open up valuable questions about the complex ways in which identities are constructed and mobilized, and taken up in practices of representation. I want to explore the extent to which jazz might be understood in the context of contemporary theoretical accounts (of race, gender, ethnicity, and of language and its relation to structures of power) which unsettle received notions of identity, and to consider jazz in the context of broader efforts (in music, in literature, in theory, in the public sphere) to articulate the processes through which communities and alliances of misrepresented peoples struggle for access to self-representation. If, as Mercer, Brantlinger, Stuart Hall, and other cultural theorists have suggested, identity formation depends on and is determined by complex struggles over relations of, and access to, representation, then the historical and cultural force of jazz, it seems to me, may well reside not only in its interventions into ongoing debates about the political function of music, but, perhaps more notably, in the ever-changing interpretive frameworks it has sought to establish for articulating the terms of its own self-representation.

Those frameworks find an instructive parallel in contemporary literary and cultural theory. By tracing particular aspects in the history and development of jazz from its origins to the present day, we can observe the ways in which fundamental changes have taken place both in theories about jazz and in theories about language (and its relation to social realities). Similar kinds of reorientations of interpretive strategies in these adjacent (and, indeed, interpenetrating) discourses of jazz and literary theory suggest to me that much might be gained through a rigorous attempt to theorize the history of jazz in relation to the broader debates about language, culture, and identity that get played out in the history of contemporary critical theory. Merod suggests that though "[t]he world of critical theory may appear to be a universe distant from the high-spirited environment of the jazz musician," jazz, nevertheless, "is a unique North American cultural energy that . . . reflects both the cultural opportunities and the social traumas of this century; the very interests and circumstances addressed by critical discourses are no less addressed by the jazz musician's stylistic changes" ("Resistance," 190). In the space of less than a century, the histories of both discourses—jazz and critical theory—have betrayed steadily changing characters. They have been marked less by an evolutionary unfolding than by the kinds of changes I alluded to earlier. For example, jazz, developing from the early diatonic (and, if I can put it this way, realist) styles of ragtime, New Orleans, and Dixieland, has moved through the chromaticism of bebop and the modernism of atonality and free collective improvisation into what might be seen as more recent (postmodern) attempts at rehistoricization: I'm thinking, for example, of the models offered by the Art Ensemble of Chicago, with its renewed engagement with history and black traditions (discussed in chapter 2), and by Sun Ra and what, in chapter 4, I will call his postcolonial pedagogy of cultural resistance.

Scant attention has thus far been paid to the historically complex ways in which jazz intersects with these broader debates about language, identity, and representation. Though there seems to be an evolving body of critical work that foregrounds for reflection the social, cultural, and ideological implications of jazz, it is only in recent years that writers have, in any kind of sustained way, heeded Krin Gabbard's salutary call for the field of jazz studies to avail itself of the "discourses developed by cultural historians and literary theorists" ("Writing," 1). Gabbard is, I think, right in pointing to the tendency for "jazz writers . . . to ignore . . . extramusical aspects of jazz by conceptualizing it as a safely autonomous domain, more dependent on rhythmic innovation than on social change" (3). Indeed, a number of recent studies have taken issue with this general tendency in musicology and music theory: Richard Leppert and Susan McClary, for instance, in their Introduction to *Music and Society*, tell us that "[f]or the most part, the discourse of musical scholarship clings stubbornly to a reliance on positivism in historical research and formalism in theory and criticism" (xii). Edward Said, similarly, writes, "the roles played by music in Western society are extraordinarily varied, and far exceed the antiseptic, cloistered, academic, professional aloofness it seems to have been accorded" (*Musical,* xvi). And Joseph Kerman, writing in 1985, suggests that "nearly all musical thinkers travel at a respectful distance behind the latest chariots (or bandwagons) of intellectual life in general. . . . Semiotics, hermeneutics, and phenomenology are being drawn upon only by some of the boldest of musical studies today. Post-structuralism, deconstruction, and serious feminism have yet to make their debuts in musicology or music theory" (17). Arguably, there has been some change in the decade since Kerman wrote his influential *Contemplating Musicology*, yet when one looks at the current state of jazz criticism, there is, I think, more than a little relevance to his claim. Consider, for example, Gunther Schuller's account of his own methodology in the Preface to his 1989 book *The Swing Era*: "I imagined myself coming to jazz without any prior knowledge or preconceptions and beginning, *tabula rasa*, to listen to the recordings—systematically and comprehensively. . . . This kind of systematic/comprehensive listening to the recorded evidence—often the only reliable information the jazz historian has—puts things in true, sometimes glaring perspective" (ix–x). Schuller's history of jazz, of which *The Swing Era* is the second volume, is, as John Gennari puts it in his excellent account of the history and development of jazz criticism, "the field's authoritative work" (452). Though Schuller remains aware of the fact that "[n]o art or act of creativity stands in isolation, self-contained and uninfluenced by its times, its social and cultural environment, and its own history" (x), the influential statement of methodology which I've quoted might well be said to bear some responsibility for the continuing institutionalization of formalist models of inquiry in jazz criticism. As Gennari rightly notes, "Schuller seems to be advocating a critical approach along the lines of literary New Criticism, which would approach individual works of art as self-contained, self-defining objects to be elucidated as autonomous aesthetic works rather than understood as documents created in specific socio-historical contexts. If the tenets of the New Criticism have proved excessively confining for most literary critics," he continues, "its narrow injunctions are of especially dubious value for critics of jazz, whose texts are in a constant state of revision, and whose historical significance to African-American social identity is simply too compelling to disregard" (450).

It may, indeed, seem odd that a music so clearly rooted in social processes, in struggles for access to representation and identity formation, should give rise to such formalist models of aesthetic analysis. Jazz, after all, is, as Martin Williams puts it, "the music of a people who have been told by their circumstances that they are unworthy. And in jazz, these people discover their own worthiness" (267). Asian-American baritone saxophonist and activist Fred Wei-han Ho more explicitly points out that jazz, in fact, ought to be seen as an attempt to "dismantle the entire institutional power structure of white supremacy and Eurocentrism" (135), and he is adamant in his attempt to reinvigorate our understanding of the social function of music. Jazz, says Ho, needs to be read and heard in the context of oppressed peoples who "suffer from their history, identity, and culture being defined, (mis)represented and explicated by [their] oppressors" (133). Cornel West makes a related point about contemporary black struggles for identity, dignity, and validation in his important essay "The New Cultural Politics of Difference": "The modern black diasporan problematic of invisibility and namelessness can be understood as the condition of *relative lack of black power to represent themselves to themselves and others as complex human beings, and thereby to contest the bombardment of negative, degrading stereotypes put forward by white-supremacist ideologies*" (*Keeping Faith,* 16; emphasis in original).

The struggle to define worth, for these writers, is thus a struggle to overcome the denial of access to self-representation for oppressed groups. If, as postcolonial critic Ashis Nandy puts it, "[t]he recovery of the other selves of cultures and communities, selves not defined by the dominant global consciousness, may turn out to be the first task of social criticism and political activism and the first responsibility of intellectual stock-taking in the first decades of the coming century" (264–65), then the study of jazz has a role to play in retooling academic models of inquiry to ensure purposeful trajectories of intervention. One critic, Burton Peretti, has, in fact, pointed to the ways in which recent "scholarship on jazz brings new modes of inquiry to the study of the music and helps to clarify how jazz might be viewed as a paradigm for students of postcolonial culture." Peretti argues that this scholarship demonstrates how "the African-American creators of jazz, descended from victims of colonization, displacement, and enslavement, belonged themselves to generations which continued to suffer from injustice and to seek healing" ("Plantation Cafés," 90). Moreover, jazz is, as one of the leading historians of our generation and, to boot, a self-professed member of "the underground of . . . academic jazz-buffs" (xxxvii), Eric Hobsbawm, has put it, "one of the most significant phenomena of twentieth-century world culture" (xxiv). One particularly instructive way to account for that significance, I have been suggesting, is to theorize jazz in relation to the contexts that have helped shape and define some of the key arguments and debates in contemporary literary and cultural theory.

Indeed, Hobsbawm's own example provides a telling point of entry into some of the matters I want to touch on in this introduction. It too, somewhat after the fashion of the Sidney Poitier movie whose title I borrowed earlier, charts a kind of narrative of acceptance. When Hobsbawm's book, *The Jazz Scene*, was first published in 1959, it appeared under the pseudonym Francis Newton. As Hobsbawm tells us in his introduction to the 1989 edition of the book, the pseudonym "was . . . intended to keep the author's writings as an historian apart from his writings as a jazz journalist" (xxiii). He goes on to tell us, however, that "[t]he attempt did not succeed, so it is now republished under my own name" (xxiii). Though Hobsbawm admits in his introduction to the 1992 edition that even today "a historian who also writes about jazz is still considered in many quarters as freaky" (xviii), the fact that he can now attach his name to recent reprintings of the text may suggest that jazz is poised to overcome its "longstanding institutional neglect" (Merod, "Jazz as a Cultural Archive," 3), a neglect that, in another critic's words, is "one of the great intellectual crimes of the century" (Lock, *Chasing,* 15).

There are a number of things worth commenting on here. First, I am tempted to sketch a parallel between the conditions that might have led Hobsbawm to attach his own name to his writings on jazz and those that sparked a rethinking of my own interpretive habits and practices. I spoke earlier about how, because of my particular academic training, I had not wanted to interview the very author whose texts were the subject of a book I was writing, and about the fact that now, in contrast, I found myself wishing I *had* conducted interviews with musicians who had performed at our festival. Like Hobsbawm's willingness to allow his name to stand, my new take on the value of interviews as models of cultural inquiry says something, I think, about how we mustn't allow our interpretive procedures to settle into an orthodoxy. Here, again, jazz offers an instructive model: just as, in Gennari's words, "jazz's articulation of an ever-changing, multi-layered, and infinitely wondrous African-American aesthetic . . . ensures that no jazz critic has the final word" (510), so too do the shifting rhythms, emergent energies, and complex histories of momentum that characterize contemporary critical theory suggest that our interpretive frames of reference must be subject to continuing forms of self-scrutiny and reassessment.

Second, something needs to be said about the institutionalization of academic objects of study as legitimate fields of endeavor: Why is it that a renowned historian writing about jazz—indeed writing a kind of social history of jazz—would have felt compelled to keep his academic work separate from his work on jazz? Once again, Merod is helpful here: "intellectual effort," he reminds us, "is routinely thought to be distinct from the world of entertainment. The critical theorist and the teacher operate in the realm of 'high' culture; the jazz musician, perhaps the jazz critic too, operates in a lower cultural orbit. The separation between 'high' theoretical discourse and 'low' entertainment reinforces a political stratification built not only on racial and professional lines of exclusion but also on a less visible inability to imagine the common circumstances that they share" ("Resistance," 191). Though Merod, like Gabbard (in the passage I quoted earlier), is making a general point about the need to challenge received models of institutional containment, his call for a reassessment of the academic status of popular forms of cultural expression such as jazz provides an instructive context for understanding Hobsbawm's initial efforts to keep separate his writings on history from his jazz journalism. Merod's comments might also be helpful for understanding why, even when academics and theorists such as Theodor Adorno did in fact discuss jazz, they tended to dismiss it as an example of the standardized workings of the Culture Industry.

I'll return later in this book to jazz's complex relation to the popular, but for now I want rather to point to some of the ways in which Hobsbawm's example itself touches on many of the main debates and issues which I have set out to trace. In addition to opening up purposeful questions about what we consider worthy of debate and inquiry (and why), the publication history of Hobsbawm's *The Jazz Scene* offers us a glimpse—even if only an indirect one—of how jazz studies have been enlivened by the new methodologies that have emerged out of literary criticism and cultural studies. If the initial pseudonymous publication of *The Jazz Scene* came at a time when it became axiomatic for historians to expunge all sources of authorial subjectivity from their texts, then the later editions of the text, issued under Hobsbawm's own name, force us to recognize the extent to which (to borrow New Historicist Louis Montrose's words) "our analyses and our understandings necessarily proceed from our own historically, socially and institutionally shaped vantage points . . . the histories we reconstruct are the textual constructs of critics who are, ourselves, historical subjects" (23). No longer able to keep his academic writing apart from his popular journalism, Hobsbawm now explicitly invites his readers to reflect on the very impossibility of erasing the site of production from the writing of history.

Such a recognition that history cannot unproblematically be seen as an isolated source for the rehabilitation of past meaning, indeed, is particularly interesting in the context of a discipline—music—that, as Said, Gabbard, Kerman, and Leppert and McClary point out, has been slow to respond to theoretical realignments which, in adjacent disciplines, have made clear the need to rethink received strategies of interpretation. Hobsbawm's newfound willingness to attach his name to the book, in effect, might suggest that jazz can no longer be seen as (for example in Schuller's formulation) a distinct and autonomous form of cultural practice, that established musicological models of inquiry need to be supplemented with, if not supplanted by, a broader social and cultural narrative that reveals the extent to which our modes of comprehension and representation are themselves historically contingent.

I'm conscious here (as I am elsewhere in the book) of foregrounding critical formations over and above performance practices. Given the concerns I've been expressing about the ways in which our critical frameworks might be at odds with the lives and music we seek to describe, this is, perhaps, a point worth belaboring. In relation to the lived realities of performance (what it meant for Billie Holiday to be performing in the racist South, for large black orchestras to be playing in white communities, for Paul Robeson to perform in *Show Boat*, for trombonist Melba Liston to break into Dizzy Gillespie's all-male big band, etc.), the publication history of a jazz book by a marquee figure from white British academic discourse (no matter how sympathetic and how astute) is, admittedly, a minor issue. Yet if one of this book's central tasks is to inventory the complex (and often contradictory) ways in which the politics of representation have been played out in both jazz and contemporary cultural theory, then the critical reception of the music certainly needs to be considered for its role in shaping our understanding and assessment of jazz's representational force. What's more, as I'll argue in later chapters, an understanding of representationalism in jazz isn't simply a function of inherent qualities in the music itself, but, more suggestively, of the institutional formations of criticism.

If the concerns that emerge from a consideration of Hobsbawm's methodological interventions still seem worlds away from the lived realities of jazz performance, then let me try to illustrate some of the things I have in mind by turning to another example, this one more clearly rooted in questions about the social meanings of musical practice. When Duke Ellington felt compelled to comment on the condition of black Americans, he would, perhaps unsurprisingly, frequently turn to music to demonstrate the African-American struggle to achieve identity and self-representation. "That's the Negro's life," he would explain, playing a dissonant chord on the piano. "Hear that chord. That's us. Dissonance is our way of life in America. We are something apart, yet an integral part" (quoted in Ulanov, 276). While in later chapters I'll be troubling the assumptions of cultural totality and expressive unity that might be said to underwrite Ellington's demonstration, I refer to it here because it seems to me rather eloquently to grasp, both structurally and historically, the complexities of music's involvement with processes of identity formation. Attuned to the institutional power structures that have denied legitimacy and recognition to African Americans, Ellington offers his dissonant chord both as a representation of a deplorable condition and as a strikingly innovative and enduring response to that condition. Oppression, after all, is itself a space of dissonance, for it means being out of tune with naturalized assumptions about social structures and categories. Jazz musicians, as Ellington's demonstration suggests, have turned that space of dissonance into something profoundly empowering. Trombonist and cultural theorist George Lewis puts it this way: "For African-American improvisers . . . sonic symbolism is often constructed with a view toward social instrumentality as well as form. New improvisative and compositional styles are often identified with ideals of race advancement and, more importantly, as resistive ripostes to perceived opposition to black social expression" (94). Landing on the wrong note, in short, can be a politically and culturally salient act for oppressed groups seeking alternative models of knowledge production and identity formation.

During the half century that has passed since Ellington's demonstration, the nature of that debate about music's social meanings and representational power has, however, changed dramatically. While Ellington's insistence that we interpret dissonance in a social context calls attention to debates about music's referential meaning—assuming, that is, that Ellington meant something representational with his chord, as opposed to something unspeakable or unresolvable—dissonance itself, as I'll argue in chapter 1 when I look at Ornette Coleman's free jazz, would, in later years, become a model for the celebration of jazz's movement *away* from representationalism, of its intrinsic meaning as a self-contained cultural practice. That dissonance could be dragooned into service for such widely differing attempts to theorize music's relation to social realities suggests not only that jazz, in Gennari's words, "is a rich, multi-layered culture that has created and communicated its meanings in a myriad of ways" (449), but also that the basic trajectory of jazz history might suggestively be read in the context of the broader debates about language, representation, and identity that have shaped literary and cultural theory. Specifically, the changing ideology of dissonance, like the publication history of Hobsbawm's book, reminds us of the need to interpret both the production and the reception of jazz in terms of the material and cultural conditions of its historical moment.

Taken together, the two examples I have cited—the publication history of *The Jazz Scene* and the changing ideology of dissonance—might, along, perhaps, with my own changed attitude toward interviews, generally be seen to be symptomatic of the way in which, as Rey Chow puts it, referentiality, though having been thoroughly problematized and suspended by contemporary theory, "has not exactly disappeared" (xiii). Hobsbawm, of course, has all along been attending to the social and historical specificity of jazz forms and developments, but the paradox of the initial publication resides in its deployment of a strategy that signaled the author's attempt to "disappear" from his own work—this at a cultural and institutional moment when analogous kinds of disappearances in the writing of history were axiomatic (even if not in the case of Hobsbawm's own maverick histories). The ideology of dissonance, as it modulates from Ellington's socially grounded interpretation—"Hear that chord. That's us. Dissonance is our way of life in America"—into the ahistorical and modernist implications of Ornette Coleman's revolutionary forays into atonal jazz, similarly fails to settle into an axiology. Indeed, the epigraph with which I began the previous section points to the fact that even Coleman, an artist whose music, in many ways, provides an exemplary instance of the way in which jazz came to problematize our understanding of referentiality, was not immune from having his work interpreted according to representational theories of art.

The structure of this book as a whole reflects the complexities of debates around jazz and its relation to theories of representation. Here, in abbreviated version, is the narrative I'll sketch. The opening chapter, "The Poetics of Jazz: From Symbolic to Semiotic," suggests that the movement in jazz from the diatonic music of Louis Armstrong to the atonality of Ornette Coleman finds a parallel in the history of contemporary literary theory as it moves (via Saussure) from an interest in the relationship between words and things to an interest in the relationship between words and words. This chapter, unlike the others, functions almost as a kind of historical survey, establishing the theoretical frames of reference for the contemporary case studies in the chapters that follow. Chapter 1's emphasis on musicological forms of analysis also sets it apart somewhat from the more culturally focused models of inquiry evident in the book's other chapters. I should, as well, say something here about how the format of that chapter sets it apart from the rest of the book. While the original version of the argument presented in chapter 1 was written well over a decade ago, in revising it for this book I've come to question some of the very premises that shaped my thinking at that time. I think that a willingness to subject our critical practice to an ongoing process of inquiry can be genuinely salutary; consequently, in an effort to preserve a sense of my own discordant responses—over ten years ago and now—to the music, I've interpolated several revisionary arguments in the form of sidebars which constitute a kind of critique of my own metalanguage. Rather than revise the chapter in ways that might suggest the possibility of a seamless fit between then and now, rather than offer a new argument that attempts to harmonize these often conflicting positions, I've sought to discover a form that prods us to consider how dissonance might itself function as a model for critical practice.

Chapter 2, "The Rehistoricizing of Jazz: Chicago's 'Urban Bushmen' and the Problem of Representation," explores the ways in which the city of Chicago has become the site of a new model of jazz activity: a sustained effort to rediscover the role of black tradition and history. Emerging in response to the kind of formalism that had come to characterize jazz in the early '60s (particularly the "free jazz" discussed in the book's opening chapter), members of the Chicago-based AACM collective (Association for the Advancement of Creative Musicians) have sought to combine their own interests in black heritage with the seemingly contradictory teachings of the formalists, who showed us that jazz was finally unable to posit a reality *outside* its own language.

In the third chapter, "Performing Identity: Jazz Autobiography and the Politics of Literary Improvisation," I turn to one variant of what Gabbard calls jazz's "other history" to look at how three well-known jazz autobiographies (Charles Mingus's *Beneath the Underdog*, Duke Ellington's *Music Is My Mistress*, and Billie Holiday's *Lady Sings the Blues*) also engage—this time in *literary* terms—with that very problem of representation. If, as Henry Louis Gates Jr. argues, "[t]he will to power for black Americans was the will to write; and the predominant mode that this writing would assume was the shaping of a black self in words" ("Introduction," 4), then these three jazz autobiographies clearly need to be read in the context of what one critic calls autobiography's "democratic potential" (Folkenflik, 23), that is, its ability to enable oppressed groups to achieve access to self-representation and control over the processes of literary production. As Christopher Harlos notes, "for jazz musicians, the turn to autobiography is regarded as a genuine opportunity to seize narrative authority" (134). Here too, after a fashion, my interest is in dissonance, in identities that might be said to be "out of tune" with the white literary institutions within which they've been constructed. While the "real" has, perhaps by necessity, an important role to play in facilitating our understanding of autobiography's democratizing effects, the identities fashioned in these particular texts compel us to ask hard methodological questions about the very status of the real: How are we to assess the role that white institutions and editors have played in shaping these particular black identities? Is autobiographical identity best understood as a function of referentiality? of textuality? of social construction? (see Folkenflik, 12) or, indeed, of performance and improvisation?

The fourth chapter, "'Space Is the Place': Jazz, Voice, and Resistance," provides an inventory of some of the ways in which Sun Ra looked to jazz as an important arena for redefining the possibilities of social transformation, for, in Amilcar Cabral's formulation, examining the role of "culture as a factor of resistance to . . . domination" (53). Ra's texts (performances, recordings, writings, and even films) all work to contest and reconfigure, in highly interesting and innovative ways, the relations of power that have been inscribed and institutionalized as commonsense notions of identity.

Chapters 5 and 6 augment the consideration (in previous chapters) of musicians and the complexities of representation with an analysis of the material conditions of the music business and the ways in which identities get co-opted and represented by the social presentation of music and the institutional workings of the jazz industry. By writing as an academic *and* as a music programmer, I hope in these chapters especially, but also more generally throughout the entire book, to live up to the task that John Corbett, himself both an academic and a music journalist, has set for himself: to "inspire unpredicted ways of thinking about music and the issues it raises, and simultaneously, [to] denature the mythology that locates musical truth in one discourse rather than another" (2). Both chapters, as I've already mentioned, focus in part on The Guelph Jazz Festival.

Chapter 5, "Nice Work If You Can Get It: Women in Jazz," cowritten with Gillian Siddall, uses the festival's "Women in Jazz" theme in the 1997 season as a test case for thinking through the representation of gender in jazz and the problematics of programming a season dedicated to women performers, composers, and arrangers. By looking at some of the artistic and material considerations that have arisen from our thematizing of the festival, we explore the extent to which women's relationship with jazz has been and continues to be dictated by their social identities. Why, for example, are so many women in jazz still confined to the conventionally prescribed roles of singer and piano player? Finally, does our own thematizing of the festival redress the historical marginalization of women in jazz or exacerbate it? These questions, arising from an intensely local model of social practice, are framed in the broader context of the ways in which the very language of jazz (both the musical conventions within which it operates and the discourses that are produced about it) might be said to be gendered. To what extent and in what ways, we ask, are women in jazz engaged in fostering alternative models for thinking about gender? Complicating the book's overarching assessment of the political efficacy of dissonant models of music making is a recognition of the fact that women have historically and institutionally been encouraged to play only certain kinds of more traditional jazz.

Chapter 6, "Capitulating to Barbarism: Jazz and/as Popular Culture," addresses the vexed question of jazz's relationship to popular culture. There, I consider the life and music of John Zorn, whose remarkable ability to court different sides of the popular music industry seems, in so many ways, to be at odds with the profoundly uncompromising nature of his avant-garde aesthetic. How does one become so popular playing dissonant, edgy, and abrasive forms of music? I also reflect once again on my experiences as a festival programmer, and ask how my attempts to present innovative, cutting-edge music in a local community setting have both shaped and complicated my understanding of what it means to be "popular." Taking up Theodor Adorno's notorious denunciation of jazz as a form of barbarism, as an example of the standardized and commercialized workings of the Culture Industry, I argue that both Zorn's lifework and the activities of the festival (and indeed its very structure of organization) illustrate the problematic nature of Adorno's high art/popular culture divide. Rather than being defined by way of pre-given qualities in the music, the popular, I maintain, is constructed through the complex ways in which the music is presented to and received by a public.

Chapter 7, "Up For Grabs: The Ethicopolitical Authority of Jazz," looks at the ways in which the reemergence of ethically valenced models of inquiry in the context of scholarship and critical practice in literary studies (a reemergence magisterially documented in Wayne Booth's *The Company We Keep*) might be seen to intersect with jazz studies. If, as I trace out in the previous chapters, jazz's cultural politicization has become increasingly evident through the ever-changing interpretive frameworks it has established, then one might be tempted to argue that jazz, given both its developing cultural history and its origins, is, perhaps by necessity, a particularly resonant site for adumbrating a model of ethical criticism of music: Isn't jazz, after all, an exemplary ethical music? But what are we to make of jazz that, whatever its artistic merit, is, at some level, "built on beliefs that go beyond (or sink beneath) what we can or should tolerate" (Booth, 377)? By turning to the difficult case of contemporary free jazz artist Charles Gayle, I want to open up questions about jazz criticism's role in adjudicating complex ethical debates: How, in Gayle's case, do we weigh the music's salutary aesthetic qualities against Gayle's deplorable public statements (presented as part of his musical performances) about, for example, the sinfulness of homosexuality? Gayle's music and pronouncements—or, rather, the complex ways in which they intersect—seem to me to offer a direct invitation to confront ethical questions in music seriously and rigorously. The ethical challenges faced by listeners of Gayle's performances and recordings come to a focus in resonant questions about intent and reception, about value and judgment, and about forms of responsibility (for listeners, for music programmers, and for record producers).

In the book's conclusion, "Alternative Public Spheres," I draw on the findings of the previous chapters to consider the efficacy of jazz as a vehicle for generating new social formations, for reinvigorating what Nancy Fraser has called subaltern counterpublics (14). Revisionist historiography, Fraser argues convincingly, "records that members of subordinated social groups—women, workers, peoples of color, and gays and lesbians—have repeatedly found it advantageous to constitute alternative publics" (14). It is perhaps telling, then, that poet and literary critic Kamau Brathwaite, in his analysis of the West Indian novel, turns to jazz as his model for "the delineation of a possible alternative to the European cultural tradition which has been imposed upon us [West Indian writers] and which we have more or less accepted and absorbed, for obvious historical reasons, as the only way of going about our business" (72). If, as Fred Wei-han Ho writes, "Oppressed peoples suffer from their history, identity, and culture being defined, (mis)represented and explicated by our oppressors" (133), then to what extent, I want to ask, might jazz offer an opportunity for recasting those identities and histories, and thus for diminishing the sense of misrecognition fostered through representations in the official public sphere? Emerging in response to exclusions and misrepresentations in dominant public institutions, musicians' cooperatives such as the Chicago-based AACM, self-managed record companies and music distribution networks (Sun Ra's Saturn Records), independent music festivals, and literary representations of jazz might all, to borrow Fraser's formulation, be seen as "parallel discursive arenas where members of subordinated social groups invent and circulate counterdiscourses, so as to formulate oppositional interpretations of their identities, interests, and needs" (14).

At this point, I should perhaps make clear my own assumptions about the music I discuss here, particularly the assumptions that have enabled me (often unconsciously, I suspect) to arrive at value judgments about particular kinds of art. As many critics have noted, value is a construction, and in music our judgments are especially highly contingent on an imposed set of intersecting, and sometimes conflicting, contexts: the social and historical conditions in which the music is made and received; the institutions through which the music (and our knowledge about it) gets represented, reproduced, heard, and talked about; the kinds of social, political, and artistic commitments that guide our own critical practice as listeners; and the experiences and intentions that, from the artist's point of view, may have given rise to the music in the first place. Since these are not necessarily stable formations, there are, as I'll detail later in the book, several factors that complicate our understanding and assessment of the music in question. But for now, assumption number one would be that I see value not so much as *inherent* in musical sounds, but rather as a function of the complex ways in which those sounds get taken up in specific historical contexts by specific social groups of both performers and listeners. Value, in short, needs to be seen as a synthesis of form and function, and if my own preference is for outlawed musical forms that accent timbral innovation, playful improvisation, altered harmonies, and wrong notes, then what I find attractive about such forms is in no small measure related to my sense of what, to borrow again from George Lewis, I would call the "sonic symbolism" of dissonance, that is, the social instrumentality that such innovative models of musical practice have had, in particular, for subordinated social groups seeking access to self-representation. Which brings me to assumption number two: music *does* have a social and critical force. And while that force has certainly been manifest in forms of jazz that have adhered to more conventional models of tonality, I admit to favoring music that, in its refusal of easy harmonization, encourages us to go beyond settled habits of response and judgment. The jazz that I most value, then, encourages us to query naturalized orders of knowledge production and, indeed, to spark critical debates about why we are (or why we are not) compelled to keep listening.

1

The Poetics of Jazz

From Symbolic to Semiotic

Prelude

I suggested in my introduction that evolutionary accounts of jazz history need to be interrogated for the ways in which they elide the music's history of involvement in the formation of social identities and their attendant forms of privation and struggle. This chapter, I feel compelled to admit, grew out of just such an evolutionary account, for when I began working on this project (or an earlier version of it) more than a decade ago, I myself sought to map out the ways in which the harmonic vocabulary of jazz had evolved *from its early forms of diatonic realism into a modernism of atonality. I was convinced that I saw parallel histories of momentum, resonant analogies between the ways in which representationalism was being rejected in contemporary literary theory as well as in the cultural practice of much contemporary jazz; I was convinced too that this turning away from representationalism was, in both cases, a healthy, even an exhilarating, development. As the rest of this book should make clear, there are plenty of reasons why I might now want to take issue with the latter judgments. For starters, how can I claim (as I do throughout) that jazz is embedded in social processes, in struggles for access to representation and identity formation, while also applauding its efforts to retreat from that very social world into an autonomous realm of language as a self-sufficient system of signs?*

Intellectual honesty requires that I declare my discomfort on this front. But I don't so much want to disown that earlier argument (published in a 1988 essay in Textual Practice*) , as much as I want here to open it up to its complexities and contradictions. For it still seems useful to me to rehearse that earlier work (despite its now-evident limitations) as a model for understanding jazz's shifting position in relation to the larger questions about identity, language, and representation which I'll take up in various ways through the course of this book. The present chapter, then, will bear the traces of my earlier argument, just as it will bear too the traces of the institutional conditions which gave rise to that argument. I've sought to preserve these traces because they open up purposeful and compelling questions about how jazz might be read in the context of language and its relation to the organization and mobilization of social identities. In so doing, in fact, they engage another key debate into which this book seeks to enter: the debate about our understanding of the relationship (read: split or fit?) between aesthetics and ethics.*

That relationship, indeed, is another, perhaps broader, way of indexing and reaffirming the link I spoke of earlier between academic work and community-facing activity, or, to return to Nathaniel Mackey's way of putting it, between word and world. The shifts in jazz that I will trace in this chapter are, I think, very much part of that same set of debates, for they too involve just such questions about how language (in this case musical language) might be said to be connected to the organization of (and resistance to) social relations of power and privilege. How, for example, are we to understand the ideological workings of jazz's musical properties? Is the movement from diatonic jazz to atonality and free collective improvisation really best understood as a movement away *from representationalism (and toward a modernist notion of autonomy)—as I suggested in my* Textual Practice *article—*

or might it better be described in terms of a shift to a new form of social realism, a newly articulated effort to reflect, alter, and mediate contemporary social relations?

The argument that follows is a version of that Textual Practice *piece. While the spirit and sweep of the argument remain faithful to the original, I've interpolated several revisionary arguments in sidebars that run through the course of the text. These interpolations serve both as a kind of paradigm for my own refusal to allow interpretive habits to settle into an orthodoxy and as a prod to consider how polyphony and dissonance might function as models for critical practice. The dissonances that have emerged over time in my own criticism go hand in hand with the aesthetic and political reevaluations made by many of the musicians themselves. As John Coltrane's radically different interpretations of a popular tune such as "My Favorite Things" reflect changes in his own perspectives on music in its cultural moment, so too do my reevaluations of recurrent critical themes require periodic, and sometimes radical, reconsideration.*

Much of today's jazz argot runs the risk of becoming nettled by any number of traditional emotive approaches (jazz isn't a type of music, it's a feeling!) which see forms of representation and expression inherent in musical structure. The tendency to think of jazz as a spontaneous expression of the performer's emotions clouds our awareness of the fact that jazz, like language, is a system of signs.[1] Though it is certainly not my purpose to deny the claim that music, through sound, communicates emotion, I want, in this chapter, to look at the ways in which various trends in the music have invited us to recognize the extent to which jazz as a language has found itself yielding to a formalist as well as to an emotive approach. By tracing salient developments in the history of jazz from swing to the present day, we can observe a series of fundamental changes which have taken place both in the theory of music and in the theory of language.

I begin with certain diatonic assumptions, with seven notes arranged into a scale of five whole tones and two semitones—a system of organizing tones which was held for the longest time to be the *natural* law of Western music. According to this system, one note, the tonal center or key, serves as a guiding principle, with the function of all the other notes in the scale being determined by their relationship to this one note. Diatonic music, then, proceeds by positing a variety of relationships between tones and their respective meanings. Specific intervals and isolated chords are said to represent determinate meanings. According to conventional structures of Western harmony—where the triad constitutes, as it were, the State of Nature—the interval of a major third is said, for example, to represent happiness. The minor third, by contrast, becomes a metaphor for sadness, the seventh a reflection of the state of longing. Given the "natural" state of the triad, the presence of the diminished fifth was once thought to be a sign of the "devil in music" owing to its perceived wrongness in sound (Cooke, 43). Such traditional structures of expression, however, inevitably limit the artist's ability to create.

Historically, the laws of tonality have also *invited* artists to explore other means. What's musically constraining for some artists can, in other words, become genuinely liberating for others. Within the established structures of Western diatonicism there are many composers and musicians who have created deeply innovative structures of practice. Louis Armstrong certainly comes to mind in this context, and I'll have more to say about this aspect of his work in later sidebars. It's wrong to suggest that jazz has evolved, that it has become "better" or "more sophisticated," though the sonic palette *has* widened. Of importance are the changing social, historical, and institutional contexts that have given rise to different sonic resources in jazz: instead of speaking of the ways in which laws of tonality have "limited the artist's ability to create," we ought perhaps to turn our attention to the varying contexts that governed those laws.

Within a universe of discourse dominated by diatonic rules, "[t]he presentation of musical ideas" is, as H. H. Stuckenschmidt puts it, "as thoroughly bound . . . as the words of a lyric poem are by rhythm or metre" (30). The laws of tonality—conducive to an emotive approach to music—like the laws of language, prevent the artist from exploring a broader range of potential musical options and opportunities. Deviations from the rigid rules of tonality were originally seen as grammatical errors and solecisms: "violations of the due process of composition" (Stuckenschmidt, 31).

Tonality posits a key center with tonic as home plate—tonic as womb. The desire to go back is not arbitrary. "Return to the tonic" is precipitated by the overtones heard when a given note (say a C on the piano) is sounded. Any melodic movement from one tone to another already generates a desire to return to the original tone. As we expect riddles to have answers, so we expect structures to have meanings. Diatonic music begs for completion. Its very structure is one of resolution. Similarly, the traditional realist novel, based on plot, fosters the illusion of *telos*, of order in the world, of patterned evolution toward a final goal. The heaven-on-earth endings of the Victorian novel—based on a pattern of narrative expectation—are, I want to argue, roughly analogous to the tonal expectation of a return to the tonic in diatonic music. We can see the marriages at the end of a Dickens novel, say, as being structurally related to the cadential formulas (II-V-I or IV-V-I) which govern the endings of much Western tonal music. Both marriage and return constitute order, completion, satisfaction, and harmony.

Repetition in music can never be exact because the specificity of its historic moment will have changed.

But, as Barbara Herrnstein Smith has pointed out, "we cannot ever really 'return' to the beginning point in a . . . piece of music; we can only repeat it" (27). For Smith, the same is true of poetry. Roman Jakobson has suggested that "[o]nly in poetry with its regular reiteration of equivalent units is the time of the speech flow experienced, as it is—to cite another semiotic pattern—with musical time" (358). The repetition of sounds, then, becomes important for music as well as for poetry. Jakobson's interest in small-scale similarities of syntactic and morphological elements—elements which are, as it were, beneath the threshold of consciousness—can be applied to certain cadential expectations of diatonic jazz. Reiterated patterning of notes was, indeed, one of the hallmarks of Louis Armstrong's playing. It's there, for example, in the repetition of the notes G and E flat throughout his muted quarter note solo in "Mahogany Hall Stomp," an improvisation which Gunther Schuller sees as one of the defining moments of the meaning and feeling of swing (see Schuller, 183). Similarly, Armstrong's first solo in "Savoy Blues" (Vocalion, 3217) provides another apt example of the way in which the repetition of sound patterns prepares us for resolution. Here, the final note C is anticipated by the appearance of the same note in the polyrhythmic cycle of three that precedes the last bar (Sargeant, 96–97). Linearity—a sense that we are moving from beginning to end (the solo will not just stop randomly)—is inscribed even in these improvisational passages. Music like Armstrong's, through its use of repeated melodic fragments and polyrhythmic cycles, is based on a teleological evolution toward a goal—an end, home base, the tonic.

> **The history of jazz can be told in four words, Louis Armstrong, Charlie Parker.**
>
> **Miles Davis**

There's much in Armstrong's oeuvre that threatens to break free of diatonic structure—the slides, the capacity (legendary in his performances) to spin endless breaks, the high *tessituras*, the rhythm. Indeed, Western harmony was but one of many different sensibilities at work in early jazz. My argument clearly won't hold for rhythm (which reflected an African sensibility rather than a Western teleological model of practice), for timbre, or for the non-European sonorities in the muted trumpet work of Cootie Williams and the work of some other jazz artists.

In the space of less than a century, the history of jazz has betrayed a steadily changing character. Developing from the early styles of ragtime, New Orleans, and Dixieland, it has evolved through a neoclassicist renaissance of bebop into a modernism of atonality. Louis Armstrong will always be remembered for his robust style and emphatic tone. His trumpet playing, an extension of his own voice, tastefully explored those "blue" regions—the third and seventh degrees of the diatonic scale flattened. The poetry of his horn, however, remains steeped in the rudiments of a diatonic tradition. His smooth and eloquent improvisations are defined by an "on the beat" style, and the ends of his solos, like the ends of his songs, are governed by standard harmonic progressions. His use of the familiar II-V-I cadence—often quoted precisely because the tonics of these chords are a fifth apart—recaptures the tonal bias in its attempt to provide a strong and well-founded harmony.

To the extent that Armstrong's music constitutes an attempt to imitate the singing and speaking inflections of the human voice, it reveals itself to be yearning after the illusion of presence that has traditionally been associated with speech. Such a transference of vocal inflections to the realm of instrumentation suggests, perhaps, a desire to have music represent things or emotions in much the same way that words might be said to refer to objects and ideas in the actual world. Poet/dramatist/essayist Amiri Baraka (then LeRoi Jones), in his book *Black Music*, insists that each note in an Armstrong solo "*means something* quite in adjunct to musical notations. . . . The notes *mean something*; and the something is, regardless of its stylistic considerations, part of the black psyche as it dictates the various forms of Negro culture" (15; emphasis in original). This representational dimension of Armstrong's jazz, this hankering after an essence that can be accessed only by simulating the apparent presence of speech, however, finds itself paradoxically moving *away* from representation. Armstrong's horn, though an extension of his own voice, is already once removed from it, and as such it cannot help but become the initial step in the movement toward a nonrepresentational practice of modern jazz. Despite appearing to valorize speech as a form of presence, despite playing a kind of music which, if Baraka is correct, purports to represent certain emotions or conditions, Armstrong's trumpet playing *mediates* between the human voice and any attempt at representation. It is at once an attempt to recover the illusion of presence and an admission of its distance from any sense of an origin.

Theodor Adorno, in his review of Wilder Hobson's *American Jazz Music* and Winthrop Sargeant's *Jazz: Hot and Hybrid*, claims that instrumental imitations of vocal inflections, such as those I have been examining with the example of Louis Armstrong, are forms of a "deceptive 'humanization'" (169). Rather than bringing the instrument closer to the musician, Armstrong's technique, as Adorno would have it, reveals another site of desire—a desire for mechanization: "The vocalization of the instrumental," writes Adorno, "serves not only to produce the appearance of the human, it serves also to assimilate the voice into the realm of the instrumental: to make it, as it were, an appendage to the machine" (170). If Armstrong's horn is, as Baraka would have it, an expression of a specific social or cultural attitude, then, by transferring the inflections of his human voice onto his horn, a machine, Armstrong is already caught up in what, by Adorno's account, might be seen to be a process of dehumanization. Machines, as Gilles Deleuze and Félix Guattari maintain in their *Anti-Oedipus*, designate themselves in an "overcoded" way; they symbolize human emotions which they have replaced and which are no longer necessary. The transfer, then, from voice to horn, rather than enabling the musician to recuperate the attitude that Baraka insists gave rise to jazz in the first place, serves instead to distance the performer from any possibility of self-present meaning in music.

It is the musician's very desire to represent emotion which thus becomes responsible for the "veering off of signification" (the phrase is Lacan's) in modern jazz. What I have been trying to suggest, more precisely, is that Louis Armstrong's trumpet playing, by simulating through style and pattern the inflections of his own voice, works to conceal the cultural or social attitude that it wishes rather to reveal. Already evident in a music which is seen to be reclaiming the presence of human speech is its failed attempt to idealize the horn as signifier by bestowing upon it a materiality that it does not possess. Armstrong, though an exemplary figure in the diatonic tradition, is already forcing us to question the assumptions of that tradition, to question the time-honored belief that emotions constitute the substance of musical sounds.

We are now ready to enter a new era. The fabled bop of Charlie "Bird" Parker grew out of the ennui with antecedent forms of jazz. Baraka sees bop as a reaction to the sterility of swing as it became part of the mainstream in American culture (*Black Music,* 16). Anchored in a predictable tonal groove—with a predilection for diatonic forms of resolution—jazz had become too patterned, too diatonic. Bird's flight into chromaticism thus became what we can now deem the pivotal moment in the development of jazz. As Scott DeVeaux writes, "To understand jazz, one must understand bebop" (*Birth,* 3). If Bird was, at the time of his playing, seen as an anomaly, it was precisely because he played notes in his improvisations which nobody had dared to acknowledge except perhaps as passing harmonies. The flattened fifth, for instance, the devil itself in music, became a stylistic device that characterized much of what Parker, Dizzy Gillespie, and other boppers were doing. The use of that flat fifth, along with the minor seventh, allowed soloists to break out of the constraints of the diatonic tradition. Whereas others might have played the major third, Parker was apt to explore the higher harmonics of his horn and play an augmented ninth instead. He was one of the first to begin using the higher intervals of a chord in the melody. This movement from diatonic harmony to chromaticism is reflected in any number of his tunes. In "Ornithology," for example, Parker employs half-diminished scale degrees (root, flat third, flat fifth, flat seventh) and augmented ninths in the solo structure of the song. Along with his explorations into the minor harmonics of chords, Parker's music was also responsible for junking a past which was dominated by the thirty-two-bar chorus.[2]

Music is by its essence unable to express anything—a feeling, an attitude, a psychological state, a natural phenomenon, etc. Expression has never been the immanent property of music. If, as is so often the case, music seems to express something, it is an illusion and not something real.

Igor Stravinsky

The movement from tonality to chromaticism is best understood when contextualized within the plethora of related transformations it helped engender. The awareness that each tone in the seven-note diatonic scale could be altered chromatically by raising or lowering it by a half-tone, and the explicit articulation of this awareness into the structures of jazz improvisation, brought with it a fundamental shift in perspective. Emotive approaches—jazz as representation of feeling—began to give way to a new sort of formalism that perceived jazz in a radically new light. Sound, according to this conception, is nonrepresentational matter. What becomes important for the formalist is the architectural landscape of jazz—its use of syncopation, polyphony, and polyrhythm as structures of sound—showing not so much *what* jazz means but *how* it means. The movement from Armstrong to Parker, though perhaps not even entirely audible to modern sensibilities, represents a shift into a world ready to question the view that language is merely representation, that meaning is *present* in language at the

---

Here too, the social context surrounding bebop deserves consideration. Before the term *bebop* came into use, Thelonious Monk and others asserted that this was "modern music," referring to followers of earlier jazz traditions as "moldy figs." The hipster movement that surrounded bebop was very much concerned with turning jazz into serious "Art music"— with a capital "A." This was done largely by adopting European standards of virtuosity and harmonic complexity, and celebrating the music's erudite position in relation to Benny Goodman, Glenn Miller, and the rest of the white mainstream.

---

moment of utterance. It is a movement away from the perlocutionary utterances of Satchmo's symbolic and illustrious horn toward a view of jazz as a system of signs to be deciphered.

With the publication of Ferdinand de Saussure's *Course in General Linguistics*, modern linguistic theory took a giant step forward. Prior to Saussure, words were held to be important precisely because they were thought to represent things in the external world. Meanings were privileged; language as a medium was not. Similarly, in the jazz world, emotive approaches prevailed. Jazz was a feeling more than a type of music. Armstrong's robust style, as we have seen, is often cited as having been an expression of the black psyche. With Saussure's publication, however, we were alerted to the fact that the resemblance between words and things was an illusion, the relationship between signifier and signified an arbitrary one. Charlie Parker's explorations into chromaticism brought a similar awareness into jazz, an awareness that the meaning of a musical tone rests not in the fact that the tone represents something in the external world, but in the manner by which representation has been effected. No longer content simply to express emotion, jazz, as it moved through its renaissance, sought to expose its structural constituents and call attention to its formal aspects.

According to Saussure, the linguistic sign receives value only within the total system of signs. To be more precise, its value is determined in relation (contrast and difference) to other signs. With Parker's application of previously forbidden harmonies, the resonances of sound and the dynamics of tone become more important than the meanings which these sounds and tones might be said to represent. As jazz began to utilize chromaticism, more and more musicians were forced to recognize the extent to which meanings in music did not

The formal innovations of bebop, however, need to be read in a social and cultural context. As Anthony Braxton notes, "bebop had to do with understanding the realness of black people's actual position in America" (quoted in George Lewis, 95).

exist independently. Meaning, in Saussure's terms, is perceived to be a system of differences. Identity is defined negatively:

> Instead of pre-existing ideas then, we find . . . *values* emanating from the system. When they are said to correspond to concepts, it is understood that the concepts are purely differential and defined not by their positive content but negatively by their relations with the other terms of the system. Their most precise characteristic is in being what the others are not. (117; emphasis in original)

In music, what this meant was that the note C, for instance, could only be distinguished by its difference from other notes (D, E, F, etc.) in a given musical system. Though such a discovery was obviously made long before the dawn of bop, it was Parker's desire to go beyond the limitations of a purely diatonic framework which helped call attention to the fact that relationships between tones, rather than an inherent quality in the tone itself, could give identity to a piece of music. Moreover, not being content to accept the popular assumption that each musical interval contained a particular emotional appeal, jazz, with the introduction of chromaticism, found itself problematizing the relationship between the signifier and meaning in much the same way that Saussure made us realize a word was *not* simply a thing. In this sense, jazz too began to gravitate toward a new formalism. Moving away from representationalism, it would thus leave behind its affiliations with the nineteenth-century linguistic tendency to see language as presence and words in terms of the things to which they were said to refer.

In LeRoi Jones's (Amiri Baraka's) drama *Dutchman*, the music of Charlie Parker, though never heard, plays a central thematic role. Despite the fact that the play is not explicitly about jazz, it is a useful literary text for our purposes, not only because it dramatizes many of the principles that underlie Baraka's jazz criticism, but also because it too, despite itself, is caught up in the emergent formal relations I have been examining.

Dutchman tells the story of an encounter on a New York subway train between Clay, an educated young black man, and Lula, a white woman. Underlying the whole of the drama is the Flying Dutchman motif. According to legend, the Flying Dutchman was a ghost ship condemned to sail the seas forever without hope of reaching shore. In his play, Baraka uses the subway as a kind of ghostship, with Lula, its captain, condemned to commit a ritual act of murder, and Clay, in this case, condemned to be the victim. The setting itself indicates a state of the eternal suspension of presence, a state in transit that can never finally touch the earth or clay, a state that remains eternally alienated from its origins. By incorporating the myth of the Flying Dutchman into his use of setting, Baraka is already hinting at the possibility that the play will have something to do with a search for origins. In much the same manner that Louis Armstrong, by transferring the inflections of his voice onto his trumpet, implicitly sought a reconnection with his past, so Baraka's protagonist Clay, as I'll suggest in a moment, is hankering after a sense of his own origin.

Before turning to Clay, though, let me first say something about the way in which the characters in the play are initially introduced to us. After the opening stage direction, Baraka describes a scene in which we see a man sitting on a subway seat looking through the window and exchanging smiles with a woman on the platform. The language of this set piece is telling:

> The man looks idly up, until he sees a woman's face staring at him through the window; when it realizes that the man has noticed the face, it begins very premeditatedly to smile. The man smiles too, for a moment, without a trace of self-consciousness. (4)

Clay, here, is referred to as "the man," rather than being called by his name. As "the man," he is, perhaps, a metaphor for black America. Lula, by contrast, is described metonymically in terms of her face. She is referred to not as "she" but as "it." Though Lula too may well be a metaphor herself, this initial metonymic description of her serves to associate her with a resistance to rather than a revelation of meaning. Jacques Lacan, who, following Jakobson, has linked Freud's conceptions of condensation and displacement to metaphor and metonymy, respectively, has discussed the way in which displacement and metonymy both involve a "veering off of signification" (160). While metaphor, by positing an absolute identity between two terms, serves to *reveal* meaning, metonymy, to a certain extent, functions to conceal it by suggesting that some part of an idea can be detached from that idea. Hence Baraka's initial description of Lula bespeaks a desire to partake in the reification of her personality (she, like Clay, is a "type"), while simultaneously serving to foreground her dissembling gaze. His description of Lula as "face" instead of "woman," as "it" rather than "she," permits the localization of the true site of motivation. Presumably, Clay chooses to see only her face, and in doing so he displaces his sexual energy onto the object of his gaze. Lula, then, must be reified because she cannot otherwise be situated within the context of Baraka's (and Clay's) male discourse. She can only be fetishized or turned into an object. In this initial description, nothing about her *self* speaks; only her dissembling gestures are foregrounded. Lula thus finds herself eternally alienated from *her* identity. She is condemned to remain in transit, underground in a kind of hell.

Lula's function, within the context of the play's narrative, is to shock Clay out of his bourgeois complacency. Clay, we learn, is someone whose entire life to date seems to have centered around a conscious attempt to conceal his black identity both from himself and from others. Lula's comments, then, are not entirely out of place:

> What've you got that jacket and tie on in all this heat for? And why're you wearing a jacket and tie like that? Did your people ever burn witches or start revolutions over the price of tea? Boy, those narrow-shoulder clothes come from a tradition you ought to feel oppressed by. A three-button suit. What

> right do you have to be wearing a three-button suit and striped tie? Your grandfather was a slave, he didn't go to Harvard. (18)

> Clay! You middle-class black bastard. Forget your social-working mother for a few seconds and let's knock stomachs. Clay, you liver-lipped white man. You would-be Christian. You ain't no nigger, you're just a dirty white man. (31)

As a black man living in white America, Clay finds himself confronted with essentially two options for survival. The first, as evidenced in Lula's accurate commentary, constitutes the way in which Clay has previously conducted his life.[3] He has repressed his history, concealed his blackness, and cut himself off from the past by imitating the behavior of white middle-class Americans. In short, by ignoring the past, he has done the same thing that most commentators on jazz, according to Baraka, have done. In *Black Music*, Baraka writes, "Usually the critic's commitment was first to his *appreciation* of the music rather than to his understanding of the attitude which produced it. . . . The major flaw in this approach to Negro music is that it strips the music too ingenuously of its social and cultural intent" (13–14; emphasis in original). As Baraka champions the need to reinscribe the social and cultural intent of black music into any discourse on jazz, he similarly speaks out on the necessity of having his black characters reconnect with their past. Clay, by hiding behind his buttoned-up suit and likening himself to Baudelaire, presents himself to the world as other than he really is. Anything that is repressed, however, inevitably threatens to explode, and this is precisely what happens when Clay launches into his tirade near the play's end. It is here that Clay acknowledges his *other* option:

> If I'm a middle-class fake white man . . . let me be. And let me be in the way I want. . . . And I sit here, in this buttoned-up suit, to keep myself from cutting all your throats. . . . The belly rub? You wanted to do the belly rub? Shit, you don't

even know how. That ol' dipty-dip shit you do, rolling your ass like an elephant. That's not my kind of belly rub. Belly rub is not Queens. Belly rub is dark places, with big hats and overcoats held up with one arm. Belly rub hates you. Old bald-headed four-eyed ofays popping their fingers . . . and don't know yet what they're doing. They say, "I love Bessie Smith." And don't even understand that Bessie Smith is saying, "Kiss my ass, kiss my black unruly ass." Before love, suffering, desire, anything you can explain, she's saying, and very plainly, "Kiss my black ass." And if you don't know that, it's you that's doing the kissing.

Charlie Parker? Charlie Parker. All the hip white boys scream for Bird. And Bird saying, "Up your ass, feeble-minded ofay! Up your ass." And they sit there talking about the tortured genius of Charlie Parker. Bird would've played not a note of music if he just walked up to East Sixty-Seventh Street and killed the first ten white people he saw. Not a note! And I'm the great would-be poet. Yes. That's right! Poet. Some kind of bastard literature . . . all it needs is a simple knife thrust. Just let me bleed you, you loud whore, and one poem vanished. A whole people of neurotics, struggling to keep from being sane. And the only thing that would cure the neurosis would be your murder . . . all it needs is that simple act. Murder. Just murder! Would make us all sane. (34–35)

Finally manifesting some sense of black consciousness, Clay becomes aware of the fact that it is only through violence that sanity can be restored to black Americans. Here, at last, we return to Charlie Parker. Only now he appears not simply as a musician, as the bopper who introduced chromaticism into jazz, but rather as a murderer wanting to return to the scene of the crime, to his origin of violence. Citing Bird's music, as well as the music of Bessie Smith, Clay claims that black art, in particular black music, arises only out of suffering and oppression. He insists, moreover, that the music constitutes a sublimated hatred of white people.

I have already discussed the ways in which, for Baraka, an understanding of jazz implies an awareness of the attitude that underlies its inception. Adorno has written that in music "*survives* what is otherwise forgotten and is no longer capable of speaking directly" (Adorno, *Philosophy,* 42; emphasis added). It seems to me that this is what Clay and Baraka would like to believe, that music can and does represent a specific historical attitude, in this case, the resistance to white hegemonic culture. Yet *does* that which has otherwise been forgotten, repressed, or deliberately expunged, survive, as Adorno would have it, in music?

While Clay might like to think that he is restoring Bird's music to its true origins, what he is also suggesting is that music can signify only through a kind of absence. In other words, what the music of Charlie Parker and Bessie Smith "means" is precisely that which we can never actually hear or know. The history of suffering which is responsible for the genesis of jazz exists now as an absent trace rather than as a fully articulated meaning that *survives* as presence in musical language. Clay's speech, by bringing to the fore instincts and desires that have hitherto been repressed, attempts to make present this very absence—this unactualizable sense of an origin which, in jazz, has been effaced as it is taken up in the white cultural mainstream. It is his failure to act upon these instincts and desires, his conscious rejection of the violence he knows can make him sane, that signals the ultimate impossibility, for Clay, of ever returning to his own origin:

> Ahhh. Shit. But who needs it? I'd rather be a fool. Insane.
> Safe with my words, and no deaths, and clean, hard thoughts,
> urging me to new conquests. (35)

It is interesting to note that Clay's retreat into the world of metaphors, into the "safe" domain of his words, occurs after he has already speculated on the inadequacy of his own language: "And I'm the great would-be poet. Yes. That's right! Poet. Some kind of bastard literature . . . all it needs is a simple knife thrust" (35). What seems to be implicit in Clay's commentary is an awareness that his own words are finally inadequate because they belong to Lula's world of "bastard literature." Clay, to put it another way, understands that being a poet—as he aspired to be in college—involves recourse to a language that is not his own, a metalanguage that has appropriated his origin. He becomes aware of the extent to which he is trapped in a language of the other, and realizes that anything he says stands in the way of that "simple knife thrust" that would make him sane.

The implication seems to be that if Clay's retreat into the "safe" world of words turns out to be not so safe after all, then the true expression of his black identity resides in an act of violence which he refuses to commit. Here, too, meaning is inscribed in absence, and the center of the text—Clay's expression of identity—becomes not what can be recuperated but what cannot finally be recovered. The dramatic center of the text, in other words, is displaced, and the protagonist, rather than act out the central meaning of the play, can only, before he is murdered, adumbrate the possibility that change is imminent:

> My people. They don't need me to claim them. They got legs and arms of their own. Personal insanities. Mirrors. They don't need all those words. They don't need any defense. . . . They'll murder you, and have very rational explanations. Very much like your own. They'll cut your throats, and drag you out to the edge of your cities so the flesh can fall away from your bones, in sanitary isolation. (35–36)

What happens within the context of the play, however, is clearly not an example of such change. The kind of ideological change which Clay predicts is inevitably extrinsic to representational discourse such as Baraka's drama because it is based on an assumed presence emerging *outside* representation, a violence as presence that seeks to escape the violence of language—the violence of language that Lula has become. Hence Lula, as an allegorical figuration of language itself, entering into the text as a reduction to the metonymic, displaced into a linguistic space and removed from her origin, in turn usurps Clay's origin. Language, then, murders a presence that, within the context of the drama, was always absent.

I have tried in my discussion of *Dutchman* to suggest the ways in which Baraka's play, essentially rooted in naturalism, contains despite itself a movement away from representation. What happens in *Dutchman*, in other words, is precisely what was beginning to happen in modern jazz during Charlie Parker's heyday. Yet Baraka, both as dramatist and as jazz critic, locates in Parker's music an essence which he thinks can be recuperated through representation. Lula's murder of Clay, however, is not only an example of white killing black; it is also a symbolic dramatization of a metalanguage that has appropriated an origin, a dramatization of what happens to jazz when it is taken up in the white cultural mainstream. As such, Clay's murder demonstrates the limitations and the ultimate failure of naturalism, the inadequacy of any attempt to reduce words to things. To put it another way, naturalism fails because it attempts to access a prelinguistic human essence or reality through representation, without recognizing the terms of its own existence, without realizing, as it were, that there is finally no escape from language.

I have digressed to incorporate this analysis of *Dutchman* into my discussion of jazz because the play itself illustrates the incapacity of language to represent presence. Lula, who is reduced to the metonymic; Clay, who is murdered as a result of retreating into a world of words; and the music of Charlie Parker, which can signify only through a kind of *absent* meaning—all testify to the fact that language can only "stand in the way of" rather than "stand for" presence.

To return to jazz, then, Baraka's drama, rather than legitimizing his approach to black music, seems to undermine what it has been attempting to assert. What survives in music is *not* some predetermined meaning to which we have access. By having Lula murder Clay, Baraka undermines the possibility of representational presence. Jazz ultimately functions as a self-sufficient collection of sounds rather than as a representation of a specific historical or cultural attitude. Whereas diatonic jazz attempts to posit musical language as a way of thinking about things in the real world, chromaticism begins to foreground *form* rather than *substance*. Saussure, in his oft-cited Geneva-to-Paris express example, made clear that the source of identity of the express was not the fact that it was a train, but the fact that it was *different* from all the other trains in the timetable (Saussure 108). This emphasis on form revealed the inadequacy of any attempt to use words to refer to things as if they *were*, in fact, those things. Jazz, through Parker's experimentation with chromaticism, was in the process of making a similar discovery. It was beginning to realize that it could no longer posit a reality *outside* its own language.

Within the context of African-American culture in the 1940s, this modernist quest for a self-sufficient system of signs was, in part, an attempt to subvert white culture by mastering its harmonic vocabulary and presenting it in a way that was bewildering to (white) uninitiated listeners.

The next step in the history of jazz completes a development of transition in music in much the same way that Saussure did for modern linguistics. Atonality is, of course, an extension of what Parker and others had been doing with chromaticism. The essential difference between the two resides in the fact that atonal music has no key, while notes in the chromatic scale still gravitate toward a tonal center. The shift from diatonic music to atonality finds a parallel in the movement in modern literary theory from an interest in the relationship between words and things to a fascination with the relationship between words and words. Ornette Coleman and Cecil Taylor have ushered in the age of modernism in jazz. Coleman's *Free Jazz* of 1960, christened by many as "the shape of jazz to come," constitutes one of the most important documents in the history of Western improvisational music. It is so important precisely because, as Baraka puts it, it reestablishes "the absolute hegemony of improvisation in jazz" (*Black Music,* 54). As James Joyce's *Ulysses*, for example, was to literature, so Coleman's revolutionary recording was to jazz. With Coleman's glaring solecisms—what would have been taboos even long past the Parker era (and there are still those who insist that Coleman can't play)—we are forced, once and for all, to recognize the extent to which music has ceased to be denotative and referential. Umberto Eco, in his essay "The Poetics of the Open Work," cites works by avant-garde composers Karlheinz Stockhausen and Luciano Berio (among others) as being "open" precisely because they reject the notion of a closed and well-defined message as found in traditional classical compositions (48). Instead, these works place an emphasis on the initiative of the performing artist. Eco writes of the works of Stockhausen and Berio that "the author seems to hand them to the performer more or less like the components of a construction kit" (49). With Coleman's *Free Jazz*, we are faced with a similar situation. Up until his (and Cecil Taylor's) music, most improvisation in jazz was confined to a harmonic and rhythmic framework. Then Coleman came along and swept away the set harmonic structures and tightly knit patterns—including the lines that separated bars—which had dominated the music of his contemporaries. Even Parker's music, from this perspective, was "closed." It had a set pattern—it always knew how it was going to get where it was going—and despite its innovation was still trapped within a limited framework that the soloist would never fully transcend. Performers of Coleman's music are faced with the same problems as performers of works by Stockhausen and other contemporary

The "closed" or "open" nature of the music is a matter of critical perception, not necessarily something that is inherent in the text. And "limited framework" now seems too negatively reductive for so compelling a form as bebop.

classical composers. They must complete a piece of music that is presented in only its bare essentials by the composer.

> **That sheet stuff**
> **'s a lot a cheese.**
>
> **Man**
> **gimme the key**
>
> **and lemme loose -**
> **I make 'em crazy**
>
> **with my harmonies -**
> **Shoot it Jimmy**
>
> **Nobody**
> **Nobody else**
>
> **but me -**
> **They can't copy it.**
>
> **William Carlos Williams**

Coleman's ventures into atonality constitute, in part, a desire to explore the dynamics of tone and pitch in a radically new fashion. Chords—tone clusters—are used more for their *sound* than as parts of a cadential formula. His music, no longer rooted in the diatonic tradition, does away with such considerations as triadic structures of harmony and key centres. Coleman is no longer hampered by a set of *a priori* relationships among notes. He has created a music in which *anything goes*. Rejecting those who adhere to the twelve tones of the Western "tempered" scale, Coleman has created a "non-tempered" music (Wilmer, 64). His jazz has also been termed "non-chordal." Baraka sums it up by saying that Coleman "does not limit his line to notes that are specifically called for by the sounded chord" (*Black Music,* 40). Melody, then, is privileged over harmony to the extent that the tune itself becomes the pattern of the composition. (We might be tempted here to make an analogy with Derrida's *différance,* which is understood as being at the point of juncture of the vertical and horizontal axes—but also as being neither of these axes.) Coleman's freedom—also manifest in his refusal to be limited by four-, eight-, and twelve-bar structures (Wilmer, 60)—is part of a revolt against the notion that musical language should produce stable signifieds. With Coleman's music, jazz has entered the domain of semiotics. Like language, it has become increasingly aware of its own status as a system of signs, increasingly critical of the mimetic relationship between art and life. Moving from the tonality of Satchmo's symbolic horn to the atonality of Coleman's semiotic freedom, jazz has shifted, to borrow Eco's distinction, from the poetics of the closed work into a realm of the open. Dissonance and atonality are hallmarks of modern music's polysemy. Coleman's jazz is a proliferation of meanings, a valorization of the signifier.

The trouble with this teleological narrative is twofold. First, it diminishes the accomplishments of Satchmo, Bird, and others. Surely they, too, were aware that the notes they played on their horns did not simply represent "real" things in the world.

Second, Coleman has always been paradoxically rooted in the very traditions from which he seems to depart. This rootedness—exemplified in song titles such as "Blues Connotation," "When Will the Blues Leave," "Monk and the Nun," "Bird Food," and "The Legend of Bebop"—problematizes any simple linear narrative of the music.

The temptation is great to see Coleman's music only in terms of the underlying emotions that give rise to his rantings on the saxophone. What is perhaps just as important is the fact that we have, with Coleman, completed a movement away from an interest in representation to an interest in the *means* of expression. As Saussure was interested in the linguistic units that made meaning possible rather than in things (or meanings) themselves, so Coleman is fascinated by the various tonal units and rhythmic patterns that make musical expression possible. With *Free Jazz*, music has shifted from language as perlocutionary utterance to language as a system of signs. The step into atonality is a revolt against stable meanings. The more we listen to Coleman, Cecil Taylor, and others who seek to bestow new meanings on jazz through their attempts to dislodge traditional conceptions of melody, harmony, and rhythm, the more we come to recognize the extent to which the language of jazz, far from being a body of utterance, has become rather like a puzzle: something to be deciphered.

Coleman, then, in doing away with bar lines, standard chord progressions, scales, and consistent tempo, remains fundamentally unconstrained by the formal limitations of traditional jazz. In *Free Jazz*, for instance, we will hear melodies being played by instruments that have conventionally been limited to the rhythm section, while the so-called "lead" instruments will provide stacked harmonies to create a rhythmic base. The initial difficulty that confronts someone listening to Coleman's music for the first time is undoubtedly its very emphasis on group improvisation. Coleman, in the liner notes to his 1959 *Change of the Century* recording, explains the nature of collective improvisation as follows:

> When our group plays, before we start to play, we do not have any idea what the end result will be. Each player is free to contribute what he feels in the music at any given moment. We do not begin with a preconceived notion as to what kind of effect we will achieve.

Emancipated from any sense of a prescribed scheme, Coleman's jazz poses problems for the unseasoned listener precisely because it refuses to be coded or instituted according to traditional theories of representation. The harmonic and melodic structures which might seem to make it possible to negotiate meaning in Coleman's musical world pose a tremendously difficult task for anybody who enters such a world *expecting* riddles to have answers, signs to have referents, and structure to have readily identifiable intent. The fact that Coleman's sound does not arise out of any preconceived notion of what it tries to be testifies to its antirepresentational stance.

Another proponent of the "new music" (or "new thing" as it has been called) being developed in the '50s and '60s who deserves mention here is the remarkable pianist Cecil Taylor. Taylor's unique style of pounding on the keyboard with his fists, arms, and elbows to create a variety of overtones has precipitated, as might be expected, a wide range of critical responses. He is an atonalist *par excellence*, as is evident in his ability to manipulate the piano to yield color and texture rather than conventional harmony. Like Coleman, he too finds himself playing a music that uses notes more for their sound value than for their worth as semantic signifiers. In this sense, both these modernists have, to adapt Julia Kristeva's terminology, entered into a realm of the semiotic.

Kristeva tells us that the semiotic involves "a *distinctiveness* admitting of an uncertain and indeterminate articulation because it does not yet refer . . . or no longer refers . . . to a signified object for a thetic consciousness" (133). She associates the semiotic with rhythm, sound, and instinct, and maintains that it is "heterogeneous to meaning" (133). Cecil Taylor's percussive piano playing constitutes an attempt to inscribe a semiotic practice into contemporary jazz. Similarly Coleman's music, a jazz in which indeterminacy runs rampant, belongs to the realm of the semiotic because, to adapt Kristeva's language, it "sound[s] a dissonance within the thetic, paternal function of language" (139).

Kristeva's thetic, paternal language suggests a language which is interested in meaning and representation, and which finds a parallel in the assumptions governing much of diatonic jazz. If Coleman, Taylor, and the atonalists belong to Kristeva's semiotic realm, then Louis Armstrong and other practitioners of diatonic jazz might be said to inhabit the symbolic order. For Kristeva, the symbolic is linked with the idea of language as nomination. It is an order of cultural and social meaning, an order whose language is the language of the group. Moreover, as it is a realm in which symbols have fixed, determinate meanings, Kristeva is able to associate it with the role of the father as an authority figure. Armstrong's music, to the extent that it tries to represent a specific cultural attitude, belongs to this realm because it stresses the normative aspect of musical language. It is a music which presupposes a world of shared meanings not only between musicians but also between performer and listener. Coleman's jazz, on the other hand, though also emphasizing group experience, is more like having many individuals speak at the same time: in describing his own theory of harmolodics, Coleman writes, "Harmolodic allows a person to use a multiplicity of elements to express more than one direction at one time" ("Harmolodic," 119). Rather than result in the breakdown of all possible communication, however, this multiplicity becomes a celebration of the kind of *babble* which, as recent work in feminist and psychoanalytic theory has suggested, reclaims the realm of *female* desire. If, as Susan McClary argues in her compelling analysis of the gendered legacy of the paradigm of tonality, conventional patterns of musical resolution have functioned ideologically to *contain* "whatever is semiotically or structurally marked as 'feminine,' whether a second theme or simply a non-tonic area" (15), then

Both Armstrong and Coleman have danced on the borders between diatonicism and atonality; both have been engaged in musical gestures which are as much about "things" as they are about purely musical relationships. These often unrecognized parallels in their work combat a simple evolutionary narrative of jazz.

L'écriture féminine has been a useful model primarily in the context of white-to-white culture. Something very different happens, I think, when racial/ethnic difference is so much a part of the context of the music. Also, we need to keep in mind that free jazz has historically been a male-dominated domain of cultural practice.

might Coleman's jazz, in its rejection of diatonic authority and resolution, be regarded (as James Joyce's writings have been regarded by some French feminists) as a celebratory model for *l'écriture féminine*? And what might it mean for a nonrepresentational practice of music, like Coleman's, to be thus coded, to be theorized in the context of such extramusical considerations? I'll return to these matters in chapter 5.

The history of jazz from Satchmo's symbolic horn—symbolic in the sense that it gives rise to an emphasis on the fact that the language of music affects us—to Coleman's explicit articulation of conflict as a principle of organization (dissonance, fissure, and a consistently changing rhythm, rather than triadic harmony, closure, and a steady beat) must ultimately be viewed in the light of similar developments in related disciplines. To move from diatonic jazz to atonality is to supplant the traditional fascination with that which is represented with an interest in the means of representation. It is, to use again the language of Kristeva and Lacan, to move from the symbolic to the semiotic. Diatonic jazz remains committed to the signified. It is a celebration of the satisfaction that goes along with completion and closed symbolic meanings. It speaks a language that is interested in the relationship between words and things. Atonal jazz, on the other hand, eludes precise definition by generating a theater of potential meanings. By refusing to bow to the established rule of tonality, Coleman's radical retreat from conventional sources of musical meaning alerts us to the possibility that the expressiveness of jazz can be enhanced by an exploration of its formal aspects. Tonality had reached a point of exhaustion by the time "cats" like Parker began blowing their flat fifths and augmented ninths. Diatonic jazz had become straight, stiff, square—patterned to the point of predictability. With his investigation into the previously forbidden, the darker side of jazz, Parker paved the way for the atonalists. By subdividing the tradi-

Armstrong, in his day, was also sometimes accused of performing forbidden and rebellious music.

tional seven-note scale into subpitches, Parker opened up the possibility for an exploration of nuances of sound.

Now jazz is more free than it has ever formally been. Modernism has furnished the performer with an unlimited set of possibilities—Coleman's exploration with pitch as an attempt to transcend the tempered scale—so that jazz is no longer hampered by a limiting framework. In the words of critic and fellow composer/musician Gunther Schuller, "Ornette Coleman's proposition is a very simple one: Release me from the bondage of long outdated harmonic and formal conventions, and I will take you away from the wallpaperlike clichés of my contemporaries and let you hear a world of sound which you have never heard before, which is free, and which is beholden only to its *own* innermost logic and discipline" (liner notes to *Ornette!*). Coleman's music is sheer sound and movement. His chords need no longer resolve. Often there are no chords at all, and musicians in the ensemble are forced, as in *Free Jazz*, to respond without any predetermined framework to guide them. Usually they will respond by paraphrasing or picking up on ideas introduced by the "soloist," who, in turn, may often choose to play off what he hears in the others. Solos in Coleman's music are characterized by notes that seem to have no obvious regard for *a priori* key relationships and rules of modulation. They may, in fact, never gravitate towards a source of stable meaning, never return "home" to the tonic. While an Armstrong solo—with a clearly defined sense of beginning, middle, and end—seems to posit a narrative line or conventional story logic, Coleman's irregular phrasing, and his refusal to employ such standard devices as chorus structures, would seem to suggest that he is no longer interested in simply telling a story. Atonality seeks to call into question the strength of the bond between any language and the reality which that language is said to designate.

Jazz, however, is not a reducible, coherent entity. Many would argue that jazz is now, more than ever, constrained by market forces.

Much of the disturbance occasioned by this "new thing" in jazz seems to have resulted from the widespread impression that atonality lacks "musical" content. The *real* cause for alarm, however, is the threat such jazz poses to those who subscribe to the notion that musical language should produce determinate meanings. While a belief in representation still continues to govern the practice of much diatonic music, atonal jazz, in its attempt to explore a range of musical possibilities, constitutes a movement *away* from representationalism. Atonality's obligation, then, is *not* to something outside musical language. It is interested in process rather than closure, and its commitment, as Schuller says of Coleman's music, is more to the sound and creation of music than to *what happens* once this music has been created. Having invalidated the time-honored belief in the symbolic powers of its own language, atonality is now ready to shock us with its pronouncement that "the shape of jazz to come" is, in fact, here.

Coda

What that analysis of jazz's entry into modernism lacks, I now feel, is a critique of its own metalanguage: an awareness of the extent to which the language of Kristeva and the Tel Quel group may not be fully adequate to describe the complexities of the free jazz that emerged out of the 1960s. For one thing, as Martha Bayles points out, "Modernism has never been a monolith; on the contrary, it contains opposites as extreme as any in cultural history" (32–33). It's possible, indeed, to see some of those very opposites in the debates that have evolved around Coleman's music. Robert Palmer, in his liner notes to Beauty Is a Rare Thing: The Ornette Coleman Quartet's Complete Atlantic Recordings, *puts it thus:*

> *Some took the position that the music's raw blues inflections and emphasis on the group rather than the individual represented a return to traditional black values, which made it Afrocentric. If you were a "black militant," or a white paranoiac, you could even see it as an expression of Black Power. On the other hand, there*

were those who took the many rationalized, overly intellectual analyses of the music with the utmost seriousness. They *identified Coleman's music with the fusion of jazz and contemporary Euro-classical elements, which composer Gunther Schuller called "Third Stream." If Coleman wasn't blackening jazz, they reasoned, he was undoubtedly whitening it.*

Of particular interest here is the fact that a music which I've been affirming as being inward-looking and autonomous is seen by some as reflecting traditional black cultural values, a jazz that I see as moving away *from representationalism, is—in fact has always been—at the center of compelling debates about music's involvement in the organization of social relations. My interpretation of Coleman's jazz, indeed of jazz history, in the preceding analysis suggests, perhaps, that I have been remiss in attending to the complexities of historical processes, to the ways in which our understanding of the aesthetic imaginary is, in fact, always mediated by complex ethicopolitical affiliations and questions. It also suggests, to borrow Peter Bürger's words, that although "[a]esthetic theories may strenuously strive for metahistorical knowledge . . . that they bear the clear stamp of the period of their origin can usually be seen afterward, and with relative ease" (15). I don't mean to imply that suddenly, and unproblematically, I can see clearly now; rather, I want, again, to emphasize the fact that just as the jazz tradition, "[f]ar from being an unchanging and an easily understood historical field . . . is a constantly transforming construction" (Elworth, 58), so too should our interpretive habits be subject to a continuing process of debate, critical reassessment, and inquiry. If George Lipsitz is correct to suggest that jazz has offered intellectual and moral guidance to people all over the world precisely because it privileges "relentless innovation over static tradition," then jazz, as I've already suggested, is an exemplary paradigm for thinking about contemporary critical practice.*

In my haste to read the history of jazz as an evolutionary narrative of the emergence of modernism, I admit that I have privileged the aesthetic at the expense of the ethical. Though I risk upsetting the tidy logic of the overall parallel I am drawing in this book between developments in the history of jazz and developments in the history of literary and cul-

tural theory, let me try to be more precise about what I have in mind. In the previous section, I suggested that the free collective improvisation of Ornette Coleman signalled a turn to an inward-looking music, to a notion of jazz as an autonomous system of signs. If I am now rather uneasy with that earlier argument, and though I clearly no longer hold the assumptions that once shaped my thinking about jazz, I think there is still something here that should continue to command our attention: the fact, for example, that Coleman's Free Jazz *featured a Jackson Pollack painting on its cover, that, more broadly, his radical retreat from traditional conventions and conceptions of musical meaning and practice took place within the context of related inward-looking turns in adjacent disciplines. As Francis Davis suggests in his book* In the Moment, *"With Ornette Coleman, jazz established its permanent avant-garde, its 'new' that would always remain new—comparable to the ongoing attack on tonality in classical music, on narrative in post–First World War fiction, and on representation in twentieth-century art" (145). Martha Bayles refers to this kind of inward-turning "art-for-art's sake retreat from the world" as an "* introverted *modernism" (38). She suggests that an elimination of tonality was one of the principal strategies employed by its musical practitioners (39), and she tells us also that it typically announced itself "as the only possible next step" (38). This latter characteristic too is in keeping with Coleman's aesthetic: think, for example, of some of his early album titles such as* The Shape of Jazz to Come *and* Tomorrow Is the Question.

However focused it was on inward-looking questions of form and technique, the free jazz that, like Coleman's, emerged out of the 1960s surely had its content too. In returning to that content, part of what I now want to understand is how the aesthetic self-positioning I associated with free jazz in the previous section might be seen to relate to the ethicopolitical debates about social identities and representation which I take up in subsequent chapters of this book. This relationship is, admittedly, complicated. On the one hand, for example, it is possible to suggest that the shift in jazz toward musical autonomy has its own ethicopolitical motivations, that the modernist, "art music" character of bebop, and later of free jazz, ought to be read in the context of a strug-

gle for (mainly black) artists to "declare their independence from the marketplace" (DeVeaux, Birth, *13), of their refusal to fulfill the needs and expectations of a mass (mainly white) audience. Similarly, as we have seen, free jazz's deliberate efforts to frustrate our desire to achieve conventional forms of musical coherence might also be seen to be connected with attempts to challenge the gendered legacy of the paradigm of tonality, to envision "narrative structures with feminine endings" (McClary, 19), or, more broadly, to envisage and to reflect egalitarian social orders. As several critics have pointed out, the fact that much of the new jazz associated with Coleman and others emerged in the context of the decolonization of the Third World and the radicalization of civil rights movements "provided a rich source of social and political images and conceptions" (Alan Lewis, 44) with which musicians could "articulate the socio-political aspects of their aesthetic principles" (43). Saxophonist Archie Shepp, another key figure in the new jazz movement in the sixties, puts it this way: jazz "is antiwar; it is opposed to Viet Nam; it is for Cuba; it is for the liberation of all people. That is the nature of jazz. . . . [J]azz is a music itself born out of oppression, born out of the enslavement of my people. It is precisely that" (quoted in Kofsky, 64). Read this way, the jazz of Shepp, Coleman, and others would appear to be initiating a socially progressive form of musical realism.*

On the other hand, as Henry Pleasants argues in Serious Music—and All that Jazz!, *what the inward-looking nature of free jazz represents to its practitioners is "independence from the responsibility of channeling his* [sic] *feelings—presumably genuine and intense—into the forms by which these feelings, sensations, sentiments . . . can be communicated to others" (161). Autonomous music, in this formulation,* lacks *an ethical mooring: in declaring its commitment only to its own self-sufficiency, it is seen to have isolated itself from any broader social purpose, to have, in effect, abandoned its sense of responsibility towards an audience. The evolutionary account of jazz history that I present in the previous section seems, at least in the main, to have taken for granted this kind of severing of music from the world, this splitting off of aesthetic representation from matters ethical.*

As the subsequent chapters in this book should make clear, however, the assumptions that underwrite the judgments we make about aesthetics are, indeed, predicated on the history of materialities governing the conceptual procedures through which we construct our ethicopolitical frames of reference. Most of the material in section one was, for instance, written under the era of high theory, an era in which ethically valenced models of intellectual inquiry commanded little, if any, institutional status. That material, in fact, comes directly out of my interest in the kinds of theories about textuality that were then being privileged during the heyday of semiotic structuralism and deconstruction. If chapter 1 bears the traces of the influence of one of textuality's most prominent theorists, Jacques Derrida—whose courses I had, at the time, been attending at the Institute for the Study of Semiotics and Structuralism in Toronto—the argument that gets played out in the rest of this book undoubtedly bears the mark of "worldliness" that might be said to be one of the defining concerns in the work of another one of my former teachers, Edward Said. The next chapter, in fact, turns to jazz to focus on that very relationship between text and world. That chapter, on the Art Ensemble of Chicago and other musicians who have emerged out of the AACM collective, seeks, in a more fully sustained way, to intervene in some of the key debates I have, if only briefly, sought to open up in this coda to chapter 1. There, in chapter 2, the riven ethical terrain of modernism begins to give way to a newly articulated and equally contradictory postmodern understanding of the music as the product of a historically particular form of cultural practice.

Notes

1. Albert Murray makes a similar comment in *Stomping the Blues*: "[Blues musicianship] is not a matter of having the blues and giving direct personal release to the raw emotion brought on by suffering. It is a matter of mastering the elements of craft required by the idiom" (126).

2. The conventional thirty-two-bar chorus consists of a head or front strain of eight bars repeated twice, an eight-bar bridge, and a repetition of the front strain. It's worth noting here that, despite his departure from the form, Bird did write several tunes in thirty-two-bar form, just as he wrote several based on chord changes taken from standards.

3. Indeed, Lula's comments are accurate to the point of omniscience. Throughout the play she tells Clay things about himself that he admits are true. At one point, Clay remarks, "How'd you know all that? Huh? Really, I mean about Jersey . . . and even the beard. I met you before? You know Warren Enright?" (Baraka, *Dutchman,* 9).

2

The Rehistoricizing of Jazz

Chicago's "Urban Bushmen" and the Problem of Representation

The teachings of Mr. Muhammad stressed how history had been "whitened"—when white men had written history books, the black man simply had been left out. . . . The teachings ring true—to every Negro. You can hardly show me a black adult in America—or a white one, for that matter—who knows from history books anything like the truth about the black man's role. In my own case, once I heard of the "glorious history of the black man," I took special pains to hunt in the library for books that would inform me on details about black history.

Malcolm X, *The Autobiography of Malcolm X,* 175

As a signifier in jazz, the city of Chicago has come to be associated with two movements that, at least ostensibly, have little, if anything, in common. When jazz historians speak of the "Chicago school," they are referring to a group of white Dixieland musicians who were prominent during the 1920s in Chicago. The label "Chicago school," however, is at best misleading because, in its association with the city's white jazz movement, it works to exclude (or at least deemphasize) the "overlapping histories and intertwining experiences" (to use Edward Said's formulation) concurrent with the development of this putative school. More precisely, Chicago in the 20s was not only the center of activity for a community of young white jazz players but also the home for many black New Orleans musicians displaced by the government's closure of Storyville during the First World War. After the secretary of the navy had the brothel district shut down for fear that its activities would pose a threat to the morale of his troops, many of these black musicians moved north to Chicago. What's interesting is that the musicians who developed the Chicago style were "so inspired by the greats of New Orleans jazz that they wanted to emulate their style" (Berendt, 13). The music that came to represent the Chicago school, in other words, was modeled largely on the jazz of the displaced New Orleans musicians living on the south side of Chicago. Insofar as "Chicago school" may have been part of a pattern of designation that appropriated black music by assimilating it into the white cultural mainstream,[1] Chicago itself emerged in the '20s as the site of a struggle for representation. The first movement, the Chicago school, thus fractures in half to reveal its dependence on and derivation from that which its title would efface: black New Orleans jazz. Or, to put it slightly differently, New Orleans jazz, despite its title, actually had its heyday in *Chicago* in the 1920s.

More recently, Chicago has become the site of a new breed of jazz activity: a sustained effort to rediscover the role of black tradition and history. Emerging in tandem with the kind of formalism that, as I suggested in chapter 1, had come to characterize jazz in the early '60s (particularly the "free jazz" associated with Ornette Coleman), members of the Chicago-based AACM collective (Association for the Advancement of Creative Musicians) sought to combine their own interests in black heritage with the seemingly contradictory teachings of the formalists, who showed us that jazz was finally unable to posit a reality *outside* its own language. The result of that particular, if problematic, juxtaposition will form the basis of this chapter.

Indeed, one of the most striking features of the music that has emerged out of the AACM is its attempt to retain a kind of formalist aesthetic of autonomy while simultaneously (and paradoxically) calling our attention to the ways in which that music is historically situated and culturally produced. I want to suggest here that this interplay of "textuality" and "worldliness" (to borrow again from Said), or "word and world" (in Mackey's formulation) can be purposefully understood if placed in the context of broader debates about representation, specifically debates about how artists, critics, and theorists from minoritized cultures have sought to redefine the processes through which knowledge is produced, distributed, and legitimized.

I'm thinking, for example, of the profoundly influential work of Stuart Hall, a theorist who, like Said, has pointed to the complex ways in which "machineries of representation," supported by dominant spheres of knowledge production, work to promote and consolidate commonsense notions of identity. Hall's work shows us what is at stake in practices of representation, and asks us to attend with rigor to the ways in which representations are often taken for granted, naturalized, and accepted as self-evident. Cultural studies pedagogy and methodology, Hall and others have cogently argued, have to be concerned with representations and, in particular, with how representations construct meaning, identity, and history, and with the question of whose interests representations serve and have served. How and why, that is, is knowledge produced and maintained? What kinds of things count (or don't count) as knowledge? Who has the power to determine what counts as knowledge? How do we understand the complex relations among knowledge, power, and history? As Hall writes in his essay "New Ethnicities": "[H]ow things are represented and the 'machineries' and regimes of representation in a culture do play a *constitutive*, and not merely a reflexive, after-the-event, role. This gives questions of culture and ideology, and the scenarios of representation—subjectivity, identity, politics—a formative, not merely an expressive, place in the constitution of social and political life" (443).

The AACM is a musicians' cooperative established in 1965 by pianist Muhal Richard Abrams and others to encourage innovative black musicians to create their own opportunities to play their music. "Although music was the primary concern of the AACM," writes Alun Ford, "its basis was fundamentally ethical" (39). Collective member Joseph Jarman puts it this way: "An organization like the AACM gives a plan, a program, a power, an approach away, not only for black people but for all American people, further, all *world* people, to reorient themselves towards social values that can be useful and functional" (quoted in Mandel, "It *Can* Be Done," 41). If jazz itself, as I suggested in the introduction, has historically been a process-oriented model of performance that, with its focus on improvisation, has emphasized communal interaction, responsibility, and mutual forms of tolerance amongst both its practitioners and its listeners, the AACM has sought to extend the cooperative principle beyond music and "into the realm of practical life" (Rockwell, 169). AACM member and tenor saxophonist Edward Wilkerson Jr. puts it this way: "It's a tradition in black music that it has certain social implications, purposes beyond 'good music.' It has function in people's lives" (quoted in Corbett, 120). The organization, from its very inception, has had precisely such a social function: it has helped set up concerts, recordings, and teaching sessions, and also sponsored a free training programme for young players in inner-city Chicago. Its work attests to the capacity of non-market-driven institutions in the black community to generate access to self-representation. Jazz writer Joachim Berendt describes the AACM as "a grouping of musicians which has had much significance, not only musically, but also in terms of consciousness in the self-identification process of black musicians" (359). In seeking alternative models for the presentation, production, and distribution of its music and the administration of its cultural activities, the AACM, as many of its members have stated explicitly, needs to be understood in the context of aggrieved peoples seeking to reclaim their history and their identity. Abrams and John Shenoy Jackson make explicit the sociopolitical function of the organization in a 1973 report:

> The AACM is attempting to precipitate activity geared toward finding a solution to the basic contradictions which face Black people. . . . [It] intends to show how the disadvantaged and the disenfranchised can come together and determine their own strategies for political and economic freedom, thereby determining their own destinies. This will not only create a new day for Black artists but for all Third World inhabitants; a new day of not only participation but also of control. (Quoted in Radano, *New Musical Figurations,* 91)

Another collective member, drummer and percussionist Don Moye, corroborates this view. "The main purpose [of the AACM]," he says, "is the dissemination of 'great Black music.' To further the music on our own terms, without the intervention of the normal industry manipulations" (quoted in Green, 16). In his book on AACM innovator Anthony Braxton, Graham Lock situates the emergence of the AACM within a broader sociohistorical context: "[T]he AACM's political goals, notably their emphases on independence, self-help and researching black culture, exemplified the mood of an era when the struggle for Civil Rights and the aspirations of black nationalism were at the forefront of events" (*Forces,* 34). He goes on to argue that "[t]he additional factor that really underlined the AACM's status as a turning-point in the evolution of African-American music was their experimental approach to sound, space, structure. In Chicago, the outlines of new musical languages were beginning to take shape" (34).

Lock's comments, however, do more than simply affirm the fact that the music coming out of Chicago in the '60s reflected a context outside itself; more importantly, I would argue, they tell us that the emergence of this music was intricately caught up in a sophisticated network of other social, political, and musical factors, none of which unproblematically engendered the others. So, rather than preserving an opposition between text and context, rather than seeing the AACM's music as a reflection of, and thus something distinct from, the sociohistorical conditions of the day, Lock signally leads us to recognize that the music was itself *part* of the creative process of history.

In light of these comments about the relationship between text and context, or, roughly summarized, between music and history, I would like now to turn to the texts (performances, recordings) of the Art Ensemble of Chicago, an AACM group which perhaps best exemplifies the tension between a nonrepresentational theory and practice of music and a burgeoning interest in historicism. Made up, until his recent death from liver cancer in November 1999, of trumpeter Lester Bowie, bassist Malachi Favors, horn player Roscoe Mitchell, drummer Moye, and, until 1993, horn player Joseph Jarman[2]—all, in fact, remarkable multi-instrumentalists—the group has come to be recognized as the main proponent of a new musical genre, a genre, indeed, which it has helped to define. While the ensemble's music is notated, artistically arranged with internal structural and thematic logic, critics have repeatedly focused on its improvisational character, perhaps drawing too heavily in their reviews on the seemingly unwrought and abstract quality of the band's proceedings.

By now, the Art Ensemble of Chicago has become increasingly well-known for incorporating various black influences, traditions, histories, and forms into its music. Moye puts it thus: "We try to deal with forms that go back to the very foundation of what our music is about; coming out of the African heritage" (quoted in Green, 18). Favors, Moye, and Jarman usually perform in primitive garb and face paint, and a typical Art Ensemble concert tends to be something of a quasi-theatrical romp (complete with pantomime, flag waving, minstrelsy, staged pandemonium) through jazz from its earliest forms to its more recent manifestations: in short, a kind of abridged history of accomplishments in black music. The ensemble's slogan—"Great Black Music: Ancient to the Future"—sums up the philosophy of these musicians and makes explicit their effort to expose the African roots of their music. "Great Black Music," in itself, is a telling motto because it forces us to recognize the extent to which the quintet is engaged in an attempt to destabilize received notions of genre in music. In an interview published in 1984, Lester Bowie emphasized the fact that the Art Ensemble of Chicago remains "one of the only groups of musicians that [has] labelled [its] own music" (quoted in Green, 17).

The right to name their own music: this is what these musicians have been struggling to achieve. It is perhaps not surprising, then, that members of the Art Ensemble resent the attempts made by some critics to see commonalities between "Great Black Music" and the "new music" associated with European or American avant-garde composers. For one thing, as Moye's comments quoted above should make clear, the Art Ensemble's music is decidedly not "new." Such comparisons are also seen as part of an imperializing need on the part of these critics to locate white cultural precedents for black music. In Bowie's words, the critics are "afraid" to refer to Great Black Music: "This just goes to show you how racist some of these publications are" (quoted in Green, 18).

In its insistence on naming its own music, on asserting the right to reclaim its own cultural history and identity, the ensemble is engaged in creating institutions and practices that counter the devastating and dehumanizing effects of misrepresentation. It's perhaps worth noting here that while the AACM is perhaps the most hugely influential and most amply documented organization of its kind, it is not the only (or even the first) artist-run collective in jazz: four years before the formation of the AACM, for example, Los Angeles–based pianist Horace Tapscott founded the Underground Musicians Association, soon renamed the Union of God's Musicians and Artists Ascension (UGMAA) and the Pan Afrikan Peoples Arkestra, to nurture local talent in the African-American community. Also worth mentioning is the fact that the members of the Art Ensemble have certainly not been alone in their efforts to thematize African history in music: Randy Weston, John Carter, John Coltrane, Sonny Rollins, Abdullah Ibrahim, Horace Tapscott, and Sun Ra (to whom I'll return in chapter 4) have all, to cite some of the more well-known examples, turned to Africa to seek both inspiration for their music and alternative sources for knowledge production. In his book on the role that the idea of Africa has played through the course of jazz history, Norman Weinstein discusses some of these musicians, telling us that:

> African-American artists produce art in the context of combating centuries of racist-constructed imaginations of Africa. Faced with centuries of distorted visual and written accounts depicting Africans as uncivilized ape-men inhabiting a savagely dark continent, faced with the horrors of the slave trade and European colonialism and neo-colonialism, Africans and many African Americans have developed a counter-racist imagination of Africa. (11)

While Weinstein does not mention either the AACM or the Art Ensemble of Chicago, his comments are helpful because they situate the AACM's work within the broader context of subjugated peoples struggling to achieve control over the ways in which their histories, epistemologies, and identities are institutionalized, represented, and codified. Muhal Richard Abrams, suggests Radano, was himself so enormously influential precisely because he "underscored the AACM's intent to correct the persistent negative stereotypes of the jazz musician, which had defamed the black heritage and hindered artistic growth" ("Jazzin' the Classics," 85). Recall too the comments I quoted from Fred Wei-han Ho in my introduction:

> Oppressed peoples suffer from their history, identity, and culture being defined, (mis)represented and explicated by [their] oppressors. The struggle to redefine and reimage our existence involves the struggle to reject the stereotyping, distortions, and devaluing embodied in the classifications of conquerors and racists. In essence, the struggle over how to describe past and present reality is to change reality. (133)

The ensemble's use of alternative models of performativity and signification in music is, I'd like to suggest, part of a black institution-building strategy whose aim is precisely "to change reality," to reimagine, reinvent, and reclaim histories that have hitherto been represented and constructed in the service of dominant models of knowledge production. "Black folks got to change the ways / take in their hands the facts of life," writes Jarman in his lyrics to "U.S. of A.—U. of S.A." (*Art Ensemble of Soweto*), making explicit the ensemble's politics of self-determination. In his book *Crusoe's Footprints*, Patrick Brantlinger makes a related point about black culture in relation to the struggle for access to self-representation and identity formation, reminding us that "the struggle for Afro-American literacy and literature (and all art forms) has been a struggle against the powerful, white voices, discourses, and disciplines that at first sought to deny the black writer the very instruments of writing, then later sought to deny to his or her writing either authenticity or the status of literature or both" (154).

Reading the Art Ensemble's work in this context, we find ourselves confronting a variant on the problem of representation with which I inaugurated this chapter, and, once again, the city of Chicago is the site of the struggle. Now, however, rather than nurturing white musicians, who, however innocently, replicated the form but denied the content of the music of their black counterparts,[3] Chicago has, in effect, become the home of the resistance movement. As if to signal that change, the group names itself (Art Ensemble of *Chicago*) and its music (Great *Black* Music) in such a fashion that the illustrious history of black music in Chicago becomes an undeniable reality.

Despite this concerted effort to reclaim the origins of Great Black Music, the ensemble remains uncomfortable with the possibility of a wholesale recovery of the past through representation. This discomfort is registered in a number of different ways, and through an enormously wide-ranging set of representational practices. It's partly there, I think, in the fact that Lester Bowie frequently performed not in face paint and African garb but rather sporting a lab coat, "as if," in Aldon Nielsen's words, "to emphasize the experimental nature of [the ensemble's] music, and wearing a hard hat, as if to underscore the danger implicit in such experiments" (240). Implicit in Bowie's choice of onstage attire seems to be a self-conscious awareness of the extent to which the ensemble's reconstruction of the past is informed by its own historically situated, culturally produced position in the present. The lab coat, too, might be read as a parody of rational, racist white culture, and the hard hat a critique of the constructivism that sets up white culture as a false historical norm. Roscoe Mitchell too, it should be noted, performs *sans* face paint and African garb; unlike all the others in the group, in fact, he usually performs in casual attire, "as if," to quote Nielsen again, "he had paused in the course of his ordinary day to play some of this extraordinary music" (240). In contrast to Jarman, Moye, and Favors, Mitchell, in his ordinary clothes, foregrounds the present, reminds us that the ensemble's engagement with history is not simply an unproblematic representation of the past, that, indeed, their involvement with the past is predicated on a simultaneous commitment to perform and, perhaps, to transform the history of the present.

The discomfort is also there, of course, in the music's structure. Rather than following standard chord progressions and traditional solo structures, large portions of the ensemble's repertoire are devoted to impromptu explorations of a semiotic freedom. These freely improvised passages bespeak a reliance on a kind of formalist aesthetic: jazz as a system of signs with no necessary relationship to anything outside itself. Notes are played not so much for their worth as semantic signifiers, but rather for their sound value. Listen, for example, to the ensemble's "Old Time Southside Street Dance," from the 1980 recording *Full Force*. Although an uninitiated listener might be apt to dismiss this piece as little more than excessive noodling, I'd like to suggest that it does more than simply confirm one writer's suggestion that the ensemble employs sound for sound's sake (Grindley, 274). While certainly indicative of the group's penchant for free improvisation, this musical moment—and others like it—suggests the extent to which history, for the Art Ensemble, is not simply a realm of recoverable facts. The title of the piece, "Old Time Southside Street Dance," invokes history; it generates expectations of musical referentiality. But the piece itself, I think, does little to fulfill these expectations. The improvisational and experimental stretches seem new (rather than old), and the very thought of someone even *attempting* to dance to this music seems far-fetched. The ironic gap between what the title of this piece leads us to expect and what the piece itself delivers is evidence of the band's awareness that any representation of the past, any evocation of "old times," is inevitably a reconstruction informed by the present.

This music, thus, engages past and present in a kind of healthy and inquisitive dialogue, a dialogue that approximates intellectual historian Dominick LaCapra's goal for historical studies: "[T]exts . . . should be carried into the present—with implications for the future—in a dialogical fashion" (63). For LaCapra, what such dialogue means is a recognition of the impossibility of both "the purely documentary representation of the past and the 'presentist' quest for liberation from the 'burden' of history through unrestrained fictionalizing and mythologizing" (63). Familiar historical genres in music—ballads, marches, blues and gospel numbers, even rock, ska, and funk—are, throughout the ensemble's repertoire, reencoded, parodied, undermined by painfully long silences, and often disrupted by a self-consciousness that takes the form of sounds and noises from any of a number of "little instruments" which have become the trademark of the new Chicago school: car horns, conch shells, whistles, sirens, street-corner noisemakers. By subsuming familiar, historically laden sound sources within the context of a newly articulated musical idiom, the ensemble unsettles any assumptions we might have about ready access to the past. Even in the representationally driven "U.S. of A.—U. of S.A.," the opening track from their 1991 collaboration with Soweto's Amabutho Male Chorus, for example, the more accessible sonorities and familiar calypso-like rhythms give way, before long, to squawks, whoops, whistles, growls, free breaks, and the ensemble's trademark crescendos of noise. "Theme for Sco," from the 1982 release *Urban Bushmen*—an album title that itself calls attention to the interplay between past and present characteristic of much of the group's work[4]—offers another apt example of what I have in mind. This time the genre is clearly recognizable, but both the marked rhythms and the familiar melodies of this march are parodied by frequent blurts and beeps from the ensemble's "little instruments."

These "little instruments," in fact, might be seen as a kind of microcosm for the problem of representation that the band, as a whole, poses. Though, as I suggested a moment ago, these instruments function to problematize various forms of representation and expression in the ensemble's repertoire, they paradoxically serve to call our attention to the music's origins. They are, as Valerie Wilmer points out, part of a tradition "that started with children banging on washboards and tin-cans, blowing down pieces of rubber-hose and strumming wires stretched between nails on a wall, a tradition deeply rooted in Africa" (112). Radano too suggests that these instruments "recall the makeshift sound sources of an earlier time in black history" (*New Musical Figurations,* 107). Here, then, we arrive at the crux of the problem, to what Linda Hutcheon sees as the paradox of postmodernism: the juxtaposition of "that which is inward-directed and belongs to the world of art (such as parody) and that which is outward-directed and belongs to 'real-life' (such as history)" (*Politics of Postmoderism,* 2).

The new Chicago jazz, despite its indebtedness to and involvement with black tradition, then, refuses simply to posit history as a kind of autonomous and recuperable narrative. By problematizing and parodying past texts and genres in the history of jazz, members of the AACM urge us to examine the ways in which we make meaning in culture. Or, in Hutcheon's words, representation "now self-consciously acknowledges its existence as representation—that is, as interpreting (indeed as creating) its referent, not as offering direct and immediate access to it" (34). What, though, in the ensemble's case, are the ethicopolitical implications of such self-consciousness? And how does an aesthetics of parody and intertextuality—cited by Hutcheon as two defining features of postmodernism—figure in terms of the AACM's involvement with an institutional politics of self-determination? How might the inward-looking strategies of parody, self-consciousness, and intertextuality be seen to intervene in our understanding of outward-looking historical processes?

The debate about the ethicopolitical efficacy of an avant-garde aesthetic is, of course, not a particularly new one. Christian Wolff, in his essay "On Political Texts and New Music," for example, takes up the question of whether the ivory-towerism associated with the avant-garde "makes impossible the wider communication necessary for political content" by pointing to the difference in attitude between two politically motivated composers: Cornelius Cardew, who insisted "there can be no politically effective avant-garde art" and Luigi Nono, "who composes in an uncompromisingly advanced manner" (195). I touched on a related set of matters in the Prelude and Coda to chapter 1, where the free jazz of Ornette Coleman offered a point of departure for reflecting on the ideological workings of jazz's musical properties. The Art Ensemble of Chicago, given its explicit involvement in attempting, institutionally and musically, to intervene in contemporary social relations, requires, I think, a slightly different framework of understanding. Unlike Coleman, after all, its members are adamant in their insistence that we interpret their music in relation to the experience of social alterity. If Coleman's ventures into free improvisation were largely propelled by aesthetic considerations derived from the inward-looking teachings of modernism, then members of the AACM, as Radano notes, made use of "the abstract, nontonal sound world of modernism" (*New Musical Figurations,* 108) in order actively to "recast [its] dominant styles into a personal musical vocabulary that placed the black musical legacy at the forefront" (111). And their deliberate efforts to draw upon, parody, and rework traditional, historically laden sonorities, I'm suggesting, function to alert us to what is at stake in representations of history, to broaden our understanding of how and why we represent the past, of whose story counts as history. "As the AEC disinters, resuscitates, rummages, and rearranges rhythms, melodies, and sounds from the past," writes Don Palmer in a recent feature article on the group in *JAZZIZ* magazine, "it creates music that's more syncretic and idiosyncratic than exotic. . . . Certain elements of tradition aren't just rediscovered, but are transformed and made relevant for the present and future" (52). That relevance, it seems to me, arises out of the challenge the AEC's texts pose to the homogenizing tendencies in dominant history-making traditions. In contrast to the institutionalized silencing of dissident voices in canonical representations of history, the process that Malcolm X, in the epigraph with which I began this chapter, called "whitening," the ensemble cleverly and deliberately introduces noise into hegemonic, historically laden sonorities. It deploys nontempered sounds and intonations in an effort to create a space for the articulation and revaluing of dissonant histories. Musically, but also ideologically, then, dissonance can be heard both as a marker of the AEC's self-conscious problematizing of history and as a strategic intervention into dominant social relations.

History-making too, as they remind us through their emphasis on play and performativity, is a theatrical experience. Historian Greg Dening, in his recent, aptly titled book *Performances*, would seem to concur: he argues, in fact, that "[a]cademic history has lost its moral force because it has been subverted by its own reality effects and has lost its sense of theatre" (126–27). For Dening, the act of restoring to history-making its sense of theatricality, performance consciousness, and self-awareness will work to re-ethicize the discipline. Indeed, the ensemble's effort to reclaim history as a performative model of agency and intervention rather than as a master narrative that offers unproblematized access to information about the past puts ethical pressure on dominant spheres of knowledge production. It does so, as I have argued, by participating in an attempt to redefine the processes through which knowledge is produced, distributed, and legitimized. The ensemble's conception (and practice) of performance opens up resonant questions about history, identity, and the cultural politics of knowledge production, and the dilemma at the heart of their work (what I'm here calling "the problem of representation") is one that, more generally, might be said to characterize most politically inflected forms of contemporary performance. The tension in their texts between, on the one hand, reclaiming black history and cultural identity and, on the other, self-consciously undermining (and parodying) any such efforts to reclaim that history finds a parallel in much contemporary performance. As theater historian and performance studies critic Marvin Carlson notes, politically oriented performance is frequently forced to negotiate the tension between "the desire to provide a grounding for effective political action by affirming a specific identity and subject position, and the desire to undermine the essentialist assumptions of all cultural constructions" (182). Such performance, says Carlson, slips "back and forth between claiming an identity position and ironically questioning the cultural assumptions that legitimate it. The goal is not to deny identity, but on the contrary to provide through performance alternate possibilities for identity positions outside those authenticated by conventional performance and representation" (183).

The kinds of alternate possibilites that emerge out of the ensemble's performances invite recognition of the extent to which cultural identity needs to be understood as a contextualized social process rather than a timeless and unchanging essence. James Clifford, taking up the relational notion of authenticity, suggests that "[g]roups negotiating their identity in contexts of domination and exchange . . . patch themselves together" (338). Now "patching," perhaps, seems too haphazard a metaphor to account for the Art Ensemble of Chicago's politics of identity formation, or to describe its intensely self-conscious involvement with history. Clifford's comments, nevertheless, do seem to me to be helpful for getting at the ways in which the AEC's performance practices, with their improvisatory impulse, their tactical sensitivity to the needs and desires of the moment, can restore and reinvent history. For if a performance's ethical dimension is best understood not in terms of its commitment to empirical verifiability or to conventional models of historical representation, but rather to the presentation of "alternate possibilities,"[5] then the ensemble's efforts symbolically to recover, retell, and reconstruct black histories and cultural traditions have the salutary effect of reinvigorating our understanding of art's role (and it is perhaps no coincidence that "Art" appears in the ensemble's name) in the complex relationship between social praxis and the construction of cultural identities. Art, that is, does not simply reflect external reality; rather it plays a formative role in the constitution of social life, in the ways in which people take responsibility for creating their own histories, for participating in the management of their own social and political realities. Whether it's the car horns, kazoos, gongs, and noisemakers that buck the accepted standards of embodied systems of knowledge, value, and culture, or the long stretches of—sometimes raucous, sometimes subtle—free playing that characterizes much of the ensemble's work, what's at issue in the music is an insistence that these musicians are defining their own identity, and doing so on their own terms. Appropriately, on a cut such as "U.S. of A.—U. of S.A.," the explicit statement of self-determination that I quoted earlier—"Black folks got to change the ways / take in their hands the facts of life"—is voiced not in the context of the boisterous calypso rhythms and catchy melodies that dominate the piece, but rather on the heels of a moment during which the group is engaged in all-out experimentation with a range of tonal effects including squawks, sirens, whoops, whistles, and blurts of low-register horn sounds. The kind of taking-in-hand the group has in mind, then, involves both the reclamation and the transformation of historically laden sound sources. Of importance here (and indeed throughout the Art Ensemble's repertoire) is what Samuel Floyd Jr., enlarging on the work of Henry Louis Gates, calls "musical signifyin(g)," the deployment in African-American music "of preexisting material as a means of demonstrating respect for or poking fun at a musical style, process, or practice through parody, pastiche, implication, indirection, humor, tone play or word play" (8). "U.S. of A.—U. of S.A." is, indeed, exemplary as a signifyin(g) act, for here the familiar sounds of calypso are reconfigured through performance practices that accent the very ways in which black folks can, to borrow a phrase from later in the same song, "take up the power / take over the show."

As strategies for social and political intervention, the Art Ensemble's eclectic historicism, its playful and parodic revoicings of familiar musical genres and traditions, and its self-conscious problematization of and signifyin(g) on the very histories it seeks to rehabilitate point to the fact that black cultural repertoires (to borrow from Stuart Hall) need to be "heard, not simply as the recovery of a lost dialogue bearing clues for the production of new musics (because there is never any going back to the old in a simple way), but as what they are—adaptations, moulded to the mixed, contradictory, hybrid spaces of popular culture. They are not the recovery of something pure that we can, at last, live by" ("What Is This," 471). Hall is not talking here about the Art Ensemble of Chicago, but his comments about black popular culture seem very resonantly to speak to some of the issues at stake in the ensemble's engagement with history. His suggestion that we cannot simply or unproblematically go back to some pure or essential past, for instance, provides a useful context for helping to clarify our understanding of why these musicians, so committed to reaffirming black histories, also feel compelled to be self-conscious about their art, to deploy a formalist emphasis on nontonal sound structures to foreground their own roles in reconstructing past traditions and to insist on the situatedness of their own representations.

What the ensemble is after, I'd like to suggest, is not a reclamation of some pure lost past, but rather something that all jazz musicians, in effect, might be said to push us toward: a recognition of the extent to which knowledge (including our knowledge of the past) is more performative than informative. It's such a recognition that leads the British cultural materialist critic Terence Hawkes to take his methodological cue specifically from jazz. Hawkes, in *That Shakespeherian Rag: Essays on a Critical Process*, suggests that because jazz performance involves the act of "[r]esponding to, improvising on, 'playing' with, re-creating, synthesizing and interpreting 'given' structures of all kinds" (118), rather than the simple transmission and replaying of received texts, it offers a resonant model for contemporary critical practice. Indeed, the altered set of methodological imperatives implied by this recognition that knowledge is performative seems very much in keeping with the kinds of theoretical debates and critical perspectives that have, in recent years, emerged to redefine our understanding of the process of historical inquiry. Contemporary theoretical work by thinkers influenced by postmodern theory (I'm thinking, for example, of the cultural materialists and their American counterparts, the New Historicists) has profoundly unsettled traditional assumptions about the relation of interpreters to the pasts that form their objects of inquiry and analysis. Such work has been particularly useful for oppositional critics who have sought to challenge the cultural and political force of hegemonic systems of representation. The Art Ensemble of Chicago's self-consciousness in this context would again appear to have a salient political function: it serves not only to call our attention to the constructedness of history (and to encourage consequent questions about the interests served by those constructions) but also to provide a performative enactment of the complex and contradictory role that the process of identity formation plays for black Americans in the disruption of dominant social relations. At a cultural moment when the teachings of black history have been subjected to an institutional process of "whitening," the ensemble's performances and recordings made clear the ethical necessity for African-American artists to engage in struggles over identity politics as a way of providing a grounding for resistance to forms of oppression and domination. Yet to engage in that struggle without theoretical self-consciousness, without recognizing that identities are not fixed or pure essences naturally defined by the objective character of particular social groups but rather cultural constructions and performances, some of which become politically meaningful in different historical contexts, would be counterproductive: in short, there can be no easy return to essentialized notions of identity.

For all the ensemble's efforts to reclaim black history, to assert control over the ways in which black cultural identities are constructed, mobilized, and taken up in practices of representation, questions also abound about the appropriateness of their chosen musical idioms for expressing the struggles and the energies of misrepresented peoples. Again we're stumbling here on the kinds of broader questions about ethics and aesthetics that I've broached, if in slightly different terms, earlier in the book. Does innovative and challenging music of the sort that emerges from the AACM lend itself to advancing a political goal of black self-determination, or have these artists been limited in their ability to facilitate social change on a broader scale? Is there a correlation between artistic form and political efficacy? Do simplicity of form and accessibility of style better enable a progressive political consciousness? Have collectives such as the AACM achieved their ethical goal of wresting black music from the control of white Eurocentric institutions and discourses? Is it possible for uncompromising artists such as the Art Ensemble of Chicago to have a transformative impact, to achieve the kind of wider accessibility that might be needed for an effective politics? Interestingly, as AACM board member Carol Parks notes in an essay, "Still in the Blood," published in a program book celebrating the collective's twenty-fifth anniversary, AACM members have sought to confront "the drawbacks of experimentation at a time when they wanted to make their music more accessible" (quoted in Mandel, "Sheltering," 56). Bowie and others in the AACM have been known to bemoan the lack of audiences for innovative music, and the lack of opportunity in their own Chicago forced the Art Ensemble for a time, just as it forced Anthony Braxton, to abandon the AACM's community-building ideals in their hometown of Chicago in favor of professional opportunities in Europe (see Radano, *New Musical Figurations,* 140).

While debates continue about the political impact and efficacy of the AACM's strategies, the Art Ensemble, which recently celebrated its thirty-third anniversary, has released a new recording, *Coming Home Jamaica*, its first in nearly a decade. The recording appears on a major label (Atlantic), and, what's more, it's perhaps one of the group's most accessible outings to date. From the boisterous, rhythmically charged opening rhythm and blues number, "Grape Escape," to the wistful eloquence of "Malachi," to the hard-driving, catchy calypso piece, "Lotta Colada," which closes the set, *Coming Home Jamaica* reveals precisely what we ought to expect from a group that has worked together for so long: a collective wisdom and energy. Missing, though, is much of the innovative edge that has characterized the ensemble's playing for all these years. In "Grape Escape," for example, the rhythm section seems surprisingly static: bassist Favors never wavers from his simple Willie Dixon walking bass line, even during his "solo" spot, while drummer Moye, likewise, holds fast to his frenzied Bo Diddley two-beat shuffle throughout the entire piece. In short, there's little here in the way of the kinds of disruptions and digressions that we have come to expect from these musicians. And even the parody and self-consciousness would seem to be at a minimum: the historically laden sound sources that dominate the album (calypso in "Lotta Colada," reggae in "Strawberry Mango") appear here relatively unfiltered. How, then, might we understand this move toward greater accessibility?

Certainly there's nothing unprecedented about innovative jazz artists opting to record or to perform more accessible kinds of music: think, for example, of Lester Bowie's own solo projects with his Brass Fantasy, a group that revamps not only familiar soul and funk numbers, but also pop tunes by, among others, Michael Jackson and Whitney Houston, or of the massively influential freewheeling saxophonist David Murray, whose recent recordings include a funk date and a Grateful Dead tribute album. Think too of critics such as Stanley Crouch: once a proud champion of innovative music (and a huge supporter of some of David Murray's early "out" offerings) and now a staunch guardian of neoconservative jazz and the Marsalis revival. What makes the Art Ensemble's current forays into more accessible forms of musical expression particularly interesting is the fact that the group's intrepid spirit of innovation and experimentation has always somehow seemed politically driven. Now music and politics, as the previous chapter suggested, have a complex working relationship, and there is, as we have seen, no easy correlation between particular styles of music and sociopolitical moorings or affiliations. It does, however, seem tempting in the case of groups such as the Art Ensemble of Chicago to argue that political dissidence and musical dissonance go hand in hand, to suggest that critical opposition to dominant models of knowledge production takes as one of its salient manifestations an allegiance to forms of artistic expression that cannot readily be accommodated into our received frames of reference. This, in effect, was Theodor Adorno's argument about the critical force of avant-garde classical music. Adorno, of course, despised jazz, and it might, indeed, seem odd to invoke him in the context of the present discussion (I'll be returning to Adorno on jazz in chapter 6); nevertheless, his insistence that the very inaccessibility of modern works of art needed to be seen as intricately connected to their ability to oppose the dominant workings of culture commands our respectful attention here. Does the oppositional force of the AEC's music, then, reside (at least in part) in its inaccessibility? Or, alternatively, should we understand the recent move toward more accessible forms of music to mean that the group may finally be positioned to reach the kinds of audiences that might enable it to disseminate its political message on a broader social scale?

Both of these conclusions, it seems to me, are inadequate; both fail to engage the complexities of the Art Ensemble's music and performances. For one thing, history has recorded salient instances of political dissonance being achieved through an attempt to "pass" as nondissonant (think of Houston Baker's notion of the "mastery of form" in his book on the Harlem Renaissance).

And for another, who is to say that accessibility of form necessarily equals efficacious dissemination of a political message? A superficial listener who hears the AEC's more accessible music may be no more politicized than a deep listener who listens to their inaccessible work. The AEC has always walked a fine line between innovation and tradition, and much of its critical edge has been lodged precisely in the ability of Great Black Music to confound the capacities of dominant systems of classification and knowledge production to come to terms with it. Trombonist and longtime AACM member George Lewis makes a related point about the ways in which the musical interaction that takes place between musicians during an Art Ensemble performance raises havoc with our settled habits of musical understanding: "One thing to remember about the Art Ensemble is how they use sound to signify on each other. . . . A reverent spiritual texture offered by one musician will be rudely interrupted by an *ah-ooh-gah* horn or a field holler from another. The ability of the Art Ensemble's Great Black Music to laugh at itself makes stiff, corporate, and self-appointed guardians of black musical tradition suddenly seem faintly ridiculous" (quoted in Don Palmer, 51–52). Lewis has in mind here the specific challenge that the ensemble's inventiveness and self-consciousness pose to the neoconservatism associated with Wynton Marsalis and the Lincoln Center, but I want, more generally, to extend his analysis to point to the ways in which the Art Ensemble, as I've been suggesting throughout this chapter, encourages us to conflate its repertoire of insurgent musical practices with its cultural politics, to consider its sonic innovation in the context of complex levels of interaction among history, representation, collective identities, and agency. I want too, despite my strenuous objections to the elitist assumptions governing both Adorno's denunciation of jazz and his celebration of modern art's inaccessibility, to hold onto his assessment that innovation is the key to genuine social change.

Yet, if radical democratic practices are to be built not from an emerging elite of insurgent thinkers touting self-determination for black avant-garde musicians but from a broader participatory social base, then it should, perhaps, not surprise us to hear that the AEC's latest recording may well be designed to court popular appeal. Such appeal does not necessarily mean an abandonment of the group's politics. Indeed, it behooves us to recognize that the ensemble's music has always been contextually nuanced, its interventions understood as the varied tactics of a complexly situated social group. We need, for example, to recall that its ideological and musical deployment of strategies of exception and difference occurred at a historical moment when black popular culture was being colonized by the culture industry: specifically, as we have seen, the AACM's politics of cultural self-expression and self-determination was, in the '60s and '70s, a response to the perceived need to struggle for access to self-representation. In an essay on the marketing of black popular music, Reebee Garofalo notes that during the '60s "African American artists were simply swept away in the wash of more marketable (read white) performers" ("Culture," 278). Frank Kofsky makes a similar point in *Black Nationalism and the Revolution in Music*, suggesting that "ownership of the leading economic institutions of jazz [was] vested in the hands of entrepreneurs whose preeminent goal [was] not the enhancement of the art but the taking of a profit" (60). Kofsky goes on to argue that such institutional consolidation over the modes of cultural production would continue to be detrimental for black jazz musicians "as long as the artists do not themselves exert any control over the nightclubs, booking agencies, recording companies and, in short, the terms of their collective employment" (60). I've suggested here that the AACM played a hugely influential role in exerting precisely this kind of control (and I'll make a related argument for the importance of Sun Ra in chapter 4). While the blossoming of innovative arts organizations such as the AACM during the '60s helped create access to public life for blacks to forge what, in the book's conclusion, I'll call an alternative public sphere, the question that, I think, needs to be asked about the Art Ensemble's *Coming Home Jamaica* is whether the apparent lack of an avant-garde aesthetic on this latest recording may have something to do with the way in which changing conditions of production work to reconstitute both context and agency: might the fact that there are now, in the late '90s, more blacks working as promoters and presenters of music and occupying management positions in the recording industry suggest that an avant-gardist position is no longer politically necessary? Is *Coming Home Jamaica* inviting us to recognize the extent to which a strategy that was once politically efficacious may now, from our contemporary perspective, look like elitism?

Or is the Art Ensemble just having fun, teasing its longtime listeners by doing what it's done all along (unsettling our assumptions about the music they perform) while hooking first-time listeners with catchy melodies, infectious rhythms, and a glossy, consumable product? The group's latest move, however we might choose to interpret its political resonances, puts me in mind of a related set of matters I've myself had to grapple with as the artistic director for The Guelph Jazz Festival. Indeed, one of the problems that presenters of leading-edge jazz and creative improvised music have frequently had to confront is the question of how best to "finance" performances by artists who aren't likely, because of the innovative (and frequently challenging) nature of what they do, to draw either sponsorship support or significant revenue at the box office. I'll turn to this question (and how Guelph has sought to respond to it) in more detail in chapter 6, but for now what interests me is the extent to which the AEC's latest recording might, in fact, be read in terms of a similar dynamic of operation. For years, as the group's members have often reminded us, the group has suffered neglect; now, with a glossily packaged accessible new recording on a widely distributed major label, the group is poised to garner more performance opportunities, to command higher fees, and to work in front of larger audiences. Just as music festivals are often forced to compromise their artistic mandate by booking large-appeal popular artists in order to "pay for" performances by lesser-known innovative players, the accessibility of the AEC's latest recording might be seen as providing the opportunity to finance the more adventurous projects of group members (Roscoe Mitchell solo outings, for example) as well as the exploratory possibilities and risk-takings of live Art Ensemble of Chicago performances. There has been substantial debate about the political implications of innovative black music's crossings into the commercial mainstream (see, for example, Garofalo, "Black Popular Music"). *Coming Home Jamaica*, clearly, will not resolve those debates: while the recording may invite us to recognize the extent to which the AACM's ability to sustain localized, non-market-driven modes of production and distribution is in jeopardy, it might equally herald a salutary attempt to augment the reach and political force of Great Black Music.

I began this chapter by using jazz's renewed engagement with history to open up questions about the politics of representation, and I've ended by reflecting on the ways in which the most recent recording from the Art Ensemble of Chicago confounds our ability to clarify the political effects of the group's avant-garde aesthetic. At issue here too, I want to suggest, is history: not just the history that's invoked sonically by the AEC's performances and recordings, but also that of our own current institutional moment. For *Coming Home Jamaica*, I think, focuses our attention on the institutional apparatuses through which the Art Ensemble of Chicago is marketed, packaged, represented, and made available to us. It reminds us, in effect, that alternative public spheres necessitate a newly articulated understanding of the relationship between markets and identity, between the historical processes of cultural production and distribution and the representational strategies to which these processes give rise. In the next chapter, I'll suggest that the black identities fashioned in well-known jazz autobiographies need to be read in the context of an analogous set of intersecting frameworks of interpretation.

Notes

1. William Howland Kenney notes that "South Side musicians of the twenties referred to white musicians as 'alligators,' exploiters who copied black musical inventions in order to profit from them" (111).

2. In 1993, Jarman retired from the Art Ensemble of Chicago to devote his energies to being a Buddhist priest. See Blumenfeld, "Joseph Jarman's Longest Leap."

3. Writing about black music, Chris Cutler makes a related observation: "We know how the white music industry has tried to take these musics over, how in its early days it was abetted, sometimes innocently, by white enthusiasts & opportunists (who keenly reproduced the *forms* while missing or deliberately obscuring the *content*)" (55).

4. The title *Urban Bushmen* is part of a network of similar juxtapositions or groupings (ancient and future, primitive clothes and lab coat), that characterize the ensemble's efforts to redefine the nature and scope of historical inquiry, to enable an assertion of the sound and space of an African ancestral past to be played off against car horns, sirens, and other markers of a contemporary urban landscape.

5. See Alan Read's suggestion in *Theatre and Everyday Life: An Ethics of Performance* that theater's commitment is not to "the reflection of an 'existing' proposition as though it were fact," but rather to "exemplary and radical" alternatives and possibilities (90).

3

Performing Identity

Jazz Autobiography and the Politics of Literary Improvisation

The burden of black autobiography in America is to *tell* freedom, not just tell *about* freedom.

William Andrews, "Toward a Poetics of Afro-American Autobiography," 90

In his Preface to *The Slave's Narrative,* Henry Louis Gates Jr. refers to the "revolution in historiography" set into motion by John Blassingame's book *The Slave Community.* Blassingame's book, says Gates, marked a watershed in contemporary historiography because it signally challenged the prevailing critical assumption that saw slave narratives as inauthentic autobiographies, as being either too subjective or too heavily edited by white amanuenses to be regarded as offering accurate insights into historical reality. By dedicating *The Slave's Narrative* to Blassingame, a critic "who restored the black slave's narrative to its complex status as history and as literature,"

Gates and his coeditor Charles Davis intend their volume to stand "as a record of the history of the interpretation of, and a necessary step in the academic revaluation of the slave narrative" (xii). The interpretive debates that critics, in responding to slave narratives, have generated around questions of authenticity and verifiability find a rough, but perhaps telling, approximation in debates surrounding social identities and the changing interpretive frameworks of jazz.

I'm thinking, for example, of the differing ways in which jazz critics have sought to assess the value and status of what musicians say about their own work. Ingrid Monson, for example, in implicitly responding to the kind of formalist methodology institutionalized in jazz studies by Gunther Schuller, puts it this way: "It seems to me that watching videos, listening to records . . . can never really replace the obligation to document actively the everyday life experiences, histories, opinions, self-representations, and practices of real people" (*Saying Something,* 212). Jim Merod and Paul Berliner, as I suggested in the Introduction, have made similarly compelling arguments for the ethical obligation to take seriously insider perspectives in jazz, to recognize that the critical frameworks we impose upon jazz may be at variance with the musics, lives, and experiences we seek to describe and represent. And Christopher Harlos, in an important essay in Krin Gabbard's *Representing Jazz* on the ethos of the musician-as-historian, has commented on how jazz autobiography has worked to counter the misrepresentations fostered by institutionalized histories of the music. "If there is an overarching sentiment that a good deal written about the music does not necessarily correspond with the sensibility or even lived experience of the musicians themselves," Harlos writes, "then it seems reasonable to conclude that within the burgeoning collection of autobiography there exists a significant alternative to 'mainstream' jazz history" (137). In the previous chapter, I looked at the texts of the Art Ensemble of Chicago to open up questions about the musical forms that such alternatives to dominant systems of history writing and knowledge production might take. I want now to turn to *literary* acts of self-representation and, in particular, to jazz autobiography, and to join with Harlos in an effort to restore to that genre what, borrowing from Gates and Davis, we might call its "complex status as history and as literature."

But first, let me be more precise about methodology. Lest I seem to be unproblematically championing (and uncritically assuming the validity of) jazz musicians and their self-representations, giving undue weight and authority to intentionalist theories of musical practice, I ought, perhaps, to make clear my sense that the best writing on jazz has to involve a rather tricky balancing act, a complex set of negotiations between on the one hand the teachings of critical theory—especially its dismantling of socially produced assumptions about meaning, identity, and knowledge—and, on the other, a recognition of the value and importance of documenting insider perspectives. I also want to make clear that there are limits to both of these positions. Just as it would, as I suggested at the outset of this book, be inappropriate to ignore what musicians have said about their own craft, so too it would be foolish simply to take what they say at face value. The authority that Monson grants to the words of artists may sometimes need to be called into question; nevertheless, I very much admire her efforts to reconcile ethnomusicology's traditional preoccupations with recent work in cultural studies and poststructuralism. Monson's book, like Berliner's, has evolved not out of the assumptions of orthodox anthropology but rather as part of a groundbreaking ethnomusicology series, one that, following the lead of John Miller Chernoff, has resulted in some genuinely important work in musicology and social practice. I mention this not to defend the methodologies of these books or to justify the recourse to the self-representations of jazz artists, but rather to recognize the extent to which both critics (especially Monson, I think) assume something that orthodox anthropology and "naive ethnography" often may not: the slipperiness, mobility, and inventive flexibility of the speaker's discourse.

Slipperiness, mobility, and inventive flexibility: herein lies the tale of improvisation that's alluded to in my title. Improvisation is not generally a term that's associated with autobiographical narrative traditions, yet by situating it within the context of such traditions I'm interested in testing its applicability as a model for reenvisioning social relations, for enabling us to think anew about the complex forces that produce voice and shape identity. For if, as George Rosenwald and Richard Ochberg put it in their introduction to *Storied Lives: The Cultural Politics of Self-Understanding*, "how we formulate our autobiographies is said to depend on the predicaments in which we find ourselves at the moment" (6), then improvisation seems to me to offer a particularly resonant framework of analysis for the (per)formative power of self-representational strategies.

What interests me here, in part, is the extent to which the theoretical implications of improvisation as cultural practice and social organization might provide a point of entry into contemporary accounts of identity formation and subjectivity. I want to suggest that jazz autobiography offers a unique and compelling site for such a consideration. These self-representational narratives told by musicians who are themselves well versed in improvisatory artistic practices offer new ways to think about identity production. Indeed, autobiography itself needs to be understood in the context of precisely the kinds of struggles for access to self-representation and identity formation that, as I've argued throughout this book, ought to inform any understanding of jazz. As Georges Gusdorf writes in an essay published in James Olney's important collection *Autobiography: Essays Theoretical and Critical*, "It is precisely in order to do away with misunderstandings, to restore an incomplete or deformed truth, that the autobiographer . . . takes up the telling of his [or her] story" (36).

What, then, might improvisation have to do with this autobiographical impulse for authors to take control over the production of knowledge about their own life stories, to seek to correct dominant misrepresentations through the creative act of writing? Interestingly, many theorists of improvisation are explicit in seeing a connection between improvisation and identity, between artistic processes and agency in self-representation. Improvising percussionist Eddie Prévost, for one, states flatly that "improvised music is a music of self definition" (quoted in Smith and Dean, 63). Tom Nunn, in his recent book *Wisdom of the Impulse*, similarly suggests that the practice of free improvisation often has as its impetus "a search for one's own 'original voice' where specific restrictions of form, style and technique can be dropped, leaving space for the deeper, more intuitive personality to express itself" (131). And Stephen Nachmanovitch, in *Free Play: Improvisation in Life and Art*, argues that "Spontaneous creation comes from our deepest being and is immaculately and originally ourselves. What we have to express is already with us, *is* us, so the work of creativity is not a matter of making the material come, but of unblocking the obstacles to its natural flow" (10). What all of these critics, despite their varied emphases and points of focus, have in common is their insistence that improvisation is a powerful ally in struggles for self-expression, self-determination, and self-representation.

There is no doubt that improvisation can have such power. Think, for example, of Paul Robeson's brilliant (and by now well-known) onstage improvisation during a production of *Show Boat*. By altering the words of "Ol' Man River"—instead of the scripted "Git a little drunk an' you'll land in jail," Robeson, for example, during a concert in Warsaw in 1949 sang, "You show a little grit and you land in jail" (quoted in Dyer, 107)—he managed to counter centuries of misrepresentations of African-American people, changing the "crime" from drinking to resistance. The changes that, over his lifetime, Robeson continued to make to the lyrics of "Ol' Man River" are, in the words of one critic, "interventions in one of the most popular show tunes of the time; they mark a political black presence in a mainstream (i.e., white) cultural product" (Dyer, 107). Indeed, Robeson's example seems to me to be a telling one, for his performance points not only to the political efficacy and agential function of improvisation but also to its social role, rather than simply its power of *self*-expression. So yes, while improvisation is about self-definition, about the creative powers of self-expression, it can also (as Robeson's example suggests) be about social mobility, about finding innovative ways to trouble the assumptions (and the expectations of fixity) fostered by institutionalized systems of representation.

This reading of improvisation as an interventionist strategy aligned with efforts to foster black mobility is very much in keeping with Nathaniel Mackey's suggestion that improvisation for African-Americans needs to be seen in terms of the sociopolitical implications of what he calls "black linguistic and musical practices that accent variance, variability" (266). Such practices, he tells us, "implicitly react against and reflect critically upon the . . . othering to which their practitioners, denied agency in a society by which they are designated other, have been subjected. The black speaker, writer, or musician whose practice privileges variation subjects the fixed equations that underwrite that denial (including the idea of fixity itself) to an alternative" (267). Think again of Robeson as Joe the Riverman in *Show Boat*, ceaselessly toting bales of cotton across the stage, and then subtly but powerfully rising from that toil to disempower the production's stereotypical representation of blacks through an improvisation that subjects the scripted verse (and its assumptions) to a radical alternative. In challenging socially and institutionally constituted frameworks of intelligibility, improvisation, after the fashion of Robeson's example, can offer meaningful alternatives to the fixity and to the naturalizing effects of misrepresentations which have confined African Americans to what Mackey punningly terms "a predetermined status (predetermined stasis)" (266). James Baldwin, writing in part about Robeson, puts it this way: "What the black actor has managed to give are moments—indelible moments, created, miraculously, *beyond the confines of the script*: hints of reality, smuggled like contraband into a maudlin tale, and with enough force, if unleashed, to shatter the tale to fragments" (121–22; emphasis added).

One of the points I'm making here is perhaps an obvious one: improvisation as a form of social practice derives its force from the specificities of the performance occasion. Far from being, as Nachmanovitch would have it, an expression of an autonomous identity that is deeply and naturally within us, a kind of latent creative impulse whose "natural flow" has been blocked by various kinds of obstacles, or, in the words of another critic, "a free zone in music where . . . you are responsible only to yourself and to the dictates of your taste" (Chase, 15), improvisation might be more productively understood in the context of contemporary theoretical accounts of identity formation as a social, dialogic, and constructed process. Stuart Hall, for example, is succinct on this score: the "critical thing about identity," he writes, "is that it is partly the relationship between you and the Other. Only when there is an Other can you know who you are. . . . And there is no identity . . . without the dialogic relationship to the Other" ("Ethnicity," 16). Philosopher Charles Taylor, in his extraordinary essay "The Politics of Recognition," makes a related point. "My own identity," he tells us, "crucially depends on my dialogical relations with others" (34). He continues: "On the social plane, the understanding that identities are formed in open dialogue, *unshaped by a predefined social script*, has made the politics of equal recognition more central and stressful. . . . Equal recognition is not just the appropriate mode for a healthy democratic society. Its refusal can inflict damage on those who are denied it" (36; emphasis added). Taylor, of course, is not talking about improvisation; nevertheless, his comments may well have an unsuspected resonance in the context not only of this book's overall argument about jazz identities and the politics of cultural representation but, more specifically, of the present chapter's analysis of literary self-representations in jazz. For improvisation's link with processes of identity formation and struggles for self-definition has less to do with a creative actualizing of the self as a stable origin of meaning than it does with unsettling the very logic of identity. If anything, improvisation teaches us by example that identity is a dialogic construction (rather than something deep within us), that the self is always a subject-in-process. Indeed, as Hazel Smith and Roger Dean note, "Improvisation can be seen to be consistent with the theories of Derrida, Barthes, and Foucault in challenging the notion of the creator as sole and immediate focus of meaning. . . . The emphasis in much improvisation on collaboration, or on the projection of multiple selves, radically interrogates traditional notions of subjectivity" (35).

It's possible, then, to delineate at least two frameworks of critical assumption that have evolved around the theory and practice of improvisation. The first, as represented by Nachmanovitch and others, sees improvisation as an expression of a natural identity that's always already there, deep within us. The second, by contrast, argues that improvisation, with its emphasis on dialogism and social occasion, is a process-oriented model of inquiry that radically unsettles traditional assumptions about identity. The parallel here with the frameworks of assumption governing theories of autobiography is striking. As Shirley Neuman writes, received "histories of autobiography and of its criticism construe the self as individuated and coherent rather than as the product of social construction and as a subject-in-process" (293). The cultural force of the jazz autobiographies I want to examine in this chapter seems to me to be lodged precisely in the interplay between such competing assumptions. These autobiographies are concerned, at once, with fashioning authentic identities for African-American artists who have been persistently misunderstood and misrepresented by the white cultural mainstream, and with undermining the very assumptions of authenticity to show how, historically, these artists have had to improvise their own identities in order to transgress the socially and institutionally constituted frameworks that have defined their status. In their resilient efforts to envision alternative social relations, these autobiographies, I want to suggest, offer valuable insights into the complex relations among improvisation, identity formation, and black mobility.

In this chapter, then, I'd like to turn to one variant of what Krin Gabbard calls jazz's "other history" to look at how three well-known jazz autobiographies—Billie Holiday's *Lady Sings the Blues*, Duke Ellington's *Music Is My Mistress*, and Charles Mingus's *Beneath the Underdog*—use performance-oriented models of improvisation to engage complex questions of agency and identity. If, as Gates argues, "the will to power for black Americans was the will to write; and the predominant mode that this writing would assume was the shaping of a black self in words" ("Introduction," 4), then these three jazz autobiographies clearly need to be read in the context of what another critic calls autobiography's "democratic potential" (Folkenflik, 23), that is, its ability to enable oppressed groups to achieve access to self-representation and control over the processes of literary production. Just as the "slave narrative arose as a response to and refutation of claims that blacks could not write" (Davis and Gates, xv), so, as Harlos notes, "for jazz musicians, the turn to autobiography is regarded as a genuine opportunity to seize narrative authority" (134). My interest here is in showing that while the authority attached to such authenticating narratives has, perhaps by necessity, an important role to play in facilitating our understanding of autobiography's democratizing effects, of our tendency to see the genre as offering "the most direct and accessible way of countering silence and misrepresentation" (Swindells, 7), the identities fashioned in these particular texts compel us to ask hard methodological questions about the mediated nature of these self-representational acts: How are we to assess the role that (white) literary institutions have played in shaping these particular black identities? Is autobiographical identity best understood as a function of referentiality? of textuality? of social construction? (see Folkenflik, 12) or, indeed, as a rhetorically compelling effect of performance and improvisation? In what ways do these jazz autobiographies enable us to think through the political efficacy of improvised traditions in narrative?

Writing specifically about African-American autobiography, Craig Hanson Werner tells us that "the Afro-American tradition begins with—and for the foreseeable future will continue to be informed by—an enforced awareness that the self cannot be taken for granted" (90). Mackey, in fact, makes the point that the "dismantling of the unified subject found in recent critical theory is old news when it comes to black music" (275–76), giving as some of his examples Muhal Richard Abrams's composition "Conversation with the Three of Me" and the notorious opening statement of identity from Mingus's (equally notorious) autobiography, *Beneath the Underdog*:

> In other words, I am three. One man stands forever in the middle, unconcerned, unmoved, watching, waiting to be allowed to express what he sees to the other two. The second man is like a frightened animal that attacks for fear of being attacked. Then there's an over-loving gentle person who lets people into the uttermost sacred temple of his being and he'll take insults and be trusting and sign contracts without reading them and get talked down to working cheap or for nothing, and when he realizes what's been done to him he feels like killing and destroying everything around him including himself for being so stupid. But he can't—he goes back inside himself. (3)

From moment one, Mingus's autobiography reveals itself to be engaged in a refusal of expectations of fixity, a shattering of traditional assumptions about identity as something that is stable and coherent. One critic, anthropologist Michael Fischer, suggests that Mingus's "three selves appear throughout the text as alternating, interbraided voices—like the call-and-response of a jazz session—keeping the reader alert to perspective and circumstance" (213). As Mingus self-consciously negotiates the multiple (and sometimes contradictory) selves-in-process that have shaped and determined his own life history, as he seeks, in writing, to accommodate that multiplicity with a rhythm and spirit of invention and flexibility, we recognize the ways in which the text's improvisational dynamic works both to broaden the horizon of what gets represented and imagined in autobiography and to trouble the role that the very distinction between factual and invented worlds has played in terms of our understanding of the genre. That this opening scene is part of a dialogue between Mingus and his psychiatrist is undoubtedly worth commenting on here, for not only does it open up questions about the institutional constraints that shape and determine our efforts at self-representation (the nature of the analyst/analysand narrative, after all, is heavily mediated by the "set" form of the dialogue), but also because it invites us to recognize that identity formation, like improvisation, is a negotiated process. When Mingus's doctor asks him which one of the selves is real, Mingus responds, "They're *all* real" (3), explaining that "I'm only trying to find out how I should feel about myself" (3). This striking opening of *Beneath the Underdog*—with its emphasis on dialogue between dissonant identities as a process of discovery—points to some of the ways in which Mingus's self-representational acts provide a salient forum for considering the interpretive domain of improvisational practice.

Equally worthy of attention is Mingus's unusual decision to write about himself in the third person. The text's subtitle is "His World as Composed by Mingus," and throughout the autobiography, Mingus refers to himself not in the traditional first person, but rather as "Baby," "my boy," "he," "Charles," "Mingus," or "My man." Mingus thus presents himself not as a self-willed creator with an autonomous identity, but rather as part of a complex network of affiliations among performers, family, audience, and institutions. At issue here, again, is an attempt to exit from the routine understanding of the autonomy and stability of identity as it claims to shape and determine a subject's experience. Mingus, in effect, invents a new narrator, a narrator who, to borrow from Philippe Lejeune's theoretical analysis of autobiography in the third person, "places himself between" protagonist and readers: "The autobiographer observes his own discourse instead of assuming it directly; he steps back a little and in reality splits himself as narrator" (38–39). At one point early in Mingus's narrative, for example, the narrator writes, "So Charles entered school and his problems with the outside world began. I wanted him to know that he was not alone, that I was with him for a lifetime" (12). Just how are we to understand this unidentified "I," this author-narrator who claims to be somehow distinct from the protagonist of the autobiography? The very conventions of the genre would lead us to expect Mingus's name on the front cover of the autobiography to mean that author and protagonist are one and the same person. Yet the strategic rearrangement of the traditional proximity in autobiography between narrative voice and protagonist functions here much like the multiple selves-in-process with which Mingus opens the text: it self-consciously invites us to recognize the extent to which Mingus's subjectivity—his attempt, as he puts it, "to find out how I should feel about myself" (3)—is constructed, defined, performed (and, yes, improvised) in relation to multiple identifications and negotiations.

The complexity of these negotiations around self-representation also becomes evident if we look more closely at the workings of the front cover of *Beneath the Underdog*. As I've already mentioned, the book's cover lists Mingus (as does its spine) as the author of the text. The 1991 Vintage paperback edition also displays a silhouetted photograph of Mingus and a detail of his bass as well as a quotation from *Newsweek*: "An outlandish, brilliant autobiography." The inside title pages of the book, however, though providing the full title, *Beneath the Underdog: His World as Composed by Mingus*, do not explicitly name Charles Mingus as the author of this autobiography. Unlike the cover, then, the title pages make no clear promises about the identity of the author. In fact, while Charles Mingus is not named as the proper author, the title pages *do* tell us that the text has been "Edited by Nel King." King, interestingly, is there too on the copyright page: "Copyright . . . by Charles Mingus and Nel King." And on the dedication page, Mingus writes, "I would like to express my deep thanks to Nel King, who worked long and hard editing this book, and who is probably the only white person who could have done it."

The discrepancy between the front cover and the title and copyright pages is, I think, revealing, for it raises important questions about both the methodological and the political imperatives at stake in Mingus's text. Indeed, the fraught issue of authorship that's signaled by this discrepancy returns us to our consideration of improvisation and its relation to abiding questions of race, power, identity formation, and mobility. What does it mean for Mingus to have chosen a white editor for a text that is so explicitly concerned with hegemonic structures of racism and exclusion? This is a text, after all, which points, in no uncertain terms, to the devastating consequences of white control over black musicians. Trumpeter Fats Navarro, whose (often imagined) conversations with Mingus appear throughout the text, puts it this way: "Jazz is big business to the white man and you can't move without him. We just work-ants. He owns the magazines, agencies, record companies and all the joints that sell to the public" (188). And again: "You breaking into Whitey's private vault when you start telling Negroes to wake up and move in where they belong and it ain't safe, Mingus. . . . [T]here ain't no better business for Whitey to be in than Jim Crow business" (190). In light of such concerns, how are we to assess the role that a white editor has played in mediating—and, thus, shaping—our understanding of the black subject at the heart of *Beneath the Underdog*?

I implied a moment ago that these fundamental questions about racial identity in print and the assumed power of the white editor in shaping a picture of black autobiography are, in Mingus's case, perhaps best understood if read in the context of the negotiated process of improvised creative practice and its relation to black mobility. Let me try to be clearer about what I have in mind here. If, as I've suggested throughout (and as the Robeson example powerfully illustrates), improvisation is a socially constructed act (with social issues often at stake) rather than principally a matter of individual self-expression, then the discrepancies at the heart of the writing of Mingus's autobiography provide a valuable framework for theorizing improvisation's ability to foster new, albeit problematic, etiquettes for social participation. I partly have in mind here Charles Keil's work on "participatory discrepancies," his argument that "[m]usic, to be personally involving and socially valuable, must be 'out of time' and 'out of tune'" ("Participatory Discrepancies," 275). Keil claims that "'groove' or 'vital drive' is not some essence of all music that we can simply take for granted, but must be figured out each time between players" ("Theory," 1), and he argues that the discrepancies that result from such collaborative figurings out are what make music so compelling. Christopher Waterman, enlarging on Keil's argument, puts it this way: "[G]rooves depend upon playing apart" (93).

One of the key discrepancies in *Beneath the Underdog*, as my brief account of the front cover and the title page suggests, results from Mingus's collaborative participation with Nel King: this is, after all, a book that in manuscript form was much longer than the version that finally found its way to print in 1971. Though Mingus's ex-wife Celia has claimed that he "would just write down whatever he was thinking about at the time, and then I would type it up—without editing, you know" (quoted in Priestly, 88), the very fact that the published version is considerably shorter than the thousand-plus page manuscript makes clear that there has indeed been some "long and hard" editing work involved. Janet Coleman, who'd earlier been approached to edit the book, tells us, in fact, that it had been "whitened up beyond repair" (quoted in Harlos, 139) even before it reached Nel King, its final editor at Knopf. Another of Mingus's ex-wives, Sue, has explained that Mingus's failing health forced him to be "very agreeable to many things he would not have been, had he been his normal self. . . . He got along much more easily with the editors that he met. He left a lot of decisions to Nel King that, I think, under other circumstances, he never would have" (quoted in Priestly, 180). But she also remarks that this unexpected willingness to put the decision-making in King's hands "was a good thing" for Mingus because "the book had become a huge nightmare for him" (180), implying, perhaps, that working with King was the only way Mingus would see the book (which had circulated for so many years in so many different versions) to print. Her comments invite us to return for a moment to Keil, and to ask whether the autobiography's "vital drive" might in some way be a result of the collaborative dissonances between Mingus and King.

That collaborative process, I want to suggest, is central to the text's improvisational dynamic. In their book on improvisation, Hazel Smith and Roger Dean point out that collaborative improvisation "involves the merging of the self with another, so that it may be impossible to tell who has done what" (35). The difficulty of determining just who has done what in collaborative forms of improvised artistic practice again unsettles conventional assumptions about improvisation as being deeply rooted in individual creativity. The collaborative process at work in the writing of Mingus's text suggests the extent to which identity is not fixed or prescripted, but rather constructed, negotiated, improvised, and performed in relation both to the demands of the moment and to institutionalized frameworks of knowledge production. Craig Hanson Werner's comments about audience-building strategies in African-American autobiography may also be germane here. "Recognizing the absolute necessity of attracting an audience with greater access to the sources of institutional power (which must be altered if there is to be any substantial improvement in the actual living conditions of the black community), the autobiographers," writes Werner, "employ the vocabulary of 'sympathetic' whites, who can use the text to support their own political agenda" (86). Now, I don't mean to suggest that Mingus has supplanted his own voice (or voices) with someone else's vocabulary. Yet insofar as his collaboration with editor King—whose "sympathetic" quality is registered in the acknowledgment that she is "probably the only white person who could have done it"—is an attempt to see the book to print and thereby increase access to sources of institutional privilege and power, *Beneath the Underdog* reveals itself to be a text that's strategically adept at negotiating the politics of public acts of self-representation.

It's significant that *Beneath the Underdog* ends, as it begins, in the context of a dialogue between Mingus and his psychiatrist. The setting not only reminds us that identity formation is a highly mediated dialogic process; it also, like the matters broached here relating to the editorial construction of the text, functions to call our attention to the ways in which black identities have historically and institutionally been played out through complex acts of improvised negotiation and accommodation. One critic, Thomas Carmichael, sees these acts of negotiation as offering little, if any, possibility for disrupting hegemonic relations. "For Mingus," writes Carmichael, "identity is not a subject for parody or the experience of inevitable subversion, but a tortured question of authenticity and origins. In *Beneath the Underdog*, the subject of identity is always a question of negotiating the psychoanalytic impact of the racist public sphere" (34). Carmichael, indeed, argues that "the fragmented subject and the third person narration in Mingus's African-American autobiography are not counterhegemonic ploys, but instead confirmations of the true force of the contingent formations of racism and exclusion" (39). This is, I think, a compelling argument, especially given the text's repeated insistence on the difficulties that black musicians face in seeking to exit from dominant economies of production. Yet the rhythm of invention and flexibility that's central to both the spirit and the structure of *Beneath the Underdog* encourages me to see the text's emphasis on dialogue and discrepancy as having transgressive potential. And if Mackey and others are right (as I think they are) in telling us that such a spirit of flexibility needs to be read in the context of black mobility, then Mingus's autobiography may have something to tell us about how an ability to adapt imaginatively to situations at hand can create a performative space for social change. That space has something to do with the way in which the text's discrepancies—its emphasis on multiple selves-in-process, its collaborative editorial construction, its third-person narrative—have in common with improvisational creative practice a distrust of the powers and ideology of fixity.

Like Mingus's text, Billie Holiday's *Lady Sings the Blues* can be read in the context of autobiographical accounts by historically subjugated peoples seeking access to the possibilities of self-representation and identity formation. Holiday too seeks to counter the objectifying discourses of white representations of black musicians and their art. Yet like Mingus, Holiday, as her autobiography attests, was forced throughout her life to work within and creatively adapt to the constraints imposed upon her by dominant systems of knowledge production, by white institutions such as the media, the law, and the recording industry. Angela Davis, writing about the social implications of Billie Holiday's love songs, convincingly points to the ways in which Holiday "utilized the formative power of her jazz style to refigure the songs she performed and recorded, the great majority of which were produced on the Tin Pan Alley assembly line according to the contrived and formulaic sentimentality characteristic of the era" (*Blues,* 165). She suggests that for Holiday:

> the very prospect of producing her music was contingent on her acceptance of a kind of song that not only represented a different musical tradition from the one in which she placed her-

> self . . . but that was imposed upon her repressively by the popular culture market. Had she rejected the often insipid Tin Pan Alley material, she would have denied herself the possibility of song and thus of offering her musical originality to the black community, to the dominant culture, and to the world. (166)

By choosing to work with, and yet profoundly to transform, this material produced by a rapidly developing and white-dominated popular culture industry, Holiday was able not only to secure access to broader audiences but also to reclaim that material as relevant to the political circumstances and social contingencies that characterized her own world of lived experience. It is thus that Davis invites us to see Holiday's "awesome ability to transmute musical and lyrical meaning in the popular songs she performed" as "analogous to African Americans' historical appropriation of the English language" (165).

If Davis is correct in identifying the transformative impact of Holiday's creative reworking of popular love songs, then what happens when Holiday is afforded the opportunity to fashion her own history rather than be forced to accommodate her political and cultural needs within frames of reference massively shaped by the dominant culture? *Lady Sings the Blues* is a text in which, as the back cover blurb to the Penguin paperback edition states, "Billie Holiday tells her own story." Or is it? Several commentators have suggested that the text is wildly inaccurate, awash with egregious errors of fact and deliberate exaggerations. Something similar, of course, must be said of Mingus's text. What's different, though, is that Mingus himself registers a sophisticated self-consciousness around questions of literary self-invention. Early in *Beneath the Underdog*, for example, Mingus, anticipating for his readers the description of a wild orgy that we read about several pages later (174–79), has his psychiatrist explain, "You're a good man, Charles, but there's a lot of fabrication and fantasy in what you say. . . . [N]o man could have had as much intercourse in one night as you claim to have had" (4). Like the scene in which his wife-to-be, Barbara, tells Mingus that he's "a good story-teller" (121), this comment from his psychiatrist reveals the extent to which the text contains an implicit awareness of how its improvisational emphasis on flexibility and literary invention works to trouble routine assumptions about autobiography's conventional allegiance to an aesthetics of realism.

There doesn't seem to me to be the same kind of self-conscious awareness in Holiday's text. Yet there is something of an analogous penchant for literary improvisation. One critic, Robert O'Meally, states flatly that *Lady Sings the Blues* "is not a dependable source of information. Pieced together from interviews granted over the years and from conversations between the author, William Dufty, and Holiday herself, that book," says O'Meally, "is best considered a dream book, a collection of Holiday's wishes and lies. . . . Billie Holiday herself seemed to regard such accounts primarily as publicity and as opportunities to secure quick cash" (*Lady Day,* 21). This is an interesting claim, especially in the face of the autobiography's explicit critique of the public misrepresentations of Holiday in the press and its general disapproval of those who misguidedly seek to profit from the lives of exploited black musicians: "We're supposed to have made so much progress," Holiday writes, "but most of the people who have any respect for jazz in this country are those who make a buck out of it" (Holiday, 176). Interesting also is O'Meally's refusal of the text's claims to Holiday's authorship, his outright declaration that white newspaperman William Dufty is, in fact, the author of Holiday's "autobiography." Both the cover and the title page assure us that Billie Holiday is the principal author, though they do acknowledge that she has written the book "with William Dufty." O'Meally and others have explored the fraught nature of the collaborative authorship of *Lady Sings the Blues* more provocatively and more thoroughly than I can offer to rehearse here; what interests me, though, is a variant on the question broached in our consideration of the editorial construction of Mingus's autobiography: how, that is, do we assess the role and assumed power of a white literary editor in shaping our understanding of, in this case, black female identity? To what extent might Holiday's ability to work with and improvise upon the discrepancies that result from such an editorial process find a parallel in her politically adept refashioning of musical materials from white popular culture? Can the slipperiness and inventive flexibility of *Lady Sings the Blues* be seen to have implications for our understanding of struggles for agency?

Holiday's is a fraught case, shot through with many complexities. O'Meally begins to get at some of those complexities when he explains the subtitle for his book *Lady Day: The Many Faces of Billie Holiday*: "[H]er faces were made up, invented; they were among her compositions" (21). He continues: "In the roles she created through her music, she faced the world not as victim, but as towering hero" (21). About the autobiography, he notes that:

> [o]ne of Holiday's long-term pianists of the fifties, Carl Drinkard, was one of several people close to Holiday who have said that she let Dufty do the job to get much needed cash. Despite the publicity shots showing Billie wearing glasses and typing—two things she never did before or after the photo session—she did not write the book herself. She probably never even read it, Drinkard said. (67)

In light of such assertions, it is, I think, tempting to dismiss Holiday's text as a corrupt account and to approach it with skepticism. Yet one of the things my work as a literary critic has taught me is that it is possible for imaginative writers to reclaim the world of lived experience in ways largely uninventoried in so-called factual representations. One author, Michael Ondaatje, in his remarkable novel about jazz legend Buddy Bolden, *Coming through Slaughter*, speaks explicitly in his acknowledgments about "the truth of fiction," implying that his admittedly imaginative account of Bolden may well be more narratively faithful to the complexities of Bolden's life and art than documentary or biographical representations. Writing in a different context, Rosenwald and Ochberg, in their book *Storied Lives: The Cultural Politics of Self-Understanding*, similarly argue against the necessity for allowing empiricist-laden assumptions to influence our assessment of the meaning and value of self-representations:

> Why take an interest in life stories if their truth cannot be warranted? The objection is well taken if "truth" in the realist sense

> is the target. But to the investigator of psychological or cultural representation, the object of study is not the "true" event, as it might have been recorded by some panel of disinterested observers, but the construction of that event within a personal and social history. . . . In the form a particular narrator gives to a history we read the more or less abiding concerns and constraints of the individual and his or her community. (3–4)

Far from seeing the discrepancy from the real and the role of the white editor in *Lady Sings the Blues* as announcing the autobiography's complete disengagement from Holiday's world of lived experience, we might, after the fashion of Ondaatje (or Rosenwald and Ochberg), do well to jettison our traditional assumptions about truth. O'Meally, indeed, invites us to consider how the book's exaggerations, though inaccurate and despite being highly mediated by its white editor, "do convey a deep emotional truth. They reveal the person Holiday saw herself to be, her values and sense of life" (*Lady Day,* 67).

Consider, for instance, the opening of the text: "Mom and Pop were just a couple of kids when they got married. He was eighteen, she was sixteen, and I was three. . . . Mom was thirteen that Wednesday, April 7, 1915, in Baltimore when I was born" (Holiday, 5). While the use of numbers and the exact specification of date and place lend this passage a kind of "reality effect," even these seemingly straightforward details, it turns out, cannot be taken for granted. The actual facts established in official documents run counter to the book's opening: as O'Meally notes, when Holiday was born, her mother was nineteen and her father seventeen. "Most significantly, she imagines that her parents were married. The truth is that they were never married, that they never even lived together" (*Lady Day,* 68). Holiday, in short, improvises a narrative of origins. I use the term "improvises" rather than "invents" here because I want to suggest that part of what is at issue is the text's refusal to adhere to the kind of fixed or prescripted versions of Holiday's life found in official factual accounts. Just as musicians in improvised settings adapt to situations at hand, often discovering rewarding sonic possibilities in what, in other more codified contexts, might have been deemed "mistakes" or "wrong notes," so Holiday revels in what, borrowing from Ondaatje, we might call "the truth of fiction," that is, in an inventiveness that invites a redefinition of conventional standards of coherence and judgment. The improvisational edge that characterizes the construction of identity formation in *Lady Sings the Blues*, indeed, resides precisely in the text's loose disregard for matters factual, a disregard which, like Mingus's explicit rejection of traditional conceptions of the unified self in *Beneath the Underdog*, may well be suited to serving the needs of subaltern sensibilities.

Contemporary accounts of the cultural history of African-American autobiography are forthright in arguing that there is a rhythm of movement and flexibility (and a concomitant need to unsettle an ideology of stasis) characterizing the structures of subjectivity fashioned by subordinated peoples. William Andrews, a prominent theorist of the genre, tells us for example that:

> revising the past does not necessarily mean a deviation from historical truth. Revision can itself be indicative of a historical truth, not the truth embedded in something believed to be past but the truth emerging in something the autobiographer faces in the present. It may be that the history of Afro-American autobiography has evolved through a rhythm of revisionary renewals of certain powerful myths and images of the past in response to the changing realities of the present. In any case, the dynamic principle that I see in the history of Afro-American autobiography is the revising, not the canonizing, of traditions and even texts. ("Toward," 87)

And writing specifically about how African Americans have historically resisted various forms of fixity and institutionalization, Arnold Rampersad tells the following story in his essay "Biography, Autobiography, and Afro-American Culture":

> Carl van Vechten, the tireless (and wealthy, one should add) white collector of Afro-Americana and the founder of the very important James Weldon Johnson Memorial Collection of Afro-American literary material at Yale, used to brood on how

much of invaluable black history was lost in attics and leaky basements. He was also dismayed at what he took to be the relative indifference of blacks to his efforts at Yale and Fisk, where he founded the George Gershwin Memorial Collection of Music and Musical Literature. To which Van Vechten's close friend Langston Hughes, no mean collector of papers himself, would reply soothingly that blacks were simply not interested in museums, manuscripts, and memorabilia; such conservation was simply not a part of the culture. (4)

Now by quoting this anecdote I don't mean to give the impression that Charles Mingus and Billie Holiday resist the conservational impulse altogether; the very fact that they have sought to fashion their identities in words (and, indeed, in recordings of their music) clearly suggests otherwise. The point I am making, rather, has to do with the question of whether the modes of articulation they have (albeit with their white collaborators) devised in their respective autobiographies can be understood in the context of improvisation and its relation to black mobility. Andrews, indeed, has coined the term "free storytelling" to make a point that is useful in elucidating our understanding of precisely such a context. "The history of Afro-American autobiography," he writes, "is one of increasingly free storytelling, signaled in the ways black narratives address their readers and reconstruct personal history, ways often at variance with literary conventions and social proprieties of discourse" (*To Tell a Free Story*, xi). The improvisational dynamic at work in *Beneath the Underdog* and *Lady Sings the Blues*, I have been suggesting, points to the ways in which the strategies of "free storytelling" deployed in these jazz autobiographies—their refusal to adhere to conventional standards of accepted practice—are connected with the desire for the authors of these texts to see themselves as the split or unfixed subjects of their own history rather than the settled objects of someone else's.

Ellington's *Music Is My Mistress* seems to me to be a very different kind of book. But it too—though perhaps only explicitly in its Epilogue—invites a consideration of the dissolution of received notions of subjectivity, notions that posit identity as something fixed and stable that's deep within us. The passage I have in mind, from a section of the Epilogue called "The Mirrored Self," is worth quoting at length:

> Let us imagine a quiet, cozy cove where all the senses except one seem to have dispersed. There is nothing to smell, nothing to taste, nothing to hear, and nothing to feel but the reaction to what can be seen. Nearby is a still pool, so still that it resembles a limpid mirror. If we look in it, what we see is the reflection of ourselves, just as we thought we looked, wearing the identical clothes, the same countenance. . . .
>
> Ah, this is *us*, the us we know, and as we savor the wonderful selves-of-perfection we suddenly realize that just below our mirror, there is another reflection that is not quite so clear, and not quite what we expected. This translucent surface has a tendency toward the vague: the lines are not firm and the colors not quite the same, but it is us, or should we say *me*, or rather one of our other selves? We examine this uncertain portrait and just as we feel inclined to accept it we realize that, down below this, there is still another mirror reflecting another of our selves, and more. (451)

The other selves that unexpectedly appear below the surface image in the mirror here, like Mingus's multiple identities-in-process in *Beneath the Underdog*, raise profound questions about the nature of identity formation. The uncertainty that's signaled in Ellington's epilogue, the willingness to acknowledge the ways in which certain kinds of dissonances can function to disrupt our comfortable assumptions about how we understand ourselves (and others), seems particularly pertinent in the context of Ellington's autobiography. For one of the things that's most striking about *Music Is My Mistress*, especially in comparison with the other two autobiographies I've examined here, is the fact that, with the exception of this moment in the epilogue, it shows little indication of unsettling the logic of its surface representations. Ellington's son Mercer tells us that "it is a fact that [Duke's] autobiography contains scarcely an ill word about anybody" (Mercer Ellington, 172). Duke "wanted nothing in his life ever to be that complete and final," explains Don George, a songwriter with whom Ellington collaborated. He believed that "people shouldn't be written about until after they're gone" (George, 235). And when George asked Sam Vaughn, the editor who sought in the first instance to inveigle Duke into writing an autobiography, why the book is written in such a way that "everything is moonlight and roses. Everything is great, everything is wonderful," when "it wasn't like that" (237–38), Vaughn explains, "the value of a memoir is not whether it is accurate. It's a picture of what the man wants you to think. Memoirs are all flawed by self-service, but they still have their value" (238). That value, I've been suggesting, has something to do with our understanding of the performative and improvisational aspects of projects of self-invention. William Andrews, taking up the issue of the skepticism and resistance that often greeted slave narratives, puts it in slightly different terms: "Today our sensitivity to the relativistic truth value of all autobiography and to the peculiar symbiosis of imperfect freedom and imperfect truth in the American autobiographical tradition makes it easier for us *to regard the fictive elements of black autobiography as aspects of rhetorical and aesthetic strategy,* not evidence of moral failure" (*To Tell a Free Story,* 3; emphasis added).

In this context, I find it useful, for example, to think about why Ellington (unlike Mingus and Holiday) downplays or sidesteps issues of race throughout the text. When, at a press conference in Delhi, India, during a State Department tour in 1963, Ellington is confronted by an interviewer who wants to know about "the race question" in the United States, he responds by generalizing that "[e]verywhere, there are many degrees of haves and have-nots, minorities, majorities, races, creeds, colors, and castes" (Ellington, 308). As the exchange continues, Ellington points out that "the basis of the whole problem is economic rather than a matter of color" (308). Later on in the text, Ellington generalizes again when taking up race-related questions: "I don't believe in categories of any kind, and when you speak of problems between black and white in the U.S.A. you are referring to categories again. I don't believe there is anybody in the world who has no problem. The person who has no problem has a very dull life" (378–79).

If the texts by Mingus and Holiday are provocative critiques of hegemonic structures of racism in the music business, Ellington, in his autobiography, seems repeatedly to frame his achievements precisely in the context of the dominant white social order. Much of Ellington's text, in fact, describes his hobnobbing with those who explicitly represent that social order: Presidents Nixon and Johnson, Queen Elizabeth II, the Duke of Edinburgh, and so on. The apparent ease with which Ellington moved in social settings that functioned to reinforce institutionalized spheres of knowledge production seems, at least on the surface, a far cry from the refusal of structures of fixity that we've seen in the improvisational dynamics in the Mingus and Holiday autobiographies. And Ellington's refusal to acknowledge pressing questions of race relations in America would appear to be rather a glaring omission in *Music Is My Mistress*, especially given the political realities of the day. As Mark Anthony Neal notes in *What the Music Said*, "There may be no period in twentieth-century America that witnessed more state-sanctioned repression against African-Americans than the period from 1968 to 1972. The election of Richard M. Nixon, in concert with the continued surveillance and destabilization activities of J. Edgar Hoover's Federal Bureau of Investigation (FBI), left lasting impressions on the Civil Rights/Black Power movements" (55). What does it mean, then, for an African-American artist—indeed one of the century's most illustrious and respected African-American artists—to move so contentedly amongst these people and these institutions?

The passage I've quoted from the epilogue ought, I think, to give us pause, for it troubles some of the assumptions we might have about the text's presumed unwillingness to participate in struggles for identity and voice. In encouraging us to attend to reflections beneath the surface, reflections that are "not quite so clear, and not quite what we expected" (451), Ellington, in this passage, alerts us to the possibility that the autobiography's politics may be lodged in unstressed textual moments, in dissonances, in fissures in the workings of hegemony, its social edge masked in the workings of "rhetorical and aesthetic strategy." Ellington himself, after all, was fond of subtlety and nuance, adamant in his insistence that "a statement of social protest in the theatre should be made *without* saying it" (180; emphasis added). "This," he remarked, "calls for the real craftsman" (180).

How do we begin to assess the ideological implications of what Ellington does not say in *Music Is My Mistress*? Is Ellington's craft here (and, indeed, his politics) best understood through an analysis of the text's absences? Or perhaps his politics is most purposefully understood only in terms of his music: Ellington's legacy, of course, is in his music, a music, we should remember, which, unlike the autobiography, was often conceived of by Ellington in terms of social and political issues.[1] As sheer craft, clearly, the autobiography fails to measure up to the expectations generated by the sophistication of Ellington's musical oeuvre. James Lincoln Collier has, for instance, argued that Ellington's way with words never did justice to his real-life complexities:

> The fact must be faced that Duke Ellington was a dreadful writer. It is not merely that he employs false rhymes and lines that do not scan, or that he is addicted to the obvious and cute. The trouble runs much deeper—all the way to the bottom, in fact. There is nothing in the interviews he gave, in his book *Music Is My Mistress*, which was put into shape by Stanley Dance, and in [his] lyrics . . . to suggest that Ellington was in any way the wise and ultimately sophisticated man he actually was. (*Duke Ellington,* 295)

I must confess, though, that I'm not entirely convinced by Collier's claims. Rather than dismissing Ellington's text as the product of an ineffective writer, rather than simply denying its sophistication because it, like the Mingus and Holiday autobiographies, was assembled by a white collaborator, I want, as in the case of those other autobiographies, to hold onto something potentially emancipatory here. What if, for example, we seek to understand *Music Is My Mistress* in relation to how Ellington, as a culturally and historically constituted subject, improvised his identity in ways that provided a conduit for African Americans to gain access to influence, institutional authority, and public legitimacy? Moving contentedly amongst dominant white institutions, Ellington was engaged in a form of "passing," where passing is itself subversive because it provides some measure of power, credibility, and autonomy. I partly have in mind here Andrews's readings of fictive elements in black autobiography, but I'm also thinking about Houston Baker's extraordinary reading of the Harlem Renaissance. In his discussion of some of the sounding strategies which enabled American blacks to establish their own identity, Baker identifies two strategies which, when taken together, constitute the essence of black discursive modernism: "mastery of form" and "deformation of mastery." Baker's formulation is instructive in the current context because it alerts us to the fact that a self-conscious adoption of the discourse employed by a hegemonic white culture (what he calls "mastery of form") represents a salient stage in the process of subversion ("the deformation of mastery"). In this context, the absences in Ellington's text, particularly the refusal to thematize race as a central issue of concern for African Americans, are part of the "mastery of form," part of Ellington's perceived need to compete for access and public legitimacy not by explicitly challenging dominant structures of knowledge production but by improvising *within* an already constituted system. In an era in which, as Neal writes, the government was making it clear that "being a dissenter—particularly an African-American dissenter—was very dangerous" (55), an era which witnessed the "increased militarization of the nation's law enforcement agencies as well as calculated and covert state-sponsored attacks against the black protest movement's most progressive elements" (62), Ellington's literary improvisations were very much attuned to the empowering possibilities of being part of the dominant social order.[2]

All three of the autobiographies I've touched on here seek, if in highly varied ways, to create improvisational structures for the representation (and the transformation) of black social energies and cultural practices. For Ellington, it would appear, improvisation has to do not with the more active forms of political resistance championed by Robeson's unscripted performative interventions, but with the adjustments made to enable structures of mobility *within* governing institutions. Indeed, all three autobiographers (and Robeson too, for that matter) are in varying degrees concerned with precisely such adjustments, that is, with finding innovative ways for African Americans to become active subjects in the face of various forms of institutional coercion and containment, to engage in struggles against centralized systems of power and fixity. As a structure of movement and flexibility that's central to the rhetoric of these autobiographies, improvisation plays a valuable role in alerting us to what's at stake in the debates that have evolved around African-American resistance to the white cultural mainstream and in inviting us to recognize the extent to which black cultural identities are continually being reinvented to serve the political needs of the moment.

Notes

1. Ellington tells us, for example, that "*Black, Brown and Beige* was planned as a tone parallel to the history of the American Negro" (181).

2. We can, perhaps, find an instructive contrast in the case of Robeson. Like Ellington, Robeson was, at least for a time, one of the world's most influential African-American artists. W. E. B. Du Bois, in fact, speaking in the '50s, said of Robeson, "He is without doubt today, as a person, the best known American on earth, to the largest number of human beings. His voice is known in Europe, Asia and Africa, in the West Indies and South America and in the islands of the seas. Children on the streets of Peking and Moscow, Calcutta and Jakarta greet him and send him their love" (quoted in Brown, x). In his own home country of America, however, Robeson was shunned; because of his communist sympathies and his uncompromising efforts on behalf of the social and political rights of African Americans, Robeson was severely persecuted by his government, denied his rights as a citizen, and prevented from making a living as a performing artist. His autobiographical *Here I Stand*, first published in 1958, was almost completely ignored in the mainstream press. "Only in his native land," as Du Bois put it, was Robeson "without honor and rights" (x).

4

"Space Is the Place"

Jazz, Voice, and Resistance

Place is security, space is freedom: we are attached to the one and long for the other.

Yi-Fu Tuan, *Space and Place,* 3

If you find earth boring, just the same old same thing, then come on and sign up for Outer Spaceways Incorporated.

Sun Ra, "Outer Spaceways Incorporated"

Sun Ra is not a joke!

Anthony Braxton, quoted in Lock, *Forces in Motion,* 154

When Duke Ellington, in a 1957 issue of *Down Beat* magazine, was quoted as saying that he was not interested in educating people, Sun Ra, in the liner notes to one of his earliest recordings, released that same year, responded by declaring, "I want to go on record as stating that I am" (*Sun Song*). Ra's pronouncement, I'd like to suggest, constitutes an explicit invitation for us to reflect on the social function of art and in particular on his own music's participation in and engagement with what, following Edward Said, I'd like to call the worldly context of human struggles and aspirations. Ra's comment also forces us to rethink our understanding of the places where we look for knowledge. If only implicitly, that is, it issues a challenge to the institutionalization of knowledge: it encourages us to ask: What does it mean to educate people *not* through academic institutions but through music, and in particular, through jazz? To what extent can jazz—and Ra's jazz specifically—be seen as providing the conditions for the production of learning? In "studying" Ra's texts (his recordings, his performances, even his films), are we also engaging in the process of promoting social change?

Ra's insistence that we take him seriously as a kind of educator is evident in any number of his pronouncements, and it is these pronouncements which have led me to situate his art within the contexts I sought to establish in my introductory remarks. "The real aim of this music," he tells us, for example, on the liner notes to *Pictures of Infinity*, "is to coordinate the minds of people into an intelligent reach for a better world, and an intelligent approach to the living future." And, in an interview in 1965, Ra said, "I would hate to pass through a planet and not leave it a better place. It's ridiculous to spend all that time and energy and then leave it the way it was" (quoted in Litweiler, 141). In his biography of Sun Ra, John Szwed points out that during rehearsals with his various groups (rehearsals which "were the stuff of musicians' legends" [*Space*, 111]), Ra (who had in fact studied to be a teacher) was notorious for lecturing his performers "on the history of black people and their role in the creation of civilization" as well as "on the use of music in changing the world" (98). "My business," Ra unequivocally declared, "is changing the planet" (quoted in Szwed, *Space*, 84). Ra's musicians, too, repeatedly speak about him as an educator, as someone who sought to mobilize knowledge in ways that would reduce the effects of oppression. Baritone saxophonist Pat Patrick, who has called Ra a "strict teacher" with "very high standards" (quoted in Wilmer, 85), puts it this way: "Sun Ra was another kind of being. He was educational, he helped you to grow and develop. He was a black self-help organization run on a shoestring. Blacks don't have many people like him. If he could've had the resources, the planet would be a better place. That's all he's done: tried to make life better" (quoted in Szwed, *Space,* 89).

As such comments make clear, Ra believed that jazz could be a vehicle for social betterment. Burton Peretti, drawing on the work of Edward Brathwaite, has made a somewhat similar point, suggesting that jazz, broadly speaking, ought to be viewed as "a paradigm for students of postcolonial culture." His argument is that "the African-American creators of jazz, descended from victims of colonization, displacement, and enslavement, belonged themselves to generations which continued to suffer from injustice and to seek healing" ("Plantation Cafés," 90). What makes Sun Ra a unique figure in the history of jazz, though, is not simply his insistence that jazz has a political function, that it can and should actively intervene in the production and the distribution of knowledge in ways that counter oppression and injustice. Other artists (I'm thinking, for example, of Max Roach, Bill Dixon, Archie Shepp, and members of the AACM) have certainly looked to jazz as an important arena for redefining the possibilities of social transformation, for, in Amilcar Cabral's formulation, examining the role of "culture as a factor of resistance to . . . domination" (53). Indeed, as Frank Kofsky suggests in his book *Black Nationalism and the Revolution in Music*, Shepp, Roach, and others have forced a recognition of the extent to which "a certain residue of protonationalist thinking . . . has always been present in jazz, even to the point of influencing the timing and the direction of stylistic innovations" (27). While Sun Ra was always on the forefront of stylistic innovations in jazz—as Graham Lock points out, Ra was "one of the most radical forces in creative music. A pioneer of synthesizers and electronic keyboards, of modal music, of looking to Africa for inspiration (and finding chants, raps, polyrhythmic percussion), of reasserting pride in black music and black culture" (*Forces,* 13)—his legacy, I think, resides not only in his interventions into ongoing debates about the political function of music but, to return to a distinction I made in the book's Introduction, in the interpretive framework he sought to establish for articulating the terms of his own self-representation.

That framework, evident in my title, "Space Is the Place" (also the title of an album, of one of Ra's most well-known compositions, of a film in which Ra acted and for which he wrote and performed the soundtrack, and, more recently, of Szwed's biography), ought also to be evident in the comment I quoted earlier, where Ra talks about passing "through a planet." Ra, it's worth noting here, speaks of "*a* planet," rather than "*the* planet," as though he has passed through several planets, and his rhetoric, I'd like to suggest, is carefully chosen. For Ra repeatedly insisted that he was not of this planet (see, for example, Rusch, 62), and his song and album titles, the theatricality of his concert performances, the course he taught when he was invited to be a lecturer at the University of California in Berkeley—"The Black Man in the Cosmos" (Szwed, liner notes)—and the space-age attire which he was seen to sport not only on stage but also in supermarkets all work to reinforce Ra's otherworldliness. Listing Saturn as his place of birth, Ra was frequently dismissed by both musicians (including black musicians) and critics as a charlatan. Betty Carter, for one, was famously nasty in her response to Ra: "Sun Ra. . . . He's got his metallic clothes on, his lights flashing back and forth, and he's got the nerve to spell orchestra a-r-k-e-s-t-r-a. It's supposed to have something to do with stars and Mars, but it's nothing but bullshit. Sun Ra has got whitey going for it" (quoted in Szwed, *Space,* 265). Indeed, even before he talked about being from Saturn or changed his name, Sonny Blount (as he was known in his Birmingham, Alabama days) was dismissed and disliked by the more traditionally minded musicians in his hometown.

Numerous other artists—among them John Coltrane, Anthony Braxton, and even Herb Alpert— have, however, recognized Ra as an enormously influential figure in the history of jazz. And, as Chris Cutler suggests in *File Under Popular*, Ra is perhaps best understood not strictly as "an entertainer, a band-leader, an eccentric 'personality,' but [as] an Elder, a filter of wisdom, a chief guildsman, active in the presentation & preservation of the Mystery of his guild craft" (64). "None of [Ra's] visual paraphernalia or mythology will make much sense to a passive observer," Cutler admits, "but, at a concert, & for a willing audience, it does help to suspend for a while our habitual cultural sense of isolation. . . . Indeed, everything which helps prevent us from getting a foothold in the familiar, from *consuming* rather than *participating*, will help us . . . to get nearer to the heart of [Ra's] music" (66).

As a kind of cultural text himself, Ra ought to be of interest to us precisely because of the problem of interpretation that he poses, and, perhaps, demands: if, as Cutler suggests, the process of defamiliarization at work in Ra's performances and in the conceptual thinking that animated these performances constitutes an invitation for us to participate in a newly articulated understanding of musical meaning, then how are we to respond to that invitation? How, more precisely, do we make sense of Ra's pedagogical project in light of the glittering space robes and hats, the rhetoric of space and interplanetary travel, the cosmic mythology? Can we take seriously the claims to educate people from someone who told us that he was from another planet? Can we—and need we—reconcile Ra's otherworldly claims with his situatedness in worldly circumstances and struggles? When Ra and his Arkestra (more about the Arkestra in a moment) told us, as they did in "Enlightenment" (which for a time was something of a signature song at Ra's performances), that they were "inviting" us into their "space world," were they in fact trying, as the song title implies, to educate us in some way?

Saxophonist Anthony Braxton explicitly situates Ra's work within the context of an oppositional pedagogy that interrogates the forces that have shaped the production and the distribution of knowledge: "To examine the work of Sun Ra," says Braxton, "is to see his attempts to uncover the information that was lost in the last 3,000 years and to transmit that information to the public" (quoted in Lock, *Forces,* 155). If, with Jim Merod, we see "jazz as a cultural archive of the Black community which has marked the entire social logic of twentieth-century life in North America" ("Resistance," 193), then Ra's jazz and its transgressive energies are perhaps best understood as attempts to articulate the complex processes through which communities and alliances of misrepresented peoples struggle for access to self-representation. Just as, in R. Radhakrishnan's words, "Contemporary theorists of subjugated subject positions (feminists, ethnic theorists, critics of colonialism and imperialism) have contested the necessity to conceive of their positions as 'lacks' and 'absences' within the dominant structure" (33), so Ra worked to contest and reconfigure the relations of power that have become inscribed and institutionalized as knowledge. I'd like to spend the remaining time in this chapter attempting a rough inventory of some of the ways in which these processes of articulation are encoded in Ra's music, and showing how, at least insofar as Sun Ra functions as a signifier for the cultural history of jazz, and thus in Merod's formulation, for the social logic of North America, he was engaged in developing a pedagogy of resistance.

There is, of course, a substantial—and growing—body of writing on resistance and counterdiscourse, but I can't pretend to do justice to it here: I'm thinking, for example, of Cabral, Frantz Fanon, and Edward Said in postcolonial theory; Barbara Harlow and Richard Terdiman in literary studies; Jean Comaroff and James Scott in anthropology; bell hooks in black feminism; Ray Pratt and John Street in music; and the work of the Subaltern Studies collective in historiography. What interests me for the purposes of the present discussion is the extent to which we can see, read, and hear resistance not simply as a site of figural contestation but also, in Said's terms, as "an alternative way of conceiving human history" (*Culture and Imperialism,* 216). Ra's jazz, in such a context, seems to me to offer a particularly resonant way of thinking about the expressive possibilities of human and imaginative agency. His mythology and uninhibited vision, I want to suggest, speak powerfully to the ways in which African Americans have elaborated empowering strategies of signification.

Consider, for instance, the nature of a performance by Ra and his Arkestra. Although, as Ra discographer Robert Campbell documents in his book *The Earthly Recordings of Sun Ra*, there are several hundred recordings of Ra's music, few of these succeed in capturing the energy and the variety of a live performance. For the music of any given performance by Ra and his Arkestra trafficked in and emblematized a complex set of cultural and historical moments, ranging in reference from ancient Egypt (which Ra, along with George G. M. James, maintained was a black civilization) to outer space. A typical concert by Sun Ra (like an Art Ensemble concert) tended to be something of a spectacular theatrical romp through the history of jazz from its earliest forms (swing) to more recent manifestations (bebop, free jazz) and beyond: as with the Art Ensemble, a kind of abridged history of accomplishments in Black music. As one writer puts it, behind Ra's music "stands the whole black tradition: Count Basie's Swing riffs and Duke Ellington's saxophone sounds; Fletcher Henderson's 'voicings'; old blues and black songs; African highlife dances and Egyptian marches; black percussion music from South, Central, and North America, and from Africa" (Berendt, 337–38).

Ra's performances (with their range of geopolitical reference) sonically approximated the periods of transition that might be seen more generally to mark postcolonial cultural production. Frantz Fanon and others have made the point that reclaiming history is often a necessary first step for oppressed peoples seeking access to a postcolonial subjectivity. "Colonialism," Fanon writes, "is not satisfied merely with holding a people in its grip and emptying the native's brain of all form and content. By a kind of perverted logic, it turns to the past of the oppressed people, and distorts, disfigures, and destroys it" (210). In the context of such a claim, Ra's rehabilitation of swing-era tunes, his reworking of traditional jazz forms such as stride, stomp, and blues, as well as his attempt to reclaim ancient Egypt as a black civilization have the pedagogical effect of encouraging a radical rethinking of institutionalized history. That such cultural reclamation was part of his pedagogical plan is also apparent in the texts Ra chose to put on his reading list for the course he taught at Berkeley: among those texts, for example, was Theodor P. Ford's *God Wills the Negro*, a text whose very subtitle, *An Anthropological and Geographical Restoration of the History of the American Negro People*, points to Ra's involvement in recasting, now from a black perspective, the kinds of notions of the past that had been authorized and institutionalized as dominant fields of knowledge. Ra's reclamation of ancient Egypt, indeed, prompts us to reconsider history in ways that are akin to the teachings of important African scholars such as Cheikh Anta Diop and Theophile Obenga, both of whom, as Molefi Asante and Abu Abarry point out in the introduction to their monumental source book, *African Intellectual Heritage*, "attacked the central thesis of much Eurocentric scholarship on ancient Egypt. They argued that the European writers attempted to make the ancient Egyptians white in order to discredit the civilizing role of the African continent" (3).[1]

But for all his interest in revising our cultural understanding of the past, Ra too, of course, was fond of blasting off into the future. If the thematic emphasis on the past functions in Ra's art to create a space for the apprehension of alternative histories, to enable us to hear other kinds of historical rhythms, then Ra's forward-looking vision seems to be about the creation of a genuinely independent postcolonial future for American blacks. Ra's innovative handling of electronic (or what he was fond of calling "intergalactic") instruments, his insistence that blacks "take advantage of new discoveries in science and technology" (Lock, *Forces,* 15), his participation in what some have called a secret society on the South Side of Chicago which, in Robert Campbell's words, "preached an unusual variety of Black Nationalism, admonishing Black men to recognize the importance of outer space if they were to better their lot in the future" ("From Sonny Blount to Sun Ra"), and his wigged-out space themes all suggest a desire to opt out of the very codes of representation and intelligibility, the very frameworks of interpretation and assumption, which have legitimized the workings of dominant culture. Ra's space-age futurism, I'm thinking, may well mark a shift in postcolonial struggles for identity formation: rather than critically interrogating the dominant ideology's misrepresentation of black history (and consequently seeking to correct the historical record), Ra's space sounds, philosophy, and paraphernalia invite us to envision new models for an aesthetic of resistance, to generate a space outside the very framework of domination. If Arthur Jafa is correct to suggest (as I think he is) that there has been a tendency in black music to "treat notes as indeterminate, inherently unstable sonic frequencies rather than . . . fixed phenomena" (254), and if, as I suggested in the previous chapter, such refusal of structures of fixity has provided African-American performing artists with purposeful alternatives to socially and institutionally constituted frameworks of intelligibility, then Ra's patented use of the synthesizer to create futuristic bursts of sound, his manipulation of pitch, tone color, and noise (listen, for example, to "When Spaceships Appear" from a 1985 Saturn recording that has circulated under various titles),[2] can be seen as part of his attempt to remake music to his own specification. Read as postcolonial discourse, Ra's texts, I'm suggesting, might be heard as a condensed historical resounding of the interplay between the constraints of inherited systems of history writing and knowledge production (and their concomitant representations of otherness) and the independence associated with imaginative, future-oriented processes of inquiry. "Instead of being/Nowhere here," Ra wrote, "Let's go/Somewhere There."

One of the recordings that *does* seem to me to do justice to the energy of Ra's performances is *Sunrise in Different Dimensions*, recorded live in Switzerland in 1980. Featuring a scaled-down Arkestra, with Ra playing only piano and organ, the recording highlights material ranging from thunderously intense free-blowing sessions and forward-looking space anthems to carefully orchestrated arrangements of swing-era tunes. The opening number, "Light from a Hidden Sun," is a solo piano piece which, in miniature, seems in some ways to exemplify the range and scope of Ra's musical vision: there's beauty and elegance here, a compelling sense of swing, too, even in the freest moments. Listen, too, to Ra's rendition of Fletcher Henderson's "Big John's Special," a song that would have been part of Henderson's repertoire in the 1930s. Ra himself emerged out of the black big band tradition, having played with Henderson in the '40s. Robert Campbell tells me that while Ra's arrangement of the tune is nearly a straight transcription of Henderson's original, with John Gilmore (heard on clarinet here) and some of the trumpet players deliberately copying solos off the 1934 recording at Ra's behest, Ra also included instruments not in Henderson's lineup, and he sneakily retouched the harmony. Worth noting in Ra's rendition is the way in which he enlarges on the call-and-response figure as a development of big band sound: listen, for instance, to the interplay between Ra's piano and the horn arrangements. Henderson, famous for employing call-and-response patterns in his approach to ensemble playing, was probably the single most important big band leader of his time; nevertheless he remains something of a neglected figure. This neglect stems largely from the fact that the swing era, which Henderson himself inaugurated through his arrangements for Benny Goodman, became a white phenomenon: Goodman, as one writer puts it, "happened to be the symbol of the age [the King of Swing], but this came about, at least in large part, as a result of the artistry and craftsmanship, born of twelve hard years of musical experience, that Fletcher Henderson brought to him at just the right moment in history" (Hadlock, 217).[3]

While this is not the place to do a detailed reading of the way in which black art forms were co-opted by the white cultural mainstream (see also Fanon on bebop, 243), I allude to Henderson's "lack" or "absence" in the institutionalized production of knowledge about jazz history to make the point that Ra's rollicking interpretation of this tune from Henderson's repertoire is itself an attempt to reclaim a misrepresented history. Indeed, in the 1980s Ra used to append a sermonette to "Enlightenment." It was a catchy ditty called "Strange Mathematic Rhythmic Equations" and part of it was explicitly about reclaiming the past through schooling:

> They tried to fool you,
> So I've got to school you
> About jazz
> About jazz.
>
> Bessie Smith, now that's jazz.
> Billie Holiday, now that's jazz.
> Duke Ellington, now that's jazz.
> Fletcher Henderson, now that's jazz.
>
> If it ain't got that swing
> It don't mean a thing.[4]

If, as Patrick Brantlinger puts it in his book on the emergence of cultural studies, "[t]he struggle for Afro-American literacy and literature (and all art forms) has been a struggle against the powerful, white voices, discourses, and disciplines that at first sought to deny the black writer the very instruments of writing, then later sought to deny to his or her writing either authenticity or the status of literature or both" (154), then the narrative trajectory that is traced out through Ra's music and his career is, if only implicitly, emblematic of that very history of domination and resistance. Ra, of course, was a musician and not (or at least not primarily) a *littérateur*, yet Brantlinger's comments are, I think, relevant here, for they provide a salient context for understanding Ra's attempt (like the attempt of members of the AACM) to enable African-American artists to become active subjects of their own histories, epistemologies, and experiences. The inclusion in Ra's repertoire of "Big John's Special" and other tunes from the Henderson era plays an important role in this pedagogy of resistance: such an inclusion approximates in miniature what, in Cornel West's estimation, is the central task for black intellectuals: "to stimulate, hasten and enable alternative perceptions and practices by dislodging prevailing discourses and powers" (*Keeping Faith,* 83). What Ra promotes, then, is a change in the nature and the orientation of the very frame of investigation: Ra's tributes to Henderson's swing era tunes constitute an attempt to read against the "white" grain of institutionalized jazz history, to reveal the extent to which swing has been commodified in the service of dominant white interests and to reclaim that history in the context of black cultural practice.

Henderson's approach to ensemble playing is of particular importance to Ra largely because of the political philosophy of big bands and the tradition that it exemplifies. As Francis Davis points out, "a big-band *sound* is less important to [Ra] than the blueprint for black solidarity he understands big bands to embody" ("Hottentot," 24). One of the amazing things about Ra's various Arkestras is that though the names may have changed (Solar Arkestra, Astro-Infinity Arkestra, Myth-Science Arkestra, Intergalactic Space Arkestra, Cosmo-Love Adventure Arkestra, etc.),[5] the musicians, many of whom played with Ra for some four decades (and lived with him in a communal setting), remained committed to the principle of the big band in an era when smaller groups (quartets, trios) have become the rage. In his interview with Bob Rusch, Ra spoke of the way in which the growing preference for small groups destroyed the cooperative spirit and energy of big bands. "As a result," said Ra, "you destroy initiative and cause total chaos and confusion in the Black communities" (Rusch, 68).[6] What Ra was suggesting, I think, is that he was drawn to big bands, and the black tradition out of which they emerge, because they constitute "collective forms of oppositional consciousness" (Pratt, 13). As if to signal that oppositional role, Ra, who apparently loved to scour the Bible for hidden meanings, named his band the Arkestra, thus alerting us to the possibility that music can function as a vessel of salvation, that it can preserve communities of meaning from the forces that threaten to destroy them. Pianist Vijay Iyer, in an essay on African-American music collectives, points out that the Arkestra "presented and maintained a revolutionary, separate totality that had its own powerful, unique voice. Sun Ra's pervasive use of the 'outer space' metaphor," Iyer adds, "reinforced the group's separateness, its otherness, in an active sense that resists interpretation or domination by mass culture. The Arkestra relished the marginalized position, the outer space, by actively defining its collective identity."

This naming, this active insistence on articulating the terms of his own self-representation (something that, as I suggested in chapter 2, was also to become a central concern for the Art Ensemble of Chicago), is reflected too in Ra's awareness of the need to maintain control over the production of his music. As numerous commentators have pointed out, Ra played a key role in pioneering the concept of the artist-owned record company by recording and distributing (often in the most amateur way)[7] most of his music on his own Saturn records. At the time that Ra registered his artist-run company with the Musicians Union in 1956, "the idea of any musician, black or white, being able to produce and sell his own records was," in Szwed's words, "so daring, so unprecedented, as to be heroic in the music business" (*Space,* 152). Just a few years earlier, Charles Mingus had set up his own record company, Debut, so that, as Frank Kofsky writes, "he would no longer have to suffer the fate of a pawn in the game of the white-controlled jazz record industry" (51). Later, in 1960, Mingus would again seek to find ways for musicians to take control over their art, this time joining forces with Max Roach to stage the Alternative Newport Festival. The blossoming of organizations such as Debut and Saturn in the '50s, and the AACM, Alternative Newport, and Horace Tapscott's Union of God's Musicians and Artists Ascension in the '60s provided a resistance to existing white-dominated institutions and values while also suggesting theoretical and institutional alternatives to dominant models of cultural production. At stake in such organizations is a vision that seeks to extend the possibilities for creating an oppositional black public sphere. Kofsky has argued that "regardless of what many black musicians may believe, their suppression is due less to competition from white players than to the fact that ownership of the leading economic institutions of jazz are [*sic*] vested in the hands of entrepreneurs whose preeminent goal is not the enhancement of the art but the taking of a profit" (60). By exerting control over the production and distribution of his own art, Ra not only ensured that his music is amply documented, but also worked to map out a pedagogy of resistance. This process of self-documentation, in fact, is very much a part of Ra's broader pedagogical game plan: his insistence on independence of movement and on "the creative construction of alternative identities and renovated social possibilities" (Corbett, 8).

Ra's pedagogy, I've been trying to suggest, is about the need to deterritorialize institutionalized forms of cultural domination. But it also points to the possibilities of both individual agency and collective solidarity. If, with bell hooks, we agree that "[a]wareness of the need to speak, to give voice to the varied dimensions of our lives, is one way [to] begin the process of education for critical consciousness" (13), then Ra's achievements speak directly to the need to reclaim voice, to ensure access to the possibilities of self-representation and self-determination. Through his music and his example, his critique of the complex dynamics of institutional power structures, Ra offered a particularly resonant variation on what Cornel West has called the "basic orientation in New World African modernity": the need "to flee the widespread victimization of Euro-American modernity . . . and to find a 'home' in a safe and 'free' space" (*Keeping Faith,* xiii), to forge "a sense of possible momentum and motion for a temporal people with few spatial options" (xiii–xiv).

This sense of the need to generate social momentum and to foster black mobility is, perhaps, one of the most enduring of Sun Ra's lessons. Ra's work and his vision, indeed, are very much in keeping with the compelling emphasis on movement that has historically animated the narratives, struggles, and improvisations of African Americans. Szwed is correct to situate Ra's vision in the context of "the theme of travel, of journey, of exodus, of escape which dominates African-American narratives: of people who could fly back to Africa, travel in the spirit, visit or be visited by the dead; of chariots and trains to heaven, the Underground Railroad, Marcus Garvey's steamship line, Rosa Parks on the Mobile bus, freedom riders" (*Space,* 134). Space, in this context, functions as a metaphor for possibility (or, perhaps, for doing the impossible), for alternatives to dominant systems of knowledge production, "a metaphor of exclusion and reterritorialization, of claiming the 'outside' as one's own, of tying a revised and corrected past to a claimed future" (*Space,* 140). Or perhaps more simply, it is, as John Corbett writes, a metaphor for "being elsewhere, or . . . making this elsewhere your own" (18).

The 1974 film *Space Is the Place*, starring Ra and directed by John Coney, develops many of these ideas. "Part documentary, part science fiction, part blaxploitation, part revisionist biblical epic" (Szwed, *Space,* 330), the film offers a twist on the familiar African-American theme of flying as a trope for liberation and freedom, and is explicit in theorizing outer space as a site of resistance for African Americans. "Everything you desire upon this planet but never have received," says Ra at one point in the film, "will be yours in outer space." The film shows Ra alighting on earth after having traveled the spaceways for some time, seeking to lead those willing to follow him into outer space: his goal is to set up a new planet in outer space for black people, to "see what they could do with their own planet, without any white people." Ra lands in early '70s Oakland, the very place "where in real life the Arkestra was staying and where the Black Panthers were under attack by the police and the FBI" (Szwed, *Space,* 330). In the film, Ra too, as it happens, finds himself under attack by the FBI. Ra tells members of a local black community center whom he hopes to lead into space that, on Earth, black people don't exist except as myths because they have been denied rights and status. "Astro-Black mythology," explains Szwed, "was what he had to develop: black people are not real in this society. They exist as myths, but other people's myths" (*Space,* 315–16). There is a clear link here, as indeed there is throughout Ra's philosophical musings, between race and space, between African-American struggles for rights and citizenship and outer space as a place of liberating possibilities.[8] Ra used space iconography, in John Corbett's words, as a "platform for playful subversion, imagining a productive zone largely exterior to dominant ideology" (8). Countering the dominant myths, values, and behaviors that have become institutionalized, authorized, and naturalized in American society with a radical revisioning of black history and culture, Ra thus sought to generate new models of knowledge production. Space becomes a site for the recovery and the articulation of other histories, epistemologies, identities, and possibilities.

Speaking of the new planet where he plans to "teleport" the earth's blacks "through music," Ra tells us in the film that "the music is different here, the vibrations are different, not like planet earth." And, indeed, the music *is* different. Unlike the stride piano Ra is shown playing at a Chicago nightclub in 1943, where his music causes a riot (well, almost stride: let's call it stride with an edge), when Ra's in space, the film's music becomes decidedly free and futuristic, mysterious, and, yes, even spacey: the soundtrack is awash with lower-register sonorities and heavy percussion, with distant horns that sound as if they're being played in an echo chamber, with wonky harmonies, with intense collective improvisations (indeed, another of Ra's contributions to the music was his sustained attempt to integrate free collective improvisation into large ensemble playing), and, of course, with Ra's wild flights of fancy on the Moog synthesizer. It's tempting to draw an explicit analogy here between the space philosophy and the music's attempt to push the outer limits: as Corbett puts it, a "connection is established between 'going way out' (a common phrase in jazz for a solo that transgresses a widely held musical code, such as the established harmonic framework), and leaving Earth.

Tradition = earth; innovation = outer space" (17). Others, like Amiri Baraka, are even more explicit in linking Ra's music and his rhetoric of space travel with black political struggles against oppression and injustice: "What Trane spoke of, speaks of, what Ra means, where Pharoah wd like to go, is clearly another world. In (w)hich we are literally (and further) free" (quoted in Szwed, *Space,* 210).

Ra clearly identified with the aims and struggles of black nationalism and was involved in various kinds of black causes; yet to align his art solely with black nationalism or to see it primarily in terms of the free music associated with other prominent (and politically motivated) black musicians in the '60s would, I think, be a mistake. Although Ra participated in the now-famous October Revolution in Jazz (1964) spearheaded by trumpeter Bill Dixon, and in fact later joined the Jazz Composers Guild which emerged out of that festival featuring the leading free jazz players of the day, he soon left the guild, saying of two of its prominent members, Archie Shepp and Cecil Taylor: "They were doing their thing, but they were not talking about Space or Intergalactic things. . . . They were talking about Avant Garde and the New Thing" (quoted in Jost, 181). Ra's discomfort in being associated with '60s free jazz (and its politics) suggests that we need to be cautious in making assumptions about the connections between "out" jazz and the rhetoric of outer space, or more generally, between specific styles of music and particular kinds of political allegiance. Tempting as it is, for example, to hear insurgent energies in jazz's timbral dissonances, or to read the explicit violation of musical etiquette as a critique of dominant social relations, I'm forced, again, to consider the extent to which my interpretive frameworks may be at odds with the lives and the musics that I seek to describe and analyze.

There's much in Ra's legacy specifically that resists neat frameworks of analysis, that forces us to interrogate our critical assumptions about his cultural work. Most notable, as I've been suggesting, is the music, with its quirky dissonances and its extraordinary geopolitical range (from Egypt to outer space). We should note too that it's not just the "out" tunes in Ra's repertoire that deal with space: space thematics also figure in more traditionally oriented big band pieces such as "Saturn," as well as in some of the Arkestra's catchiest chants and anthems ("We Travel the Spaceways," "Rocket Number Nine," "Saturn Rings"). My discussion of the political implications of Ra's Astro-Black philosophizing also admittedly requires some qualification, especially given the more troubling and authoritarian aspects of his personality described in Szwed's biography. Furthermore, for all his insistence that African Americans turn to outer space to seize control of their futures, to assert their role in the narrative of science and progress, and, in effect, to decolonize planet Earth, Ra himself uses the word "colony" in the film *Space Is the Place* to describe the separate planet he plans to set up for blacks. I was initially tempted to ignore Ra's use of the term, to see it as an oversight (even Sun Ra makes mistakes!) or as something that could be explained in terms of his claim that the music and vibrations would be different on this new planet: colonization too, I was tempted to reason, would, in Ra's space world, somehow be vibrationally different, somehow nonoppressive. But Ra's use of such a historically laden word here forces me to confront the limits of my own analysis. Further, it leads me to re-ask a question which has sparked much debate among postcolonial theorists: To what extent can complete resistance to dominant systems of thought ever be a possibility. Can genuinely oppositional postcolonial work ever entirely exit from the narrative and history of colonization? And what, then, should we make of the fact that while Ra sees in outer space the possibility of resistance to hegemonic social relations, his rhetoric, perhaps despite itself, in some ways echoes the very rhetoric of colonization that more generally surrounded the American space program? Recall, for example, President Nixon's comments to the astronauts on board the historic Apollo 11 space mission, comments which suggest that the exploration of other worlds is part of a larger desire to colonize the unknown: "Because of what you have done," Nixon told the astronauts, "the heavens have become a part of man's world" (quoted in von Braun, 360–61). And recall too, as interactive multimedia artist Colette Gaiter, creator of "SPACE|R A C E," reminds us, that "Media accounts of the moon mission made endless comparisons" to another act of colonization, Columbus's voyage. Ra, who in so many ways sought to stand outside such dominant models of thinking, and who instead looked to the parameters of the possible (indeed the impossible) to expand opportunities for independence and self-determination, seemed, perhaps uncharacteristically, to fall back on the very frameworks of assumption that he was elsewhere so quick to reject. What Ra seems to teach us here is that even the rhetoric of resistance is imbricated in hegemonic formations.

Also complicating our attempts to understand Ra is the very stuff of his everyday life. Eager as I've been to assimilate Ra's lifework into debates emerging out of the struggles of subordinated social groups, there is still much that remains untold here. For Sun Ra, as Robert Campbell, John Gill, and others have implied, was not only black, but gay. While Ra identified with some kinds of black causes, he never overtly engaged in gay activism or was seen supporting gay causes. How do we understand Ra's support for black causes but not for gay ones? "[I]t is saddening," writes Gill in *Queer Noises: Male and Female Homosexuality in Twentieth-Century Music*, "to think that Sun Ra could be out about so many things—not least his regal ancient Egyptian ancestors, and the fact that he didn't come from this planet—but not about his sexual orientation" (60).

Ra, in addition, would often go out of his way to conceal much about his family or his early years on Earth, and, as Robert Campbell pointed out in his 1995 address to the Alabama Jazz Hall of Fame, the cosmic philosopher was deliberately vague about when exactly he had arrived on the planet: "maybe in 1055, he would say, maybe a few thousand years before that" (Campbell, "From Sonny Blount to Sun Ra"). Ra would also often insist that he was "never really named Herman Blount, that he had always used other names, that the name [Herman Blount] 'didn't have no rhythm' anyhow" (Campbell, "From Sonny Blount to Sun Ra").

Szwed's biography makes clear that there has always been something of the trickster in Ra, something that makes it difficult to pin him down, to know with certainty that we've understood what he's about. Even those close to him couldn't know with certainty how to interpret his claims. Once, for example, in Berlin in the late '80s, Sun Ra was allegedly kidnapped. Ra's account of the incident is oddly reminiscent of the scene in the film *Space Is the Place* where Ra is kidnapped by the FBI. In Berlin, Ra recounted, he was taken to a planetarium by people who wanted to learn the secrets of the black space program: "They started asking me questions, strange questions, like how did I intend to get black folks off the planet. What kind of ship was I going to use? What kind of fuel was I going to use in the ship?" (quoted in Szwed, 359). Writing about the incident, Szwed remarks, "some of the band complained that it was a setup, another one of [Ra's] jokes. But who could be sure? The line between the mundane and the theatrical was sometimes very fine with Sonny" (359).

In keeping with the spirit of Ra's lifework, I want to end with a joke—at least I think it's a joke—that has become part of the legend that has evolved around Sun Ra and his art. It goes, at least in one of its versions, something like this: Sun Ra is stopped at the border by a customs official.

> Customs official: Where are you from?
> Ra: Saturn.
> Customs official: Come on. Where are you from?
> Ra: Saturn.
> Customs official: I'll ask you once more. Where are you from?
> Ra: Okay, okay. Jupiter.

It's true that I may be making Ra's joke bear awfully heavy freight. But I'm wondering whether encoded somewhere in this little example might be a model for cultural listening. For isn't Ra, in refusing to homogenize frameworks of knowledge, pushing us here, as in his music, to recognize the importance, indeed the *necessity*, of crossing cultural borders? Isn't he, in effect, pushing us into a mode of thinking that not only reconceives spatial options for African Americans but also attempts to create a space for cultural resistance in general, for the apprehension of alternative histories and epistemologies? I'm aware here that such a statement appears to fly in the face of postcolonialism's critique of universalism, that it runs the risk of suggesting that our ability to cross all boundaries enables us to transcend (or perhaps forget) differences and cultural specifics.[9] While my own commitment to postcolonial theory certainly encourages me to be critically suspicious of universalist claims and methodologies, trickster Ra, whose art and pedagogy would seem in so many ways to offer a resonant fit with some of the most pressing tasks and concerns of postcolonial thinking and stock-taking, has once again succeeding in confounding my critical assumptions. Ra's project has always been to force us into rethinking our understanding of perspective, to broaden our focus of attention (are humans necessarily the center of the universe?), and to push us into a consideration of the ways in which forms of respect and tolerance can be achieved both within and between constituencies. Despite his nationalist inclinations, and the extreme rarity of white musicians in the Arkestra, Ra's aims and methods were often unabashedly universal, his sermons and jeremiads addressed to Planet Earth as a whole. On his 1956 recording *Super-Sonic Jazz*, we are told that the compositions on the recording "are universal in scope. . . . THIS IS A UNIVERSAL MUSIC. A FREE LANGUAGE OF JOY" (*Super-Sonic Jazz*). Ra's space rhetoric suggests to me that although his ideas frequently depend on and are determined by a specific set of moments in black cultural history, his vision ultimately remains more inclusive: his achievement, I think, resides precisely in what postcolonial theorist Diana Brydon has called "the search for non-repressive alternatives to the present organization of knowledge and its limiting representations of otherness" (110).

Ra's legacy, I have been suggesting, needs to be understood in the context of the social processes and institutional dynamics that have shaped (and continue to shape) the production of knowledge, his musical aspirations reconfigured as part of a broader sense of pedagogical purpose. Let's recall here that we're talking about someone who states flatly that he arrived on Earth from space in order to save humanity and to bring harmony to the world. Ra himself has, to use his own *parlance*, left the planet now, but his lifework—with its ongoing participation in the transformation and reinvention of musical and conceptual categories, its continuing efforts to put critical pressure on dominant spheres of knowledge production, its salutary commitment to enabling oppressed peoples to become subjects of their own histories and futures, and its capacity to function as bearer of the cultural desire to fly beyond possible limits—has gifted us with a jubilant choreography of mobility and social momentum.

Notes

1. George G. M. James makes a related point: "The true authors of Greek philosophy were not the Greeks; but the people of North Africa, commonly called the Egyptians; and the praise and honor falsely given to the Greeks for centuries belong to the people of North Africa, and therefore to the African Continent. Consequently this theft of the African legacy by the Greeks led to the erroneous world opinion that the African continent has made no contribution to civilization, and that its people are naturally backward. This is the misrepresentation that has become the basis of race prejudice, which has affected all people of color" (7). See also Martin Bernal's critique of the process by which African history was whitened to serve colonial interests (Vol. 1, 241): "If it had been scientifically 'proved' that Blacks were biologically incapable of civilization, how could one explain Ancient Egypt—which was inconveniently placed on the African continent? There were two, or rather, three solutions. The first was to deny that the Ancient Egyptians were black; the second was to deny that the Ancient Egyptians had created a 'true' civilization; the third was to make doubly sure by denying both. The last has been preferred by most 19th- and 20th-century historians."

2. See Campbell's *Earthly Recordings* (103) for more information on this Saturn release.

3. See also Leslie B. Rout Jr. on Fletcher Henderson: "As early as 1928, this bandleader had worked out the basis of the jazz style known as Swing.

By the early thirties he had assembled an outstanding aggregation—but it was still a black orchestra. A compromise of sorts resulted: Benny Goodman became the 'King of Swing' . . . and Fletcher Henderson became his chief arranger" (quoted in Kofsky, 58).

4. Thanks to Robert Campbell for the reference.

5. See Szwed, *Space* (94–95) for a partial list of some of the names the Arkestra has taken on over the years.

6. See also Szwed, *Space* (308): "From the music he had experienced, big bands were living microcosms of government; the big bands best represented society, and harmonious relations between people. The bands' history showed what could be done. But bands also showed what could go wrong. When soloists were lured away from bands by promoters and turned into 'stars' of small combos it promoted self-sufficiency and destroyed initiative, creating chaos in black communities."

7. Ekkehard Jost has noted that the mail-order service for Saturn records "does not seem to work" most of the time, and that the "Chicago address given on some Saturn productions does not exist" (183). Many of Ra's Saturn releases, in fact, could generally be purchased only at concerts, and purchasers would, more often than not, have no clear sense of what exactly they were buying. The records were often put together in a slapdash way: covers were blank, information was scarce or glaringly inaccurate.

8. Multimedia artist Colette Gaiter sees similar kinds of links: "The civil rights movement and space program," she argues, "celebrate our most important cultural fantasies as Americans—that no goal is out of reach, that technology will improve any situation, and in spite of vast evidence to the contrary, that we are benevolent and moral." Also, for a rather different analysis of the relationship between race and space, see "The Race for Space," an essay in which Duke Ellington (who uncharacteristically seems willing here to talk about race-related issues) suggests that the American failure to stay abreast of the Russian competition in space technology is linked with the failure to transcend American racial injustice.

9. One of the most famous attacks on universalism has come from Nigerian novelist Chinua Achebe: "I should like to see the word *universal* banned altogether from discussions of African literature until such a time as people cease to use it as a synonym for the narrow, self-serving parochialism of Europe" (9).

5

Nice Work If You Can Get It

Women in Jazz

Ajay Heble and Gillian Siddall

The difficult I'll do right now, the impossible will take a little while.

Billie Holiday, quoted in Wallace, "Variations on Negation and the Heresy of Black Feminist Creativity," 62

Throughout this book, we've seen how the conceptual shifts mapped out by contemporary theory have necessitated new ways of thinking about the methodological and pedagogical implications of jazz and its relation to social identities. We've explored some of the ways in which performance, improvisation, alternative institution building, innovative strategies of public address, and, of course, the music's very spirit of sonic exploration, can unsettle dominant assumptions about history, language, identity, and agency. In this chapter, we'd like to extend these lines of inquiry by turning our attention to the surprisingly undertheorized issue of women in jazz: in what ways might the very language of jazz (both the musical conventions within which it operates and the discourses that are produced about it) be said to be gendered? To what extent and in what ways, we'd like to ask, are women performers of jazz and creative improvised music engaged in fostering new models for thinking about gender?

Scant attention has thus far been paid in jazz scholarship to the complex factors that shape our understanding of jazz's gendered legacy. While a number of critics have been engaged in the historical work of documenting the accomplishments of women performers and composers in jazz, little has been done to analyze more broadly whether gender can be seen as a determining factor in the music these women produce. There has also been a tendency (at least in jazz criticism) to neglect considering the extent to which this music needs to be understood in relation to larger cultural and institutional questions: questions, for example, about the various kinds of obstacles that have prevented women from participating more fully in the music. In her groundbreaking 1991 book, *Feminine Endings*, Susan McClary convincingly argues that "music does not just passively reflect society; it also serves as a public forum within which various models of gender organization (along with many other aspects of social life) are asserted, adopted, contested, and negotiated" (8). McClary touches on a range of musical genres, periods, and conventions, but she doesn't have much to say specifically about jazz. All the same, it seems surprising that jazz scholars haven't followed her lead, haven't sought to examine, in any kind of sustained theoretical way, how the conventions of music making in jazz might be connected to cultural assumptions about gender.

What we'd like to do in this chapter is to open up questions about how the production of new social relations through women's music making in jazz can subvert dominant ideas about gender and sexuality in the public sphere. McClary's work has been exemplary in exposing some of the ways in which conventional aspects of musical practice frequently taken for granted as natural and autonomous, are, in fact, powerfully, if not necessarily consciously, caught up in reproducing, transmitting, and inculcating prescribed cultural attitudes toward gender and sexuality. In jazz, such attitudes are not only consolidated through musical structure; they are also publicly reinforced in various extramusical ways. As Monson notes, "Male jazz musicians have not infrequently enjoyed their reputations for virility and have constructed accounts of themselves that play into the market for this image and its transgressive aspects" ("The Problem with White Hipness," 419). Monson, Christopher Harlos, and others have noted that autobiographies by leading figures such as Miles Davis and Charles Mingus contain descriptions of virility that rely on deplorable representations of women. Harlos, in fact, points out that "Miles's rendering of the time his then-wife Cicely Tyson was forced to call the police after he hit her in the face . . . was so disturbing to writer Pearl Cleage that after having read *Miles: The Autobiography* she created a performance piece in 1990, 'Mad at Miles'" (160–61). Harlos quotes the following excerpt from Cleage's piece:

> I kept thinking about Cicely Tyson hiding in the basement of her house while the police were upstairs laughing with Miles. I wondered what she was thinking about, crouched down there in the darkness. I wonder if thinking about his genius made her less frightened and humiliated.
>
> I wonder if his genius made it possible for her to forgive him for *self-confessed crimes against women such that we should break his albums, burn his tapes, scratch his CD's until he acknowledges and apologizes and rethinks his position on the Woman Question*. (161)

The ethical concerns raised by Cleage's performance piece—how do we weigh good art against oppressive social behavior?—open up a broader area of inquiry which will be addressed more fully in chapter 7. For now, though, the point that needs to be made is this: the inadequate and demeaning portrayal of women fostered in such public statements by celebrated male musicians makes clear the need for feminist analyses of jazz to counter assumptions about the taken-for-granted nature of the music. Lest our appreciation of Miles's musical genius become naturalized in ways that allow his ill-treatment of women to disappear from the critical agenda, we need to insist that gender is a necessary category in the context of the sociocultural and historical analysis of jazz. As Ray Pratt argues, "The effect of a particularly sexist kind of hegemony in analyzing popular culture is to discourage certain questions from being asked because the situations involving exclusion of women seem somehow natural" (160); consequently, we need to be vigilant in demanding a fundamental revisioning of the ways in which the music industry has oppressed and demeaned (and continues to oppress and demean) women. Indeed, if gender has been kept from achieving its own politicization not only in music theory, but also, specifically, in jazz, then this may be due largely to the tendency for those writing about jazz to separate the music from the person creating it, to fall back on the kind of received musicological wisdom that promotes music as an autonomous entity. It has been one of the tasks of much work in contemporary feminism to challenge precisely this kind of critical orthodoxy, to take issue with the assumption that an artist's personal experiences should have no bearing on our analysis of his or her works. Judith Butler, taking up the feminist slogan "the personal is the political," argues that "[f]eminist theory has sought to understand the way in which systemic or pervasive political and cultural structures are enacted and reproduced through individual acts and practices, and how the analysis of ostensibly personal situations is clarified through situating the issues in a broader and shared cultural context" (273).

The structures of masculine dominance that we see inscribed in the public culture of jazz are also, as we've implied, reinforced through the very conventions of musical practice. McClary, for instance, has pointed to the gendered nature of the paradigm of tonality, suggesting that the Other in music—dissonances, subthemes, chromatic melodies, passages in nontonic key areas—has been understood to be structurally marked as feminine. Her claim is that in traditional forms of Western music, this Other has to be contained, overcome, or domesticated in order "for identity to be consolidated, for the sake of satisfactory narrative closure" (14). This containment and domestication occurs through the restoration of order that's implied by a return to the masculine domain of stable tonalities and key centers. Says McClary, "The 'feminine' never gets the last word within this context: in the world of traditional narrative, there are no feminine endings" (16). Her point is that these often taken-for-granted conventions of musical composition and reception do powerful ideological work: "they are perhaps the most powerful aspects of musical discourses, for they operate below the level of deliberate signification and are thus usually reproduced and transmitted without conscious intervention. They are the habits of cultural thought that guarantee the effectiveness of the music—that allow it to 'make sense'—while they remain largely invisible and apparently immutable" (16).

To what extent is jazz implicated in such frameworks of assumption? And in what ways have jazz musicians (women jazz musicians in particular) struggled to overcome the gender stereotypes fostered by such structures of thought, to propagate new models of representation? What shifts in performance and composition style, in strategies of public address and self-representation, and in audience-performer relations have been enacted by women performers and composers in jazz, and how have those shifts worked to reconfigure dominant social relations?

If McClary's argument holds, and sonorities that are somehow outside of traditionally ordered structures of intelligibility in music tend to get coded as feminine, then mightn't much jazz—with its predilection for what Charles Keil calls "participatory discrepancies," its fascination with dissonances and nontempered sounds, its exhilarant use of irregular rhythms and altered chord structures—by its very nature (and despite its marginalization of women) be seen as a style of music that revalues and makes central to musical composition and performance what has traditionally been constructed and dismissed as the feminine in music? And if *that* is the case, then are women who do jazz, because of the very nature of the music, rejecting masculine hegemony? And are male jazz musicians, then, also rejecting masculine hegemony?

Or is it only "out jazz" that might be seen to do this kind of political work? Are Cecil Taylor, William Parker, and Roscoe Mitchell, for example, because they would seem entirely to avoid the return to "masculine" systems of musical order and containment,[1] even more fully engaged than other jazz musicians in musically destabilizing dominant ideas about gender, in "envisioning narrative structures with feminine endings" (McClary, 19)? And does such an argument lead us to ask the rather problematic question of whether women who perform more traditional forms of tonal jazz (Rosemary Clooney, Diana Krall, Shirley Horn, etc.) are thus somehow reinforcing a masculinist hegemony?

While there may be some validity to this line of thinking, the destabilizing possibilities of men performing "feminine" music, we need to acknowledge, are certainly limited by the fact that jazz has been discursively constructed as a male preserve. Men performing "out jazz" aren't necessarily going to bring about real-life changes for women performers. In fact, one might argue that when the so-called feminine elements in music altogether displace the so-called masculine forms, when there is, in effect, no return to tonal centers, the nontonal sonorities might no longer be seen as feminine. In other words, the possibilities for a kind of feminist reading of dissonance may well be relatively short-lived.[2] Also, we need to be aware that the kinds of questions we're raising about the links between gender politics and dissonance may run the risk of erasing the complex material factors that have contributed to the consolidation of masculinist structures of knowledge production. Indeed, one might wonder whether the reason that many women (and women singers in particular) rely fairly heavily on tonal forms is that, as we'll see later in this chapter, they have ironically (and systemically) been discouraged from composition and performance that reclaim "feminine" structures of music making.

Such issues involve us in some of the central areas of debate in contemporary feminist theory. Chapter 1 opened up a related set of concerns: that chapter looked at jazz's shift from diatonic music to atonality in the context of Julia Kristeva's distinction between the symbolic and the semiotic, and explored how the music of free players such as Cecil Taylor might be seen as approximating Kristeva's semiotic realm. Kristeva's linguistic theory has some parallels with McClary's feminist musicology in that both explore links between antirepresentationality and the feminine. Both theorists envision alternative structures of feminist discourse that seek to intervene in dominant social relations. Kristeva, claiming that the semiotic, with its antirepresentational emphasis on rhythm, sound, and instinct, "sounds a dissonance within the thetic, paternal function of language" (139), has explicitly linked feminine language with the semiotic, rather than the symbolic, which she associates with male authority and control. The semiotic, she suggests, reclaims the realm of feminine desire in its very disruption of the symbolic order of representation. Other French feminists, too, perhaps most notably Hélène Cixous, valorize antirepresentational strategies (including the writing strategies of male authors such as James Joyce) in theorizing *l'écriture féminine*. These kinds of language-centered or aesthetic arguments about what constitutes the feminine have, however, come under attack from other feminist thinkers. Catherine Clément, for instance, has pointed out that such arguments will not bring about changes in masculinist control over the modes of production, and a number of thinkers have suggested that essentialist valorizations of femininity may run the risk of ignoring important race and class differences among women. These critiques must be kept in mind, as we have already pointed out, when thinking about the gendered legacy of music.

Our consideration of the ways in which music has been gendered is certainly not meant to imply that particular musical styles possess intrinsically masculine or feminine characteristics. Rather, gendering in music, we'd like to suggest, is the product of culturally prescribed roles, assumptions, and expectations, and the kinds of institutional power and legitimacy that reinforce and get ideologically attached to them. Along with McClary, Marcia Citron is one of the few feminist critics who have extensively explored gender-related issues in the context of the language of music. In taking up the question of whether specific styles and conventions in music can be linked with gender, Citron advises us to be somewhat cautious: "while we might isolate certain tendencies that could be part of a female aesthetic, I have found no specific language, style, or dynamic that every woman utilizes." Furthermore, she tells us, "women are not raised in 'pure' female culture and will tend to express, at least in part, aspects of masculine culture" (17). Overarching generalizations about music's femininity and masculinity are clearly inadequate; yet as powerfully coded cultural conventions, musical paradigms can be analyzed to reveal "how essentialist notions of male and female [permeate] society" (21) in ways which have real material consequences for men and women performing artists.

Jazz, Women, and Pianos

Essentialist notions of gender have also been naturalized in relation to particular instruments. In *Men, Women, and Pianos: A Social History*, Arthur Loesser argues that "the history of the pianoforte and the history of the social status of women can be interpreted in terms of one another" (267). His claim is that the piano became a signifier of bourgeois domesticity and femininity—played by women in the Victorian parlor. Historically, women in all Western musical genres, including jazz, have been discouraged from playing instruments socially understood to be unfeminine. Instead, they've been encouraged to play the piano or sing, both of which have served to reinforce women's relation to the domestic sphere. One way in which this tendency to restrict women's musical activity has been rationalized is to suggest that women lack the physical strength to play certain instruments. *New Yorker* jazz critic

Whitney Balliett made this argument in 1964. Given the overwhelming evidence to the contrary (witness, for example, the exuberant drumming styles of Susie Ibarra and Cindy Blackman), we need to look more closely at the ideological reasons governing the gendering of instruments.

There is something that might be perceived as transgressive and threatening about women, especially small women like Ibarra, who, in their performance style, depart from socially prescribed notions of femininity. Furthermore, certain instruments such as drums invite stances and body movements that bear the social stamp of masculinity because they require an overt display of physical activity. Others, such as trumpets and saxophones, are more subtle, but, as Krin Gabbard notes, they too have accrued connotations of male sexuality ("Signifyin(g)"). Unlike the genteel posture associated with piano playing (whether it be in the bourgeois parlor to which Loesser is referring or in contemporary jazz settings), the customary stance required to hold and play the trumpet and, particularly, the saxophone constitutes a more explicit display of the body. Judith Butler's contention that "gender is constructed through specific corporeal acts" (272) is, we suggest, exemplified in jazz performance: the performer playing trumpet or saxophone in jazz (unlike in traditional orchestras) is usually standing up, facing the audience, moving his body to emphasize mood or rhythm, sometimes lifting the instrument high up into the air, and bending low to the ground. (We are consciously using the male pronoun here to underscore the point that such performers have usually been male.) His own body is connected to the instrument in ways that are obviously different from body positions for playing the piano: to put it bluntly, he is holding the instrument and he has it in his mouth. We'd like to postulate, then, that one of the reasons women have been discouraged from playing horns is that these instruments invite an explicitly sensual (if not sexual) kind of performance that transgresses socially prescribed notions of feminine sexuality.

While Loesser's book is concerned (as, in the main, is McClary's) with the classical tradition rather than with jazz, his comments offer a valuable point of departure for considering the history of women in jazz. Loesser's comment about the link between pianos and the social status of women highlights the extent to which women's relationship with music has been dictated by their social identities. As we've suggested, the gendering of instruments has limited and defined women's roles as jazz musicians. We need to acknowledge, however, the extent to which the tradition of jazz as a resistant form has opened up possibilities for female jazz artists that may not have been available to the bourgeois women referred to by Loesser. Early jazz women did not, after all, come from bourgeois homes, but rather, as Linda Dahl points out, from minstrel shows and from the black churches, which Dahl identifies as an early site of black social resistance that "developed the fine point of Afro-American call-and-response and encouraged the working out of rhythmic patterns, or 'riffs'—elements that would later become central to jazz" (5). There is also evidence to suggest that while most black women musicians were, like the white bourgeois, limited primarily to piano and voice, they were more active in the early New Orleans jazz bands—playing a variety of brass instruments—than history has recorded; Curtis D. Jerde, former curator of the William Ransom Hogan Jazz Archive of Tulane University in New Orleans, argues that as jazz became more acceptable to mainstream culture, women's place in it became less acceptable (see Dahl, 20-21).

Indeed, though early jazz, at some level, may have offered a site of social resistance to mainstream culture for both black men and women, the possibilities for black women to engage in political resistance through jazz were limited by the ways in which jazz discourse was becoming consolidated as a male preserve. As Burton Peretti notes in his book *The Creation of Jazz*, "Only a few jazzwomen, in a few clearly defined spheres of activity, achieved prominence" (122). He goes on to suggest that:

> singing and piano playing were virtual ghettos for jazzwomen. Their restrictions to these roles resulted from general Western traditions that encouraged women to pursue

> voice or piano, because their musical activities most reinforced women's association with the parlor, the Victorian home, and the domestic sphere as a whole. Female wind and brass players and leaders received scant attention from commercial interests. (122)

Jazz, then, from its very inception, has been a world that is difficult for women to inhabit. Women were seen to be rivals to male band leaders, and life as a jazz performer meant being on the road, away from one's family, playing in rough bars and dance halls. The public space and, concomitantly, the discourse of jazz very quickly emerged as masculine. We've already talked about the masculine body language associated with particular instruments and performance styles in jazz. Other visual signifiers associated with key moments in jazz history have also been coded as masculine. In her essay on the construction of "hipness" as a gendered and racialized phenomenon in jazz history, Monson, for instance, talks about the markers of hipness that characterized a particular kind of black male jazz artist. These markers (beret, goatee, zoot suits) came to define the image that was cultivated by some key players in the bebop tradition, most notably Dizzy Gillespie. She argues that "the 'subcultural' image of bebop was nourished by a conflation of the music with a style of black masculinity that held, and continues to hold, great appeal for white audiences and musicians" ("The Problem with White Hipness," 402). The dominance of male musicians on the jazz scene was thus only cemented by the ways in which white male mainstream culture co-opted hipness as a way of romanticizing and stereotyping the rebellious energies of black jazz movements. In short, women in jazz were not associated (either by the black male musicians or by white audiences) with innovation and political resistance. Indeed, access to hipness and thus to the visual signifiers of innovation and resistance was denied to women. Monson refers in a footnote to a book entitled *The Hip: Hipsters, Jazz, and the Beat Generation* which includes a section on "hip chicks," a designation meant to offer a female counterpart to male hipness, but which relegates women to the conventional position of sexualized object. While the hip chick referred primarily to singers, it also significantly included "kittens on the keys." These hip chicks "were shapely, decorous, wolf-whistle worthy. They all came poured into dresses that accentuated their superstructure" (quoted in Monson, "The Problem with White Hipness," 401). Monson also points out that "[t]he sartorial accouterments of the male look are absent" and that the women bear "no particular 'hip' stylistic markers" (401).

Consider also Melba Liston's account of being hired by Dizzy Gillespie in 1949. Liston, although perhaps not a household name in jazz today, was considered by many to be one of the top instrumentalists and arrangers—male *or* female—of the time. As a trombone player, Liston was one of the few early jazz women who didn't fulfill the expected roles of pianist or singer. The band that Gillespie invited her to join (as both arranger and instrumentalist) involved some of the leading male musicians of the day, including John Coltrane. As Dahl points out, "To play in that band was an honor for any up-and-coming musician. . . . For a top-ranked bandleader to sign a woman instrumentalist—much less bring one all the way across the country—was just about unprecedented" (255). Liston's own recounting of this story indicates how strongly resistant the male musicians were to having a woman join their ranks:

> Gerald Wilson brings me to New York and drops me in Dizzy's lap, with all these giants. . . . I was so in awe of all these persons, and I didn't have any idea of what I was doin' there, although I could read the music. But Dizzy had great faith in me . . . and he told me to bring at least two arrangements with me when I came.
>
> The first thing, all the guys in the band said, "Goddamn, Birks, you sent all the way to California for a *bitch*?" Dizzy said, "That's right." He said, "Did you bring the music that I told you to write?" I said, "Yes, sir." He said, "Pass it out to these muthafuckas and let me see what a bitch you are." He said, "Play the music, and I don't want to hear no fuckups." And of course they got about two measures and fell out and got all confused

and stuff. And Dizzy said, "Now, who's the bitch!" Dizzy was really something. So after that I was everybody's sister, mama, auntie. I was sewin' buttons, cuttin' hair and all the rest. Then I was a woman again. (quoted in Dahl, 256)

What's revealing about this passage is that even as Liston is telling a story that demonstrates her brilliance as an arranger, she downplays her abilities by suggesting that she is out of place amongst these jazz giants. As many commentators have noted, such self-deprecating remarks are common among women in music. One critic, Eva Rieger, notes that this kind of response "was not the result of innate feminine modesty as is often supposed; it had to be inculcated" (147). Indeed, the response of the male musicians to Liston's arrival points to the inculcation and naturalization of jazz as a male preserve. Of particular interest here is that once the men recognize the caliber of Liston's work, they rationalize her presence not by accepting her as an equal in the public world of jazz performance, but by invoking a prescribed set of gender roles that relegate her to the domestic sphere: Liston is "everybody's sister, mama, auntie." In light of the comments we've already quoted from Burton Peretti about jazz women's association with voice and piano being an echo and reinforcement of their place in the domestic sphere of the Victorian parlor, the heightened need for these men to domesticate Liston seems to have been precipitated by the fact that she played the trombone, not the piano.

Liston's final cryptic sentence—"Then I was a woman again"—exemplifies the complexities of her positioning in this male-dominated industry. It can be read as a commentary of her own awareness that she can enter this space only through the agency of male acts of domestication, codification, and naturalization. It also should call our attention to the fact that the male musicians have simply replaced one set of prescribed gender roles with another: in other words, Liston can be a woman again because she is, in their eyes, no longer a bitch. The threat she poses to the male musicians when she first arrives thus is diminished by the men's reconfiguration of her as a domestic figure.

The example of Liston provides a telling instance of Ray Pratt's assertion in *Rhythm and Resistance* that "[w]hatever area of popular music over the past century one considers, women simply do not appear to men as men do to each other, that is, as persons involved in the common construction of a particular kind of social reality, a cultural product that is itself a kind of ideological construction, a way of understanding the world" (155). He goes on to say that "[w]omen in music, as in most areas of activity, must work inside a discourse which they have little part in making but in whose terms they are judged and with which they are often in agreement" (156). Pratt's argument raises a number of interesting issues. A paradoxical feature of innovation is that it can occur only within an already existing discourse. Is it possible for a woman to be innovative in the male traditions of jazz? What, for example, is the innovative legacy of Melba Liston or of someone like Mary Lou Williams, one of the most famous women pianists in jazz history? Certainly some of Williams's high-profile male contemporaries, such as Charlie Parker, Duke Ellington, Dizzy Gillespie, and Thelonious Monk, were interested in and influenced by her work. Ellington described her as "perpetually contemporary," and his comment is echoed by a number of critics. Nat Shapiro describes her as "the best example of a musician who has refused to be imprisoned by either style or tradition" (quoted in David, 77), and the liner notes for *Embraced*, her collaborative recording with Cecil Taylor, claim that "Mary Lou Williams, pianist-composer-arranger, is the only major Jazz Artist who has lived and *played through* all the eras in the history and development of Jazz. . . . Critics, indeed have called *her* the history of Jazz. She is the only artist who has constantly changed and developed as the music grew—often pointing the way herself." All of these men characterize Williams as innovative. Like Liston, however, Williams was forced to be conscious of her gender in a way that men did not have to be. Barry Ulanov wrote in 1949 that Williams's music, while of a very high stature, "has a delightfully feminine ambiance" (quoted in Dahl, 60), and as Williams herself put it, "You've got to play, that's all. They don't think of you as a woman if you can really play. I think some girls have an inferiority complex about it and this may hold them back. If they have talent, the men will be glad to help them along. [And] working with men, you get to think like a man when you play. You automatically become strong, though this doesn't mean you're not feminine" (quoted in Dahl, 67). On another occasion Williams declared that "people were surprised to hear a little 90-pound girl play the piano like a man" (*Zodiac Suite* liner notes). Both comments illustrate the difficult space jazz women inhabited in terms of the relationship between their music and their social identity.

The fact that an innovator such as Williams characterizes her art in terms of her ability to play and think "like a man," in terms, as it were, of her success in playing the "right notes," suggests, again, just how difficult it has been for women in jazz not to frame their achievements in the context of partriarchal assumptions. But also implicit in Williams's comments is, perhaps, a profound act of resistance: by performing, and signifyin(g) on, music that has historically been seen as masculine, Williams shows us that there is nothing naturally male about the music at all. Her collaboration with Cecil Taylor, indeed, makes this point perfectly clear. While Williams and Taylor each have their distinctive styles—Williams favors a legato style rooted in stride, boogie-woogie, and blues patterns, while Taylor is well known for his thunderous tonal clusters—the remarkable thing about this recording is that it's sometimes difficult to tell who is playing what. Here, then, is a performance that complicates the essentialist assumption that particular styles of music are intrinsically masculine or feminine.

Another powerful example of the complex connection between gender and performance style can be found in the lesser-known jazz musician Billy Tipton. Tipton came into the public eye at the time of his death not so much for his music but rather because a paramedic discovered that the musician who had been passing as male for nearly sixty years was actually a woman. Born Dorothy Lucille in 1914, Tipton, in the 1930s, apparently began dressing as a man in order to get work as a jazz saxophonist in a male band. His cousin Eilene recalls:

> Some way or another Dorothy heard about a band that needed a saxophone player. . . . Back in those days you know they didn't have girls traveling with bands—it was just frowned on. Anyway, she wasn't helpless and appealing-looking like you'd expect a woman to be. So she said, "Well, if I can't go as a woman, maybe they'll take me as a young man!" She took a piece of worn-out sheet and wrapped it around her chest and pinned it real tight. . . . Dressed as a boy, she got this job and left with the band. (quoted in Middlebrook, 55)

Tipton's cultivation of a cross-dressed male identity provides another perspective on the complexity of the gendered legacy of jazz. If, as Monson argues, bebop was inextricably linked with and signified by markers of hipness that denoted an exclusively masculine identity, then Billy's move to dress as a man could be seen to show a keen awareness of the politics of gendered identities in the music industry. Implicit in the term *jazz musician,* for some of the reasons we have already touched on, is the word *male*: gender, it would seem, becomes an issue only when the performer is female. And the words *female* and *jazz musician* are at odds with each other because of this naturalized relationship between the music and masculinity. Tipton recognized that one way to circumvent the stigma of being judged as a female jazz musician was to perform masculinity. Diane Wood Middlebrook suggests in her 1998 biography *Suits Me: The Double Life of Billy Tipton,* "By 1937 [Tipton] was so practiced in moving and talking and looking like a man that the performance of masculinity came as naturally as the motion of her fingers on the keys of her instruments" (94). Middlebrook's use of the word "naturally" detracts from the very point she is making about gender being a performative act. Indeed her observation about Tipton can, we'd like to suggest, be read in the context of Judith Butler's groundbreaking work on the way in which bodies participate in the performance of gendered identities:

> That the body is a set of possibilities signifies (a) that its appearance in the world, for perception, is not predeter-

> mined by some manner of interior essence, and (b) that its concrete expression in the world must be understood as the taking up and rendering specific of a set of historical possibilities. (272)

By successfully passing as a man, Tipton challenged the notion of an interior essence of masculinity, and that challenge has become even more profound with the recent public discovery that Tipton was female. In comparison with innovators such as Mary Lou Williams or Melba Liston, Billy Tipton is, of course, a fairly minor figure in jazz history; yet Tipton's case is nonetheless compelling and instructive for the questions it raises about "what possibilities exist for the cultural transformation of gender" (Butler, 272) in a performative context.

Transformative possibilities are apparent in a very different way in the music and philosophy of composer/accordionist Pauline Oliveros. Oliveros, who is one of the most significant and widely respected women in contemporary music, isn't, per se, a jazz musician; nevertheless, her profound contribution to contemporary notions of improvisation, her pioneering efforts to push beyond received generic boundaries in music, and her innovative collaborations with leading jazz figures clearly suggest that she is an important figure for our discussion. In addition, Oliveros's music offers resonant ways of considering the role of gender in our understanding of innovation as a site of resistance. For, as Timothy Taylor notes, her very "aesthetic has been powerfully driven by a feminist consciousness" (100). Indeed, suggests Taylor, "it is possible to argue that the entire trajectory of her career has been an attempt to define and then shed the established norms of postwar composition, which she sees as overwhelmingly male" (100). In abandoning received notions of musical intelligibility in favor of what she calls intuitive and receptive models of composition and performance, she has done much to reclaim styles of musical practice that have been dismissed and undervalued as "feminine." Oliveros's efforts to promote such intuitive strategies of listening have the salutary effect of unsettling conventional distinctions between performers and audiences. At her performances, she will frequently insist that the audience is as actively engaged in the process of music making as she is. While other musicians and composers may make similar kinds of claims, few have succeeded as compellingly as Oliveros in demonstrating a commitment to working with audiences to explore precisely what it means to be "in the moment" of a performance occasion. Eschewing the kind of individual virtuosity traditionally associated with both jazz soloists and Western classical composition, Oliveros has thus sought in her own work to explore the possibilities of sound that can be produced in a given context and a given moment, and while there is no doubting her mastery of the accordion, she refuses to feature herself as a virtuosic player if the context doesn't invite it.

At a solo accordion recital during the 1997 Guelph Jazz Festival, for instance, a violent thunderstorm began at the very moment that she sat down to play her instrument. This gothic atmosphere was enhanced by the venue, which was an old stone church sanctuary with stained glass windows. Despite the crashing thunder, bursts of light, and pelting rain, Oliveros proceeded with slow, meandering, and quiet chords that explored subtle changes in sound. While some artists might have been annoyed at having to compete with the noise of the storm, and others might have succumbed to the temptation to imitate its frenzy, power, and intensity, Oliveros explored a notion of receptivity that varied from the obvious response that the storm might have seemed to call for. This performance, in fact, proved to be an exemplary demonstration of Oliveros's attempt to reclaim what she sees as a kind of feminist mode of musical practice. In an essay called "The Contribution of Women Composers"—which Oliveros originally wrote as part of a grant proposal to the Ford Foundation for Faculty Fellowships for Research on Women in Society—she wrote that "[c]ultural traditions ordain how women as well as men ought to behave. Traditionally, men are encouraged in self-determining, purposive activity, while women are encouraged to be receptive and dependent" (135). Oliveros's aesthetic of receptivity, so extraordinarily demonstrated at The Guelph Jazz Festival, rehabilitates a model of creative practice that, because of its reliance on intuition, has been traditionally devalued as "feminine." Oliveros, in "The Contribution of Women Composers," is forthright on this point when she argues for "the recognition and re-evaluation of the intuitive mode as being equal to and as essential as the analytical mode for an expression of wholeness in creative work" (135).

All four of these women—Liston, Williams, Tipton, and Oliveros—challenge gender stereotypes, and, we would argue, foster new models for thinking about women in jazz. Liston and Williams were very successful at writing, performing, and arranging a kind of music that was seen to be beyond the capability of women. Tipton, by passing as male in the jazz world, demonstrated very powerfully that the production of jazz music is not inherently masculine. Oliveros challenges the valorization of a style of music, prevalent in jazz, that has been culturally associated with men; instead, she asks audiences to listen for and learn to value the kind of music that has historically been seen as feminine.

The Problematics of Programming

In recounting this brief history of women in jazz we have been theorizing gendered identities as determining factors in the production of knowledge "about" jazz. As jazz organizers arranging a festival, we have been forced to confront the practical implications of our theoretical inquiry. We have written this chapter collaboratively because for many years we have worked together as the chief artistic and administrative directors of The Guelph Jazz Festival. As a result, we have a good sense of the complex interactions between the creative and material consequences of producing this annual event. The highly fraught nature of these interactions became particularly evident during our 1997 season, when we chose to make "Women in Jazz" the theme of our program.

Tensions between the artistic program and issues surrounding sponsorship, marketing, and the festival's role in the community became apparent in ways that had not been evident in previous years. For example, some of our long-term sponsors became anxious about associating themselves with what they perceived to be "a feminist" and thus, in their minds, a highly political and exclusionary event. Likewise, some of our regular audience members asked us whether men were welcome at the festival that year. Issues of representation became a hotly contested point of negotiation. Marketing agencies in part responsible for promoting the festival wanted to take advantage of the opportunity to represent women on posters in a sexually suggestive way that they felt would have mass appeal. Some male artists who seemed chagrined by our programming decisions told us that there simply weren't enough women musicians to make such a theme workable, implying, perhaps, that the quality of the festival would be compromised because we would be forced to hire minor or mediocre musicians. While it is true that there are far more men than women performing jazz, for the historical and institutional reasons we have already discussed, there are nonetheless many, many women performing jazz in North America and around the world. It is, as we hope our festival made clear, ridiculous to claim that there aren't enough world-class women to fill a festival program. Other men asked us when the festival would feature "Men in Jazz" as the theme. Such a question highlights some of the very issues we've been addressing in this chapter. These men seemed not to acknowledge the extent to which men continue to dominate the jazz music industry, and that most festivals (simply in terms of the ratio of men to women performers) *could*, in fact, be dubbed "Men in Jazz." Furthermore, both this question and the assertion that we wouldn't be able to fill our program with women illustrate the ways in which the dominance of men in jazz has become naturalized. Pratt's point about how the workings of masculinist hegemony make "the situations involving exclusion of women seem somehow natural" (160) is tellingly demonstrated through such examples. The phrase "Women in Jazz" is unsettling because it threatens to expose that naturalized conception of jazz as male and to call attention to the social and institutional inequalities that continue to militate against women's access to performance and recording opportunities, media exposure, and influential management positions in the music industry.

While on the one hand, we hoped as festival organizers to redress some of these inequalities, on the other hand, we also became acutely aware of ways in which we might unintentionally exacerbate them. We have been forced to recognize our role as participants in how the history of women in jazz unfolds: depending on the kinds of decisions we made about whom to program, in what context, ticket prices, marketing strategies, and so on, our interventions worked to configure and represent the role of women in jazz in particular ways. In other words, we were not simply presenting the music in a neutral or disinterested way (nor could we); instead we were fashioning a narrative around the role of women in jazz, a narrative that was inflected by our own biases, predispositions, and ideologies. As Hayden White, writing in another context, puts it, "narrative is not merely a neutral discursive form that may or may not be used to represent real events in their aspect as developmental processes but rather entails ontological and epistemic choices with distinct ideological and even specifically political implications" (ix).

Choosing a theme such as "Women in Jazz" is itself a gesture which runs the risk of invoking expectations and possibly stereotypes about female performers. We guessed that much of our potential audience would be attracted to this theme because they would anticipate a program that featured vocalists and piano players—perhaps no surprise given the institutional, ideological, and historical constraints that have discouraged women from venturing beyond these prescribed roles. While we didn't choose this theme as an explicit marketing strategy, we were certainly aware of the extent to which it would likely work in our favor by drawing audiences to our festival. Female singers, in particular, continue to be cherished in the popular imagination.

While there was a danger, then, that our choice of theme, even as it worked in our favor at the box office, might perpetuate already consolidated notions about the role that women have played in jazz, we nonetheless saw our program as an opportunity to get the public excited about the wide range of musical styles that women in jazz, are, in fact, performing, and to shake our audience's assumptions about female jazz performers. More precisely, because many women in jazz are, for reasons we've already touched on, singers, the public may well have expected a more traditional program than our festival normally delivers. We should point out here that the mandate of The Guelph Jazz Festival (as indicated in our mission statement) is to present a program "that reflects the most innovative and compelling accomplishments in jazz and creative improvised music."

The problem we faced, then, was how to negotiate between, on the one hand, a legacy that relegates women in jazz to conventionally prescribed roles and that thus diminishes the role of women in the trajectory of jazz innovation, and, on the other, a festival program that sought to present leading-edge performances by contemporary jazz women. What were the implications for us, as programmers, of the fact that, for a variety of historical and institutional reasons, most contemporary women in jazz continue to be pianists or singers or both? Did it matter if the program was heavily weighted by piano and song? How difficult would it be to program a lineup of women that *wasn't* dominated by pianists or singers, especially when the performers who don't fit those roles (drummers Cindy Blackman and Susie Ibarra, saxophonist Jane Ira Bloom, trumpeter Ingrid Jensen, accordion legend Pauline Oliveros, bassist Joelle Leandre, etc.) happen to reside in places that, because of travel costs and immigration fees, made it difficult for our small festival to afford them.

This latter concern reflects the material realities that shape our final program of events. The Guelph Jazz Festival operates on a steadily increasing but very modest budget, and we can't always afford to program exactly whom we want. Furthermore, the festival is committed to featuring Canadian artists, and while there is no shortage of excellent women jazz musicians in Canada (soprano saxophonist Jane Bunnett, vocalist/pianist Diana Krall, cellist Peggy Lee, singer Karen Young, etc.) that commitment sets a particular set of parameters on the program that necessarily limits our use of out-of-country artists. In short, our usual balancing act of fund-raising, considering our audience's needs and expectations, and fulfilling our artistic mandate came into focus in a particular way with this theme.

Another set of issues which we were forced to confront had to do with the ethics of thematizing marginality and oppression. Does a festival program that makes "Women in Jazz" its theme challenge or exacerbate existing stereotypes? As Leslie Gourse points out in her book *Madame Jazz*, "Some women never agree to play in all-women's groups or all-women's festivals out of an unwillingness to be ghettoized" (14). Indeed, some of the women artists who performed at our festival that year expressed a very similar concern, wanting to be seen as musicians period, not ghettoized as *women* performing artists. In an effort to address these kinds of concerns, we did not program an all-women festival, but rather tried to find innovative ways to present women artists while integrating them with male artists. For example, in addition to featuring a number of leading women performers such as Amina Claudine Myers, Myra Melford, Pauline Oliveros, Jane Bunnett, Karen Young, Lee Pui Ming, and Marilyn Lerner, we also invited Randy Weston to perform on one of our main stages to pay tribute to his longtime collaborator Melba Liston. Liston, having suffered a stroke, was no longer able to play, and rather than leaving her out of the program in order to ensure an all-women festival, we felt it was appropriate to have a male performer honoring her accomplishments.

Our final set of questions is perhaps the most difficult to answer. Are contemporary jazz women still functioning within a male discourse, and, if so, are they judged in terms of a male discourse of performance? Consider the comment made in 1973 by an anonymous male jazz player quoted by Dahl: "Jazz is a male language. It's a matter of speaking that language and women just can't do it" (3). Consider also another anonymous male observation, this one from 1977: "There is a difference between men and women in everything they do, if you think about it. Like, look at how a woman washes a floor, compared to the way a man does it. Somehow, the woman is more dainty. Same with music. Men just have more guts when they play. I don't know why, they just do" (quoted in Gourse, 28). A similar kind of observation was made in 1962 by Harold Schonberg, music critic for the *New York Times*: "Playing any instrument is a conflict in which the instrument must be dominated and—generally speaking—men are better dominators than women, if only by virtue of size and strength" (quoted in Dahl, 38). All of these comments, we need to note, were made more than twenty years ago. We'd like to hope that with festivals such as ours booking women in jazz, as well as material developments such as increasing numbers of women taking positions in the music industry as promoters, managers, and marketers, jazz has become a world that is easier for women to inhabit. However, we are not convinced that there has been a related shift in the kinds of ideological assumptions which underwrite popular understandings of the role and history of women in jazz, assumptions which, as we've tried to point out elsewhere in this chapter, were naturalized through hiring practices, media representations of "hip chicks," and a delineation of gender imposed by male musicians that sought to domesticate women artists and restrict them to piano and song. In retrospect, then, we recognize that our 1997 Women in Jazz program was, in the context of the history of women in jazz, both problematic and promising: because we couldn't produce the festival in a historical and social vacuum, because there is such a powerful and complicated set of social and institutional forces at work framing the very way we think about women's role in jazz, it was impossible for us to program and produce a festival that would unproblematically do the kind of feminist work we hoped it would. All the same, we remain committed to the belief that as festival organizers we are also political activists, working, even if in a very small (and utopian) way, toward "the impossible [that] will take a little while": to change the public perceptions and popular assumptions that tend to diminish the role of women in jazz, and to enable the many women who are performing and composing the music on a daily basis to gain increased access to performance opportunities and articulate alternative models of knowledge production through their music.[3]

Notes

1. In what ways does the fact that Cecil Taylor is an openly gay musician contribute to or complicate our understanding of gendered notions of musicality? Stanley Crouch has made the ridiculous claim that there is a link between Taylor's sexuality and his "inability" to play the piano properly. Such a claim shows how stereotypes about gender have been imposed onto the music. If Crouch did not know Taylor was gay, but still felt the need (as we're sure he would) to criticize Taylor's music, he would likely be forced to invent some other excuse to explain his distaste (see Gill, 61–62).

2. In fact, one could also argue the opposite here, that the short punchy sounds and quick succession of notes that characterize certain kinds of "out jazz" ought to be seen as masculine.

3. Since the 1997 "Women in Jazz" year of The Guelph Jazz Festival, we have continued to work toward these ends, and to struggle with the kinds of problems we've identified here. While we are proud of the world-class women artists we have featured since 1997, we are also forced to admit that we have fallen short of presenting a program that features as many women as men. Faced with the reality of fewer women than men in the business, and perhaps our own inability to see past culturally produced notions of innovation, we have so far been unable to redress this imbalance. Is it, for example, more difficult for our culture to accept women doing experimental music, and do they experiment with music in ways that we may be unable to discern as being innovative?

6

Capitulating to Barbarism

Jazz and/as Popular Culture

What enthusiastically stunted innocence sees as the jungle is actually factory-made through and through, even when, on special occasions, spontaneity is publicized as a featured attraction.

Theodor Adorno, "Perennial Fashion," 202

"Anyone who allows the growing respectability of mass culture to seduce him into equating a popular song with modern art because of a few false notes squeaked by a clarinet, anyone who mistakes a triad studded with 'dirty notes' for atonality," says Theodor Adorno in his notorious denunciation of jazz, "has already capitulated to barbarism" ("Perennial Fashion," 205). Adorno's attack on jazz, his insistence, in the words of Keith Tester, that "the much announced rebelliousness and originality of jazz is just a stylistic trick developed by the culture industry in order to sell more product" (44), that its vaunted improvisatory spontaneity "is in fact carefully planned out in advance with machinelike precision" (201), is part of his well-known critique of mass culture, or, to use the phrase that Adorno and fellow Frankfurt School member Max Horkheimer would themselves come to prefer, of the *culture industry*. Concerned with what happens when art gets turned into a "species of commodity . . . marketable and interchangeable like an industrial product" (Adorno and Horkheimer, 158), Adorno saw the industrialization of culture as the "means by which capitalism could erase any possibility of opposition and thus of social change" (Fiske, "Popular Culture," 324). Marxists such as Adorno were not, of course, alone, in their attacks on mass culture. Similar critiques of mass production and nostalgia for preindustrial community-based arts initiatives can also be found in F. R. Leavis's and Denys Thompson's traditionalist lament for organic communities in their 1933 book, *Culture and Environment*, as well as, more recently, in various kinds of attempts to promote independent national cultures.

I'm thinking, for example, of Canadian culture, which, during the heyday of nationalist consciousness in the '60s and '70s, would be contextualized in strikingly analogous terms, "represented readily," as one critic has put it, "as an organic 'lived tradition' facing extinction at the hands of a commercially-produced and technologically-dominated American mass culture" (Gruneau, 15). Such nationalist arguments often assumed "that Canadian culture was not yet a capitalist mass culture," and consequently that "it was necessary to defend local popular cultural forms and other indigenous cultural initiatives against the homogenizing commercial forces centred south of the 49th parallel" (Gruneau, 16). That nationalism is no longer the *dernier cri* in popular culture analysis or, more broadly, in contemporary cultural theory is a point that hardly needs rehearsing here. Angela Davis, speaking of "the kindred character of Black nationalism(s) and ideologies of male dominance during the sixties," has, for example, presented compelling arguments about the ways in which "Black popular culture may have been unduly influenced by some of the more unfortunate ideological convergences of that era" of black nationalist activity ("Black Nationalism," 317).

Indeed, work by a wide range of thinkers, including Davis, Stuart Hall, Paul Gilroy, John Fiske, Douglas Kellner, and George Lipsitz, has invited us to recognize the inadequacy of conceptual frameworks that theorize popular culture either, as has been evident in some nationalist models, as a site of indigenist resistance to *someone else's* standardized and mass-produced culture, or, as Adorno and the mass-culture theorists would have it, as the very "culture of subordination that massifies or commodifies people into the victimized dupes of capitalism" (Fiske, *Reading the Popular,* 7). In an important essay introducing the volume *Popular Culture and Social Relations*, Tony Bennett, taking his lead from Antonio Gramsci, tells us that popular culture "consists not simply of an imposed mass culture that is coincident with dominant ideology, nor simply of spontaneously oppositional cultures, but is rather an arena of negotiation between the two within which—in different particular types of popular culture—dominant, subordinate and oppositional cultural and ideological values and elements are 'mixed' in different permutations" (xv–xvi). Hall too, in much of his work on popular culture, argues for some form of critical *rapprochement* between recognizing the power of ideology to shape consciousness, to fix frames of reference, and asserting the ability of people to resist the workings of ideology. And Lipsitz, in his extraordinary analysis of popular music's potential for resistance, puts it this way: "For many musicians around the world, the 'popular' has become a dangerous crossroads, an intersection between the undeniable saturation of commercial culture in every area of human endeavor and the emergence of a new public sphere that uses the circuits of commodity production and circulation to envision and activate new social relations" (12). His point is that "[c]oncepts of cultural practice that privilege autonomous, 'authentic,' and non-commercial culture as the only path to emancipation do not reflect adequately the complexities of culture and commerce in the contemporary world" (16). What I'd like to do in this chapter, as the remarks from Adorno with which I began have perhaps already suggested, is to open up questions about the place of jazz in such debates about popular culture.

Long touted as a resistant form whose nose thumbing at bourgeois culture has inspired a wide range of oppositional artistic practices (think, for example, of Jack Kerouac and the Beat Movement, of Archie Shepp and Max Roach's relation to the black nationalist movement, of Sun Ra's pedagogy of resistance, of the alternative institution-building strategies of the AACM), jazz, as even its fiercest admirers have recently been forced to concede, has been assimilated "within the logic of our culture's economy . . . with the emergence of new interest in its archives by the Sony Corporation, with the successful development of major journals such as *Jazz Times*, and mostly with the remarkable resurgence of jazz recordings by means of the compact disc revolution" (Merod, "Jazz as a Cultural Archive," 4). Jacques Attali, in his book *Noise: The Political Economy of Music*, suggests that music became a commodity when a broad market for popular music was "produced by the colonization of black music by the American industrial apparatus" (103). Is jazz, then, as thoroughly standardized and commercialized as Adorno would have it? And how, precisely, ought we to theorize jazz in relation to the politics of the popular? Is jazz popular music or high art? Does the fraught nature of jazz's very relation to the popular itself unsettle our traditional assumptions about "proper" forms of cultural belonging?

One of the things I've been trying to think through in this book is what it might mean to postulate a theory of musical dissonance as social practice. If, as I suggested earlier, oppositional politics takes as one of its salient manifestations an allegiance to forms of artistic practice that cannot be readily assimilated using dominant frameworks of assumption, then it certainly seems tempting to link musical dissonance with social and political dissidence, to hear in jazz's sonic innovations a compelling critique of conventionally institutionalized systems of meaning and value. In seeking to understand the ways in which sonorities and musical structures that operate outside of conventional idioms of tonality might be linked with forms of critical opposition to dominant systems of knowledge production, I've stumbled across some rather large and difficult questions: Can dissonance be said to have a politics? In what ways has the relationship between dissonance and politics been played out in jazz? To what extent does the political force of jazz reside in its "out" forms, its "wrong" notes, its very inaccessibility? Can more traditional forms of tonal jazz also perform oppositional political work? And how, to revisit a specific set of questions posed in the previous chapter, has this relationship between dissonance and politics informed our understanding of the history of women in jazz? How has it shaped women's cultural production?

Indeed, whether approached in terms of issues of gender, race, history, ethics (to which I'll turn in the final chapter), self-representation, or popular culture, dissonance raises a number of important questions for contemporary cultural theory. And as with many such complex theoretical and conceptual questions, any answers we come up with are admittedly and necessarily provisional. For dissonance in jazz, as we've seen, has given rise to various kinds of (often contradictory) interpretive efforts: from my own earlier (and, in retrospect, largely misguided) desire to see Ornette Coleman's free jazz as a modernist move *away* from representational politics to the explicit attempts by musicians such as Archie Shepp, Max Roach, and Sun Ra to link the music to struggles for black nationalism. In fact, it should already be evident that the links between dissonance and dissidence that I'm now anxious to forge may not be readily sustainable. We've seen how any understanding of dissonance's political force is complicated by a variety of social, historical, and institutional factors. In the previous chapter, for example, we saw how women have historically been encouraged to play certain kinds of music (and discouraged from playing others). How, then, does *that* history influence the way we understand the politics of dissonance and innovation? Furthermore, in thinking about dissonance, we must also be careful to remember that music like bebop, which, by today's standards, may seem conventional and standardized, was once perceived by many to be intolerably dissonant, inaccessible, and incomprehensible.

Keeping these complications in mind, I want to return to Adorno. Now it should be clear from my previous chapters that I'm in strong disagreement with Adorno's assessment of jazz. Nevertheless, he remains one of the few thinkers who has managed, in any kind of sustained way, to do serious, and indeed important, critical work on music, social theory, and aesthetics, and his claims, though certainly problematic, warrant careful consideration. "In a world in which art and the aesthetic domain had been marginalised and their products trivialised," suggests Robert Witkin in his book *Adorno on Music*, "Adorno did more than any other philosopher to raise their profile and to establish beyond all doubt their right to be taken seriously, to be acknowledged as a moral and critical force in the development of a modern consciousness and a modern society" (3). Of particular relevance to the discussion at hand is Adorno's contention that music's oppositional power can be understood as a function of its inaccessibility: as Witkin notes, "Adorno saw the forbidding obstacles to accessibility in modern works of art as intrinsic to their critical force" (9). Music's "potential for critical opposition to modern society and to the ideological underpinning of that society depended crucially upon its inaccessibility" (11). Adorno, of course, did not have jazz in mind when he was celebrating the inaccessibility of modern music. Jazz, for Adorno, represented the opposite extreme; it was, he would argue, virtually indistinguishable from mainstream popular music. In the '20s and '30s, it "was a music that seemed to be part and parcel of the modern city and its leisure spaces, a music that was accessible, in its various forms, to city people everywhere; a genuinely popular modern music, sounding the dreamscape of the metropolis and reflecting the colour and pulse of life and relations in the city" (Witkin, 160). Even in the '60s, a period that saw the emergence of free improvisation and other experimental practices in jazz, Adorno's views would remain unchanged: "For almost fifty years, since 1914 when the contagious enthusiasm for it broke out in America, jazz has maintained its place as a mass phenomenon" ("Perennial Fashion," 199).

Why was Adorno so deaf to the oppositional possibilities in jazz? How could such an astute social thinker repeatedly deny the force of structural innovation in one of the twentieth century's most important cultural forms? As the epigraph and the passage with which I began this chapter both suggest, Adorno was well aware of jazz's reputation for innovation and spontaneity, of its cultural status as being outside dominant systems of intelligibility. Yet he refused to accept the fact that jazz had earned that reputation and status. "For Adorno," writes one critic, "when jazz avoids popular song forms, diatonic scales, and a monotonous beat, its 'innovations' are merely a recycling of earlier innovations that are now safe, unchallenging conventions" (Gracyk, 164). In Adorno's own words, "The most striking traits in jazz were all independently produced, developed, and surpassed by serious music since Brahms" ("Perennial Fashion," 201). Intent on insisting that jazz had nothing new, challenging, or unexpected to offer its listeners, and on arguing that what might be perceived as innovations in jazz are, in fact, an illusory product of the culture industry's attempt to interpolate individuals into the capitalist framework of mass culture, Adorno was convinced that listeners who bought into the notion that jazz was a rebellious music were passive victims of dominant ideology.

There is much in Adorno's thinking on jazz (and, more generally, on mass culture) with which we ought to take issue. His opposition between a mass culture which leaves no possibility for resistance to hegemonic practices and a high culture which, especially in its elitism and inaccessibility, is seen to house subversive and emancipatory potential is certainly problematic. Numerous commentators, indeed, have made hash of Adorno's claims for high-cultural artifacts, suggesting that we need to be rigorous in confronting the assumptions governing his various arguments for why classical music is supposedly better than jazz. Rather than rehearse some of these familiar arguments against Adorno here, I want to point specifically to the ways in which salient moments in the history of jazz compel us to put critical pressure on his valorization of high art. I'm thinking, for example, of the music of Duke Ellington, whose varied and illustrious career—as both a popular dance-band leader *and* a composer of extended large-scale compositions such as *Black, Brown and Beige*—so eloquently resisted the compartmentalization of high and low. Indeed, the controversy that evolved around the premiere performance of *Black, Brown and Beige* at Carnegie Hall in 1943 speaks volumes about Ellington's success in encouraging his audiences and critics to confront any assumptions they might have had not only about jazz as a primitivist form of popular art, but also about European models of classical music as the sole forms worthy of being enshrined in prestigious concert venues. In a series of articles published between May and December 1943 in the American magazine *Jazz* (see Tucker, 153–78), reviewers of Ellington's celebrated Carnegie Hall appearance debated what it meant for a black jazz musician to be presenting original music in a concert hall setting. As Mark Tucker notes, "Attacks came from both classical-music critics and jazz writers: the former claimed he did not measure up to standards set by European composers, the latter accused him of forsaking his musical roots and abandoning his function as a dance-band leader" (xix). Defenders praised Ellington's concert for doing what the best jazz has always done, for stepping outside the regulations of embodied systems of culture and knowledge, and innovatively testing the very limits of the genre. True, the controversy surrounding *Black, Brown and Beige* appears to relegate Ellington to a space where varied cultural forms refuse easy harmonization, but we should recall that Ellington so often reveled in just such in-between spaces, in dissonances that confound institutionalized judgments and responses.

Indeed, if Ellington's ongoing efforts to bring together popular African-American forms of musical expression with concert music played an important role in challenging the kinds of claims Adorno and others made on behalf of both jazz and high art, then another key moment in jazz history which performed a similar function was bebop. George Lewis, in his groundbreaking analysis of contemporary improvised music, suggests that the emergence of bebop in the 1940s played a pivotal role in paving the way for jazz to position itself as a "modern music" and as a high art form, but that it did so precisely in opposition to racist theories of high art which dismissed and denied the influence of African-American cultural forms. Although Lewis does not explicitly mention Adorno, his claim that bebop had a great deal to do with the musicians' "assertion of self-determination with regard to their role as musical *artists*" (95; emphasis added) does, I think, function to unsettle any easy distinctions Adorno might invite us to make between classical music as high art and jazz as mass culture. "While jazz," says Lewis, "has always existed in the interstices between Western definitions of concert music and entertainment, between the commercial and the experimental," bebop's challenge to "the assigned role of the jazz musician as entertainer created new possibilities for the construction of an African-American improvisative musicality that could define itself as explicitly experimental" (95).

There's evidence aplenty in the history of jazz to deconstruct the arguments that Adorno and others have made for high art. We could, for example, extend the analysis of the legacy of Ellington and bebop to include a consideration of more contemporary manifestations of musics (by Anthony Braxton, Muhal Richard Abrams, Keith Jarrett, Pauline Oliveros, George Lewis, Anthony Davis, Maggie Nicols, and others) which trouble Adorno's high/low distinctions. Problematic also, I think, are the race, class, and gender divisions on which his analysis of jazz is based. His very equation of atonal jazz with "barbarism"—a word that derives its origin from the Greek root for "foreign"—implicitly and unfairly demonizes black music by reducing it to a realm of primitivism. And, as Gabbard notes, while Adorno is quick to create dichotomies between a masculine autonomous art and a consumer art (such as jazz) linked with castration (*Jammin',* 158), he "ignores the patterns of racism in the culture industry that demanded the demasculinization of black jazz performers" (138).

What is of particular interest to me here, though, is Adorno's unwillingness effectively to theorize jazz in relation to his arguments about the social force of inaccessibility in modern (high art) music. Witkin tells us that "Adorno did not ever soften the savagery of his onslaught on jazz in any of his later writings even though, by the time of his death in the late 1960s, a great deal more avant-garde jazz had appeared and the jazz scene was no longer dominated by the dance bands as it had been in the 1930s and 1940s" (162). Despite the emergence of prominent innovators and improvisers such as Ornette Coleman, John Coltrane, Archie Shepp, Charles Mingus, and Sun Ra—all of whom were engaged in various attempts to liberate their music from conventional tonal structures as well as from the standard, predigested popular tunes of the time—Adorno refused to allow these or other jazz musicians entry into his select group of admired avant-garde composers and practitioners.

If inaccessibility is key to music's political edge, then shouldn't these artists be judged according to the same musical standards used by Adorno to assess his favored avant-garde classical musicians (Schoenberg, Berg, Webern)? A case can, I think, be made to suggest that the music of these jazz artists has performed precisely the kind of oppositional cultural work which Adorno sees as being achieved by classical composers such as Schoenberg. And, in fact, Adorno himself, in a passing moment in his *Introduction to the Sociology of Music,* shows a rare willingness to recognize that dissident potential in jazz:

> The social function of jazz coincides with its history, the history of a heresy that has been received into the mass culture. *Certainly, jazz has the potential of a musical breakout from this culture* on the part of those who were either refused admittance to it or annoyed by its mendacity. Time and again, however, jazz became a captive of the culture industry and

thus of musical and social conformism; famed devices of its phases, such as "swing," "bebop," "cool jazz," are both advertising slogans and marks of that process of absorption. (33–34; emphasis added)

Despite the glimmer of recognition that jazz has a resistive potential, Adorno fails explicitly to confront the places where that potential may have been realized. The casual references to swing, bop, and cool jazz seem troubling to me, not only because I'm led to wonder what exactly Adorno had sampled from these diverse traditions, but also because there seems little willingness on his part to think through the complex social, historical, and institutional locations out of which these musical forms emerged. Consequently, although the above passage might, after the fashion of important critiques of Adorno by Bernard Gendron and Mariam Hansen, provide a valuable opening to identify the traces in his diatribes of a systematic aesthetic expressly for popular art and jazz, we also need to keep in mind the considerable cultural distance that separated Adorno—a white European critic—from the music he is here so quick to jettison. What does it mean, as Theodore Gracyk asks, for Adorno to have constructed "a typology of listening that privileges knowledge of a more formal European tradition? How have we rejected the tyranny of universal norms if we judge Duke Ellington, much less Public Enemy, according to the conventions of Bach and Schoenberg?" (166). Gracyk is, I think, right to point to the homogenizing effects of Adorno's arguments, the inappropriateness of using the standards of European high art to read the texts of a predominantly African-American idiom. Still, I'm left wondering what I might have made of Adorno's arguments if he'd been more receptive to jazz, if he'd been able to marvel at its dissonances the way he could, say, at the dissonances in Schoenberg.

By this point in the book, my attraction to dissonance—both as an academic theorist trying to understand its relevance as a model for social practice and as a festival programmer presenting innovative music to community-based audiences—should hardly come as a surprise. What might be surprising, though, is that despite his wholesale dismissal of jazz, Adorno still seems to me to offer a purposeful point of entry into our consideration of jazz's relationship to popular culture. Odd though it may seem, that point of entry, I want to suggest, may well be Adorno's own championing of dissonance and inaccessibility in music. Adorno, we've seen, associates dissonance with a high-culture tradition of avant-garde classical music, and not with jazz or popular culture. I'd like to reflect on the oppositional politics of jazz's dissonances, and to do so in a way that at once problematizes Adorno's high art/mass culture divide and makes possible a significant recasting of our traditional understanding of some of the key theoretical, social, and political concerns at issue in the study of popular culture.

In gesturing toward some, however provisional, attempts to address the issues I've been broaching (is jazz high art or is it popular culture?), I want to turn to two contemporary examples. I'd like first to consider the music and career of saxophonist/composer/conductor/improviser John Zorn. Zorn's remarkable ability to court the popular-culture industry (indeed to court different sides of it) seems to me to be of particular interest here, especially given the uncompromising nature of the music he plays: how does one achieve such popularity playing a music that is, in many respects, so profoundly inaccessible? For my second example, I'd like to reflect, once again, on the institutional politics of festival programming, and to ask, more specifically, how my involvement in presenting innovative music in a local community setting has both shaped and complicated my understanding of what it means to be "popular."

But first, John Zorn. Much has been written about Zorn, especially about his penchant for genre jumping, his mischievous feats of surprise and unpredictability, his cut-and-paste compositional methodology, his chameleonlike refusal to be catalogued, and his in-your-face fondness for performing at intolerably loud decibel levels. Indeed, at most of the Zorn concerts I've been to—including the chamber music recitals!—people are almost always covering their ears throughout the performance, moving to the back of the hall, or even storming out offended. In critically acclaimed recordings in the late '80s with his Naked City ensemble, Zorn famously chainsawed his way through a host of popular musical genres (television and movie themes, country and western, surf music, and, yes, even jazz), using piercing saxophone squeals, screeching vocals, and reckless guitar noise to interrupt the narrative flow and stability associated with the familiar genres being invoked. His noisily irreverent yet brilliantly invigorating remakes demonstrated a kind of streetwise sensibility and vernacular critical consciousness, and revealed at work an inquisitive mind intent on posing troubling questions about contemporary reality, but also on posing those questions from within the very reality that was being challenged. Zorn is also an interesting figure ethnically, as much of his recent work (witness, for example, his Masada series) seems to have participated in the creation of a cult dedicated to preserving radical Jewish culture. And as a recent article in *The New Yorker* points out, his extraordinary productivity makes him a hugely compelling force on the contemporary music scene:

> Zorn is a one-man music industry. In the five and a half years since he founded Masada, he has written two hundred and five compositions for the group. He has also written dozens of very different sorts of pieces—for string trios and quartets, solo piano, woodwind ensembles, electronic grunge bands, and symphonic orchestras. Eleven new recordings of his music were released in 1998—seven of them on his own label, Tzadik, which, in Hebrew, means a charismatic leader who performs righteous deeds. In Tzadik's four years of existence, it has issued a hundred and forty-two albums, most of which are by other musicians, some of whom would have no other outlet were it not for Zorn. (Kaplan, 84)

There is, I suspect, a link to be made between Zorn's popularity and his attempt to rediscover his Jewish ethnicity. With his Masada group—a group that has been heralded as one of the freshest and most exciting ensembles in contemporary jazz—Zorn, after all, is invoking and building on a traditional Jewish music, klezmer, which has remained popular despite the test of generations. In Zorn's hands, the music, with its angular dancing lines, often sounds as much like Ornette Coleman as it does like traditional klezmer, yet there is no mistaking the Jewish musical influence. Indeed, Zorn's work with Masada and his pride in Jewish culture are, in miniature, indicative of the complex and paradoxical interplay between a profound rootedness in popular culture and a kind of slippery aloofness from the mainstream that's evident everywhere in his lifework: for all his popularity and his success in courting the popular-culture industry, Zorn, oddly enough, is someone who generally refuses to give interviews. And if the music he's drawing on with Masada has its roots in a popular-cultural tradition, then Zorn's own renewed interest in Judaism has, by his own account, been spearheaded by a sense of isolation: "I realized that a Jew is someone who naïvely believes that if he gives selflessly to his host culture he'll be accepted," he explains in a rare interview with Fred Kaplan for *The New Yorker* article I mentioned earlier. "But we are the world's outsiders. . . . This is what was attractive to me about the tribe—the culture of the outsider" (88). The choice of the name Masada—after a hill in Judea where Jewish resistance fighters chose to commit suicide rather than submit to the Romans and deny their religion—gives some sense not only of Zorn's characteristic audacity, but also of his uncompromising attachment to that outsider culture.

On the back of the Masada recordings, there's a quote from Jewish scholar Gershom Scholem:

> There is a life of tradition that does not merely consist of conservative preservation, the constant continuation of the spiritual and cultural possessions of a community. There is such a thing as a treasure hunt within tradition which creates a living relationship to tradition and to which much of what is best in current Jewish consciousness is indebted even where it was—and is—expressed outside the framework of orthodoxy. (quoted in Zorn, *Masada: Tet*)

Scholem, the renowned historian and scholar of Jewish mysticism, might as well have been talking about John Zorn here, for his words aptly situate Zorn's restless spirit of innovation within the context of traditional Jewish consciousness. Scholem's remarks, indeed, suggest that in the context of "much of what is best in current Jewish consciousness," the perceived *split* between inside and outside, tradition and innovation, popular culture and the avant-garde, can, in fact, be turned into a kind of invigorating, if not seamless, *fit*. And just as the use of that quote from Scholem attests to Zorn's own desire to articulate a scholarly and intellectual framework for his music, so too does the very naming of Zorn's label, Tzadik—whose mandate is to release "the best in avant garde and experimental music, presenting a worldwide community of contemporary musician-composers who find it difficult or impossible to release their music through more conventional channels" (http://www.tzadik.com/)—hint at the extent to which Zorn's own popularity and charisma (not to mention his righteous deeds) are founded on a rigorous intellectual (read: highbrow) background in Jewish culture and mysticism.

Moreover, as even a brief consideration of the recorded output on Tzadik would reveal, there is a link between Zorn's role as *the* key figure in the New York–based Radical Jewish Culture movement (in fact there's a series on the Tzadik imprint that bears the title) and the kind of control he has managed, more generally, to achieve over the marketing, production, and distribution of cultural knowledge. As Zorn's colleague Elliott Sharp notes, "he is very clever at the marketing of his ideas" (Sharp, "Interview with Elliott Sharp"). Indeed, many record stores have a section devoted solely to Tzadik releases. Zorn's ability to fashion a conceptual framework for Radical Jewish Culture, to inspire a whole "movement" around his own ethic of self-discovery, has, in short, given him a purposeful material base—access to media promotion, control over channels of communication, production, and distribution—for his musical activities.

Zorn's range of influence is indeed undeniable. Yet the influence he's had on a whole host of key figures in the music (Dave

Douglas, Mark Dresser, Bill Frisell, Joey Baron, Fred Frith, Tim Berne, and many others) is only part of the story. Another thing that anyone writing about Zorn is inevitably forced to contend with is his image. What's interesting is that critics who point to Zorn's abrasive, confrontational style and the delight he takes in shocking (and sometimes offending) his audiences also seem compelled to acknowledge the extraordinary impact Zorn has had on the contemporary music scene: he's a figure, in other words, who cannot be easily dismissed, despite his involvement with what some might see as a brash, heavy-handed, and over-the-top aesthetic of noise and excess. Zorn has (and rightly so, I think) been dubbed the *enfant terrible* of jazz and avant-garde music. Jazz critic Francis Davis, who confesses that Zorn is "the only musician I've ever considered suing" because "he put me and everyone else . . . at risk of permanent hearing loss by recklessly turning the volume up as high as it would go" (*Bebop,* 183), pegs Zorn as "exactly the sort of rude, overgrown adolescent you would go out of your way to avoid, if only he weren't so . . . well, interesting, important, and influential" (185). Faced with the choice of either censoring Zorn for his delight in violating the rules of public conduct and musical decorum or being a promiscuous listener, Davis (and I would tend to agree with him here) favors the latter option. In fact, as Davis and others have noted, John Rockwell of the *New York Times* has heralded Zorn as "the single most interesting, important, and influential composer to arise from the Manhattan 'downtown' avant-garde scene since Steve Reich and Philip Glass" (quoted in Davis, *Bebop,* 182–83). *The Penguin Guide to Jazz* also speaks glowingly about Zorn's music and influence. Its authors see Zorn essentially as "a 'free' player whose hectic collage-ism is only a populist version of the invent-your-own-language gestures of the free movement" (Cook and Morton, 1617). The observation that Zorn has managed to popularize modes of music making characteristic of the work of free-jazzers is an important one. What interests me about all this, as I've implied above, is that no matter whether he's performing tributes to Sonny Clark or Ornette Coleman, hardcore thrash, chamber music, klezmer, cartoon or spaghetti western soundtracks, avant-garde Japanese music, or free jazz with improvising giants such as George Lewis and Derek Bailey—indeed it's become something of a commonplace to say that listening to Zorn's music is a little like channel surfing with a remote control—his career seems to have been marked by an extraordinary ability to cut across the high art/popular culture divide by popularizing music that's edgy, dissonant, abrasive, and inaccessible.

Davis has suggested that "Zorn's breadth is such that he tends to fragment the intrepid audience he already has, which would seem to put masscult adulation out of the question" (*Bebop,* 190–91). I'm inclined to disagree. I'd argue, instead, that the ease with which Zorn cuts across various styles of music (along with his concomitant ability to get airplay on all kinds of different radio shows and exposure in mainstream media) is part of what produces his popular appeal. Here, after all, is an artist who is able to draw scores of teenagers not only to his jazz, thrash, and klezmer concerts, but, perhaps more suggestively, to his chamber music recitals—even, as at the 1998 International Festival de Musique Actuelle in Victoriaville, Quebec, to recitals at which he is conducting rather than performing. There are very few other avant-garde musicians (working in jazz or other genres) who can boast similar kinds of accomplishments in courting popular audiences. Other generically mobile artists—such as "out" jazz saxophonist David Murray, whose Grateful Dead tributes and recent excursions into funk have given him a wide crossover audience—have somehow not been as successful in tapping into the popular market.

How, then, do we account for Zorn's success? *The Penguin Guide to Jazz* seems to me to come close when its authors suggest that "[m]ore than any other individual musician, [Zorn] appears to mark the point of transition between a period of high-value technical virtuosity and a new synthesis of art that does not presume to raise itself above the throwaway, five-minute, all-tastes-are-equal, recyclable culture" (Cook and Morton, 1616–17). Indeed, if, as we've seen, the study of jazz has been bedeviled by approaches that construct the history of jazz as an evolutionary narrative—from low-class brothels and dubious night spots to high-art status and concert-hall respectability, or, to invoke once again the words of a *Good Housekeeping* article from 1956, from being "the boy with dirty hands whom you wouldn't let come into your house" to "the boy with clean hands" who can now be found in the nicest of living rooms—then Zorn's major contribution to the music may well reside in his persistent troubling of such an institutionalized narrative. In terms of both his genre-bending music and his iconoclastic public image, Zorn, it would seem, *is* the troublesome "boy with dirty hands" whose persistent attention-grabbing gimmicks (T-shirts with slogans such as "DIE YUPPIE SCUM!" [Davis, *Bebop,* 183], album covers designed to appeal for their shock value, song titles such as "Jazz Snob Eat Shit"), serve to turn institutionalized jazz history on its head, to confound the logic of respectability that many critics (and musicians such as Wynton Marsalis, to name only the most visible example) would like to bestow upon the music.

Adorno, of course, would have despised Zorn's populism, would have seen his "all-tastes-are-equal" musical approach as a debased and barbaric product of the processes of standardization and commodification. To a certain extent, Adorno's analysis would have been on the mark: Zorn's ability to popularize avant-garde music, after all, is clearly a function of his ability to court the culture industry. Yet if Adorno valued avant-garde music because its abstractness and inaccessibility provided the basis for his consideration of the ethical necessity for an autonomous art, then Zorn's fundamental revisioning of traditionally institutionalized forms of cultural division points to the impossibility of such autonomy. Zorn's refusal to comply with the conventions of established genres of music making—the fact, for example, that a work for chamber ensemble such as *Cobra* "not only uses conventional orchestral instrumentation including harp, brass, woodwind and percussion, but also incorporates electric guitar and bass, turntables, cheesy organ, telephone bells and industrial clanging" (Kevin McNeilly, quoted in Connor, 170)—works to call our attention to the slipperiness of patterns of cultural value. Instead of the elitist separation from the everyday world of mass culture that has historically tended to shape and define the workings of an avant-garde aesthetic, Zorn's explicit valorization of the everyday (telephone bells, industrial noise, cartoon music, lounge music, television shows, and so forth) sonically documents the very complexity of art's involvement with the practices and experiences of ordinary life, suggesting, in effect, as has the work of many of the other jazz musicians considered in this book, that it behooves us to study music in relation to the very contexts in which it gets performed, transmitted, and received. Zorn's attachment to popular culture, moreover, illustrates the argument from George Lipsitz to which I referred earlier, that "[c]oncepts of cultural practice that privilege autonomous, 'authentic,' and non-commercial culture . . . do not reflect adequately the complexities of culture and commerce in the contemporary world" (16).

Zorn himself implies that, for all its dissonances, his music has been fashioned with a popular audience in mind: it is, he admits in his notes to *Spillane* (again calling to mind a culture and logic of remote controls), "ideal for people who are impatient, because it is jam-packed with information that is changing very fast." (Zorn, 12). His is, in short, a musical oeuvre whose very discontinuities seem perfectly suited to a fast-paced world of commerce and information. Of interest is the way in which acts of musical transgression in Zorn's oeuvre seem to be fully coincident with a logic of consumerism: his musical struggle to run counter to the reductive purity of genre here gets figured by Zorn himself not in terms of a refusal of the culture industry's pressures toward standardization and commodification but rather in ways that highlight his own involvement in media-propagated models of conduct and response. Here, in his description of the ideal audience for his music, we may catch a glimpse of the entrepreneurial savvy that led Zorn to create his own independent record label: both his founding of (and production work with) Tzadik and his own account of the music he performs suggest his engagement with what Lipsitz calls "an immanent rather than a transcendent critique" (35) of dominant social relations. That is, for all his alternative institution-building strategies and his desire to inject musical (and other kinds of) noise into the hegemonic rhetoric of normalcy and respectability, Zorn seems perfectly happy working *within* rather than *outside* existing structures of commodity production.

One of the things that Zorn's example teaches us, I think, is that jazz's relationship to popular culture is not something that can be defined by some fixed content in the music itself. Zorn's ability to court the pop culture industry seems to be the result of several overlapping factors: his striking embrace of the everyday, his entrepreneurial savvy, his iconoclastic public image, his complex entanglement in the very system he critiques, his roots in Jewish culture, and the profound challenges that his music poses to the reductive purity of genre. Tony Bennett has made the point that "popular culture cannot be defined in terms of some pre-given sense of 'the people' or 'the popular,' for the meaning of these terms is caught up with and depends on the outcome of the struggles which comprise the sphere of popular culture" (19). Zorn's lifework, it would seem, documents some of these struggles, showing us that popular culture is not something one seeks to define as much as it is something one works to construct. Indeed, Zorn constructs popular culture by deconstructing it. What results is a form of dissonant (and dissident) knowledge, a knowledge that's "out of tune" with orthodox habits of thought and judgment even while it draws its power and force from the very logic it works to unsettle.

My second case study also suggests that popular culture is best understood as being made and in-process rather than as something that gets strictly defined according to some pre-given social script. In turning from John Zorn to the institutional politics of programming a jazz festival, I want to explore how my theoretical reflections on popular culture are grounded in an intensely local model of social practice. I'd like to suggest that the example of The Guelph Jazz Festival offers a purposeful site not only for thinking through jazz's relation to the popular but also, by way of revisiting some of the issues addressed by Adorno and Leavis, for raising pressing questions about the efficacy and the sustainability, not to mention the value, of small-scale, community-based, volunteer-run arts organizations.

The Guelph Jazz Festival, as Mark Miller points out in a review of its 1996 season, has managed successfully to make a virtue of its smallness: "It's small and proud of it. In a field where bigger is generally held to be better, Guelph offers convincing evidence to the contrary" ("Good beat"). Heralded as "the best small jazz festival in Canada" by soprano saxophonist Jane Bunnett, the festival has, from its very inception, sought to present innovative and leading-edge performers of jazz and creative improvised music in the context of a small, community-based setting. Therein, precisely, lies the rub: innovative, frequently dissonant, world-class music in a community setting. Just as the interplay between populism and an avant-garde aesthetic makes John Zorn's work rife for cultural analysis, so too, I want to suggest, does the tension between The Guelph Jazz Festival's innovative artistic vision and its mandate to stay rooted in the local community make a fitting test case in the context of a consideration of jazz as a popular art form.

On the surface, there would appear to be very little of the popular in the festival's choice (indeed, *my* choice as artistic director) of programming. Artists such as Pauline Oliveros, Myra Melford, Amina Claudine Myers, Muhal Richard Abrams, Ivo Perelman, Gerry Hemingway, Michael Snow, William Parker, Susie Ibarra, Misha Mengelberg, Joe McPhee, Lee Pui Ming, David Mott, Ned Rothenberg, Mark Feldman, Dave Douglas, and Mark Dresser (the latter four, incidentally, all part of John Zorn's circle)—all important innovators whose recordings and performances push the boundaries of the genre we traditionally call "jazz"—are certainly not household names; nor is their edgy and often challenging music likely, at least in most contexts, to appeal to large numbers of an uninitiated public. What, then, is the festival's relation to the popular arts, and in what ways, if any, might the festival's activities be seen to participate in what Adorno saw as the commodification of increasingly large sectors of artistic culture?

Jazz itself, according to a number of critics, is the music of the people. Sidney Finkelstein, in his appropriately titled *Jazz: A People's Music*, suggests that jazz "reasserts the fact that music is something people do, as well as listen to; that art is not to be limited to a specialized profession, but should be in the possession of everybody" (27). Hobsbawm says that jazz "has become, in more or less diluted form, *the* basic language of modern dance and popular music in urban and industrial civilization, in most places where it has been allowed to penetrate." He continues: "The social history of the twentieth-century arts will contain only a footnote or two about Scottish Highland music or gypsy lore, but it will have to deal at some length with the vogue for jazz" (xliv). In Guelph, the vogue for jazz, as I hope to suggest in a moment, is peculiar indeed, reflecting the fact, perhaps, that, as Hobsbawm goes on to say, jazz "has developed not only into the basic idiom of popular music but also towards something like an elaborate and sophisticated art music, seeking both to merge with, and to rival, the established art music of the Western world" (xliv–xlv).

Jazz, then, may well be the musical genre *par excellence* that breaks down received distinctions between popular culture and high art: "Jazz, of course, is a minority music," write Stuart Hall and Paddy Whannel. "But it is popular," they say, concurring with Finkelstein, "in the sense of being of *the people*" (73). Like the blues, argue Hall and Whannel, jazz is a popular music "not because millions sang or knew [it], but because [it] grew out of a common experience, an experience central to the life of a whole people, which they transposed into art" (92). They also point out that "one of the great—perhaps tragic—characteristics of the modern age has been the progressive alienation of high art from popular art. Few art forms are able to hold both elements together: and popular art has developed a history and a topography of its own, separate from high and experimental art" (84). It is in this context that an analysis of The Guelph Jazz Festival might be instructive. For the festival has been highly successful in introducing innovative musicians—musicians who, in other contexts, might be seen not as popular artists but as proponents of an elitist high culture—to wider audiences, and, as per its mandate, of enlarging the constituency traditionally defined as a jazz audience. When avant-bop percussionist Gerry Hemingway (well known in jazz circles for his work with Anthony Braxton's legendary quartet) performed a solo recital during the 1996 festival, he played to a sold-out and highly attentive audience that ranged in age from young children to seniors, an audience which, as one reviewer noted, "would have kept [Hemingway] there all night if they could have, judging by the enthusiastic response he generated" (Bali). The fact that such an innovative artist—indeed, Hemingway's was, perhaps, the most challenging concert we presented during the '96 festival—played to such a wide-ranging and appreciative audience—many of whose members had likely never heard of Hemingway before—tells us something about the festival's success in transgressing the kinds of boundaries that Adorno erected between high art and popular culture.

That success might be measured more broadly through a comparison with the ways in which innovative music gets presented at other jazz festivals. The strength of the larger jazz festivals (such as those in Toronto and Montreal, for example) seems to me to reside in the fact that they are able to offer something for everyone; they appeal to lovers of mainstream jazz and new jazz alike. Yet the DuMaurier Downtown Jazz Festival in Toronto has certainly come under attack recently for taking fewer and fewer risks with its programming (the loss of its avant-garde Next Wave series is a case in point). Even when it *does* program innovative jazz, the Toronto Festival (like so many other jazz festivals throughout North America) tends to segregate the music by confining it to late-night spots in small venues; consequently, only audiences "in the know" generally venture to attend. This kind of programming strategy runs the risk of preventing the music from being accessible and marketable to a wide listening public. By contrast, a salient feature of the Guelph festival that has enabled us to market and build a broad-based audience for innovative forms of musical expression is our educational colloquium. Audiences (both local and international) continue to tell us how valuable they find this unique component of the festival, and how the informal talks, workshops, panels, and roundtables go a long way to building an appropriate and enriching context for music that, in other settings, might appear inaccessible.

One way, therefore, in which The Guelph Jazz Festival has maintained its links with the popular is by participating in the dismantling of the time-honored popular culture/high art divide. In fact, the festival's relation to the popular is perhaps best defined not so much in terms of the specific artists or their performances (artists who, again, would traditionally be categorized as practitioners of high art), but rather through the complex ways in which these artists and performances are presented to and received by a public. Our understanding of the music's popularity, in short, is dependent on how that music gets circulated culturally and how it gets taken up by people within the culture. If as John Fiske writes, "[p]opular culture is always in process; its meanings can never be identified in a text [or performance], for texts [including performances] are activated, or made meaningful, only in social relations and in intertextual relations" (*Reading the Popular,* 3), then an understanding of the festival's popularity needs to be predicated on a consideration of the social and institutional conditions under which performances take place and are received. In what ways, we need to ask, do these conditions shape or determine our understanding of a performance's public relevance? Relevance, after all, says Fiske, "is central to popular culture, for it minimizes the difference between text and life, between the aesthetic and the everyday that is so central to a process- and practice-based culture (such as the popular) rather than a text- or performance-based one (such as the bourgeois, highbrow one)" (6). Contributing to our understanding of that relevance are material considerations such as ticket prices and the size and nature of the venue, factors such as the marketing strategies used to promote a performance, and decisions about how to contextualize the music being presented.

Also critical to our analysis of the festival as a manifestation of the popular arts is an understanding of the community-based nature of the event. One of the difficulties we, as organizers of the festival, have been facing has to do with how best to negotiate between, on the one hand, an artistic mandate which has as one of its key features the promotion of innovative forms of musical expression, and, on the other, a strong commitment to remaining a community-based festival. How, that is, do we continue to present and promote what we see and hear as being the most compelling forms of jazz and creative improvised music without, in our relatively small community, running the risk, say, of alienating audience members who might prefer more traditional forms of jazz? Indeed, there are always *some* audience members who are quite offended by the "more challenging" music, by the "wrong" notes. And if the festival's popularity depends, to a large extent, on its continuing efforts to preserve links with the community, then what, specifically, ought to be the role of the local in determining the festival's activities?

Let me try to be more precise about why I think that the festival needs to be seen as a community-based event. From its very beginnings, the festival has insisted that its activities be affordable in ways that the activities, say, of other jazz and music festivals have not always been. To this end, we have remained committed to presenting world-class artists at remarkably low ticket prices (Hemingway tickets, for example, were only five dollars) and to staging several free concerts throughout the festival, including a series of outdoor concerts in a centrally located open-air public space or beer tent in the downtown core. Indeed, our use, for the most part, of popular public spaces—outdoor squares, cinemas, churches, university campus courtyards, beer tent—rather than traditional concert halls also, I think, has much to do with the festival's rootedness in the community.

Another of the festival's key links to the community involves jazz that is performed in many of the city's restaurants and clubs, and therein lies the tale of the local. In his essay "Local Jazz," James Lincoln Collier remarks that while "[j]azz criticism and jazz history have always concentrated on the big names, the stars, and the famous clubs and dance halls where they worked . . . in fact, perhaps ninety percent of the music has always been made by unknown players working in local bars and clubs for audiences drawn from the surrounding neighbourhood, town, and country" (997). Says Collier, "there are thousands of towns in which the appearance of a star jazz musician is a rare event, but that offer local jazz bands on a weekly basis" (999). The role that these local musicians play in helping to define jazz as a popular art form cannot be overestimated. As Collier notes, "[b]ig city music clubs today often charge customers as much as twenty-five dollars admission" (1004), while the local players, by contrast, work in places that, at least in the context of the Guelph festival, have either no cover charge or a very modest one. Insofar as the local musicians perform at venues that are readily accessible to people with financial constraints that might prevent them from purchasing tickets to mainstage concerts, there might be said to be something genuinely oppositional at work here, something that, at least in terms of what Attali calls music's political economy, might, however modestly, contribute to an effort to resist dominant processes of commodification.[1] In terms of the larger artistic design of The Guelph Jazz Festival, however, when seen, that is, in relation to the innovative mainstage artists, the local artists who perform in the clubs and restaurants might be said to embody—to adapt Stuart Hall and Paddy Whannel's formulation—"the *substructure* of the popular" (82) in the overall context of a festival of high seriousness.

Now, lest I be misunderstood, let me make clear here that I do not want to reinforce any easy distinction between local artists as popular and mainstage artists as high art, largely, as I've been arguing, because the festival's attempts to intervene in the ways in which notions of the popular are negotiated and determined complicates any such binary distinction. Nevertheless, audiences attending The Guelph Jazz Festival in search of traditional forms of jazz are more likely to find what they are expecting in the clubs than they are to hear it at the mainstage concerts. In other words, if access to widespread public appeal needs to be seen as a criterion for measuring the festival's links to the popular, then the participation of the local artists ensures the festival's success even as it runs the risk of compromising the nature and scope of its mandate to alter the forces that have traditionally governed the reception of innovative forms of musical expression.

I'd like, for a moment, to return to Adorno here. When Adorno attacks jazz, saying that "[w]hat enthusiastically stunted innocence sees as the jungle is actually factory-made through and through, even when . . . spontaneity is publicized as a featured attraction" ("Perennial Fashion," 202), he is responding, in part, to what he sees as the standardization of jazz. For him, this means "the strengthening of the lasting domination of the listening public and of their conditioned reflexes. They are expected to want only that to which they have become accustomed and to become enraged whenever their expectations are disappointed and fulfillment, which they regard as the customer's inalienable right, is denied" (202). Adorno's comments, I think, speak directly to The Guelph Jazz Festival's struggle to sustain a meaningful balance between innovation and tradition. For if the wide-ranging and appreciative audience at our innovative mainstage events can be read as a measure of our success in being able to attract and cultivate listeners who think about, reflect on, are challenged by, and learn from what they have heard, rather than an audience that routinely accepts the music as a form of conventional entertainment, then the audiences who attend the more traditional events in the local clubs and restaurants are more likely to have their expectations, their desires to achieve standardized levels of musical coherence, fulfilled. What, then, is the festival's position vis-à-vis the debates that have evolved around the theories of popular culture? While at one level, its attempt to present innovative music to new audiences has enabled the festival to participate in a dismantling of the received distinctions between popular culture and high art, the very division of its events into a mainstage/local club structure forces it, at another level, to fall back on the very distinctions it has worked to unsettle.

Mark Miller, this time in his *Globe and Mail* review of the 1997 edition of the festival, remarks astutely on what he sees as the gap between the mainstage events and the community-based nature of the festival. "In just four short years," he says, "the Guelph Jazz Festival has gone from a small, community event to something rather, well, grander. The community aspect of the festival is still apparent, what with performances by local musicians in several of the city's night spots and a free, outdoor concert . . . in St. George's square downtown. At the same time," he continues, "the festival . . . has mounted an increasingly impressive series of concerts by important international figures." It is the contrast between these two aspects of the festival that interests Miller: "The result is almost a set of parallel festivals, one of mainstream jazz for passersby and the other of contemporary music for a more daring audience. The distinction between the two," he concludes, "can only grow as the festival continues to attract notice outside the immediate Guelph area with the venturesome side of its programming, inevitably drawing even more listeners for whom the rest of the music will hold little interest" ("Guelph Features").

Indeed, the festival *has* attracted significant attention outside the community, both in terms of its growing international media profile (in places such as *Down Beat*, *Coda*, *Cadence*, *The Wire*, *Signal to Noise*, and so on), and in terms, as Miller says, of the people who come from afar to attend its events. This attention has, I should add, certainly set the town abuzz: the city's merchants do a booming business during the festival, and indeed, prominent downtown business owners have told us that the jazz festival weekend in September is their busiest weekend of the year. Surely, then, this "buzz" says something about the festival's relation to the popular, its rootedness in the community. In short, as I've been suggesting, what identifies the festival as popular culture is precisely the way in which it celebrates its "festivalness"—free concerts in the downtown core, a conscious attempt to appeal to kids, food, tents, beer, nontraditional community venues, a colloquium featuring general audience talks and workshops, the participation of the restaurants, the support and enthusiasm of local businesses, and so forth. But Miller's point is that the gap between the innovative mainstage artists and the community-based (read: popular) local performers will only grow as the festival attracts wider notice, that, in effect, we are really running two festivals: one featuring high art for an international audience and the other featuring popular local artists for the immediate community. This split asserted by Miller is complicated by the fact that many members of our own local community *do*, as the Hemingway concert attests, attend and enjoy the more daring mainstage events. Am I misguided, then, in wanting to reinvigorate our understanding of the popular social function of an innovative music festival? Am I wrong to insist that, even with its progressive artistic mandate, the festival can stay rooted in the community?

I want to continue to think that the festival's activities, and the nature and scope of its overall structure, illustrate the problematic nature of the high art/popular culture model endorsed by Adorno and members of the Frankfurt School. The case of the local artists suggests, in fact, that popular culture is not, as Adorno would have had it, monolithic, that it can, in some contexts and in some ways (Zorn's work provides another case in point here), be emancipatory even as it may in other ways be reinforcing standardization and reasserting dominant models of knowledge production and consumption. I'd also like to point to the need to move beyond (while genuinely learning from) Adorno's model into modes of analysis that can apply analogous, and equally rigorous, critical methods to a range of different cultural activities. The Guelph Jazz Festival, with its own range of events, offers a unique site for precisely this kind of critical work, not only because it confronts head-on questions about jazz as a popular art form, but also because its very structure as a volunteer-based organization is of interest. Attali is, of course, right when he tells us that music "has become a commodity, a means of producing money. It is sold and consumed" (37). And jazz, as many have pointed out, has perforce become part of that very process of commodification. Yet there is something about a small, volunteer-run jazz festival that attempts, even if in highly complex and overdetermined ways, to stay rooted in the community, which makes it seem, if not preindustrial or, to use Leavis's favored term, organic, then at least somehow resisting complete entry into the economy of labor. In this context, I'd like to argue, one of Adorno's shortcomings is his failure sufficiently to theorize emergent models of creative practice in his analysis of dominant processes of commodification, standardization, and institutionalization. Too intent on dismissing *all* instances of apparent variety in popular culture (including the wrong notes, improvisations, and dirty tones in jazz) as effects of pseudo-individualization ("On Popular Music," 26), Adorno's writings omit genuine consideration of dissident forms and dissonant histories. As both the musics and the alternative institution-building strategies associated with independent record companies, artist-run cooperatives, and community-based grassroots festivals will, I think, suggest, cultural practices that are out of tune with naturalized orders of knowledge production complicate Adorno's assessment of jazz as a simple reflection (and reinforcement) of manipulative social relations and marketplace demands.

That's not, however, to suggest that such alternatives are completely divorced from the logic of the market. True, The Guelph Jazz Festival, in its first six years of operation, *has* managed to operate on the basis of volunteer commitment and direct local organization, resisting, wherever possible, forms of corporatization. But as Stuart Hall and Paddy Whannel point out in their assessment of Leavis's nostalgia for organic communities, while it may be important "to resist unnecessary increases in scale and to re-establish local initiatives where we can . . . if we wish to re-create a genuine popular culture we must seek out the points of growth within the society that now exists" (39). With evolving popularity, as The Guelph Jazz Festival has seen, come growing pains and increased budgets, and the key question confronting festival organizers as I write seems to focus on the extent to which the sustainability of our grassroots ideology may be in jeopardy when the festival ceases to be a volunteer-run organization—when it is forced, in short, to enter explicitly into an economy of labor.[2]

George Lipsitz and others have convincingly pointed to the difficulty, if not impossibility, of sustaining forms of cultural production that stand outside existing structures of commodity production. Lipsitz argues, for example, that "attempts by artistic avant-gardes to confound the logic of the art market only produced newer and more lucrative objects for collection and exchange" (35). And Steven Connor, specifically taking up some of Adorno's arguments, makes a related claim in his book *Postmodernist Culture*: "The terms of the avant-garde's seclusion from the heat and dust of history proved to be exactly the means by which art could be commodified and absorbed into professional structures of cultural publicity and management" (271). Both the examples I've touched on in this chapter, though very different in so many ways, compel us to reflect on the political implications of culture in a market economy. Despite seeking to foster alternative models of cultural production, both Zorn's work and the activities of The Guelph Jazz Festival remain committed to an involvement in constructing a popular market for an avant-garde aesthetic. In both cases, we've seen that "the popular" is not something that's intrinsically or objectively *in* particular kinds of musical texts or artistic practices, but rather something that is formed and takes shape in relation to various social and institutional struggles for control over the distribution, management, and marketing of contemporary cultural practices.

Notes

1. While offering an alternative to dominant circuits of commodity production, the jazz performed by largely unknown players in community settings also contributes to commodification by being associated with the economy of the local industry. As well, the obvious business interests of

restaurant and club owners who feature local jazz clearly need to be taken into account. Booking innovative artists into these local settings has been difficult because, at least according to the merchants, *dissonance is bad for business*. Do the bulk of local artists play mainstream jazz primarily because it's the only way for them to get a gig in town? If that's the case, they fall squarely into Attali's (and, of course, Adorno's) commodification trap.

2. In fact, one could argue that the festival has always been part of an economy of labor: an economy predicated on the work of a very small number of volunteers and, more specifically, on the extraction of a kind of surplus value from these "laborers." Exploitation, we have quickly discovered, can be (and is) a factor even in such volunteer-run settings.

7

Up for Grabs

The Ethicopolitical Authority of Jazz

I'm a believer. My hope is to be as open and honest as I can.

Charles Gayle, quoted in Baxter

In his landmark study on ethics and literature, *The Company We Keep: An Ethics of Fiction*, literary critic Wayne Booth discusses the controversial decision of the Bollingen Prize Committee in 1949 to grant the award to Ezra Pound's *Pisan Cantos,* "poems that openly expressed anti-Semitic and other fascist views" (379). Booth's purpose in citing the example is to open up compelling, and indeed urgent, questions about literary criticism's role in adjudicating complex ethical debates: how, in the case of Pound and the Bollingen Prize, do we weigh estimable aesthetic qualities against deplorable political content? Booth's book marks something of a watershed in contemporary literary criticism, for it shows us that ethics has indeed reemerged in the context of pedagogy and critical practice in literary studies in ways that those of us who were trained as postmodernists and poststructuralists could hardly have foreseen. In this chapter, I'd like to focus on some of the ways in which this newly articulated interest in ethically valenced models of inquiry might be seen to intersect with jazz studies. Booth himself broaches the issue of an ethics of music when he asks: "Are some musical forms inherently better for us than others? Is it possible to talk responsibly about the relative ethical power and value of two musical works that move us deeply. . . . Where can we find criticism that might help us answer such questions?" (19) If I've been correct in suggesting that jazz has played a valuable role for antihegemonic publics in their struggles for access to self-representation and identity formation, then does it not follow that jazz is, perhaps by necessity, a particularly meaningful site for adumbrating precisely the kind of ethical criticism of music that Booth has in mind? I know that ethics is not easily definable as an abstract, tangible form, that it is, rather, better understood as a function of human behavior and context. However, given the ways in which jazz has accented contingency, improvisation, risk, dissonance, and play to buck oppressive systems of culture and knowledge, isn't jazz in some ways an exemplary ethical music? Yet what are we to make of jazz that, say, as with Pound's *Cantos*, is, whatever its artistic merit, "built on beliefs that go beyond (or sink beneath) what we can or should tolerate" (Booth, 377)?

Now music, it's often argued, is the least representational of the arts, and, consequently, it would seem to be an unlikely place for the expression of intolerant views. Nonvocal jazz music, lacking manifest political content, hardly seems comparable to the example of Pound. But, as I hope this book has suggested, music *is* representational in that it invites us to ask questions about the very nature of representation: questions about who and what gets represented and under what conditions, about whose interests are being served, and so forth. Indeed, for theorists like Jacques Attali, the music we imbibe has profound social consequences, and theories of identity formation and social organization, he would argue, thus need to attend much more rigorously to its significance. Attali admits that we should abandon our search for music's referential character: "To my mind," he says, "the origin of music should not be sought in linguistic communication. Of course, the drum and the song have long been carriers of linguistic meaning. But there is no convincing theory of music as language" (25). Nevertheless, Attali insists on "demonstrating that music is prophetic and that social organization echoes it" (5). Despite the radical nature of Attali's insistence on "establishing relations between the history of people and the dynamics of the economy on the one hand, and the history of the ordering of noise in codes on the other" (5), there is perhaps nothing new in the claim that music plays a pivotal role in the construction of social identities. In *The Republic*, for example, Plato tells us that the guardians "must throughout be watchful against innovations in music and gymnastics counter to the established order. . . . For a change to a new type of music is something to beware of as a hazard of all our fortunes. For the modes of music are never disturbed without unsettling of the most fundamental political and social conventions" (4.424b-c). Like Attali, however, others see change to the established order of music making and to the present modes of producing, distributing, and consuming music as genuinely liberatory. I've already talked in some detail about Sun Ra and members of the AACM in precisely this context. Consider, too, the following comments from free jazz pianist Cecil Taylor: "It seems to me that in the long run your art becomes a reflection of a consciousness which, if it is powerful enough, may change the social consciousness of the people who listen to you. Great music implies a challenge to the existing order" (quoted in Willener, 255).

In this chapter, I want to turn to the difficult case of another of contemporary jazz's most uncompromising of black free jazz artists: Charles Gayle. I say "uncompromising" because Gayle has always insisted on performing on his own terms. In a 1995 *Down Beat* co-interview with fellow saxophonist David S. Ware, Gayle put it this way: "You can either play a music with someone else's rules or you can make up your own" (quoted in K. Leander Williams, 35). Gayle's make-up-your-own brand of free jazz seems in so many ways to be genuinely liberatory, to be a profound statement about the necessity for forms of self-expression in the face of industry-dominated art. In this sense, Gayle's music might be said to speak very powerfully to the cultural and political history of black music as expressed in the work of other practitioners I've considered in this book, particularly the Art Ensemble of Chicago and Sun Ra. His music, too, as his own words imply, invites analysis in the context of a politics of self-determination, of art's role in the process of unsettling historically and institutionally determined categories of thought and judgment.

While Gayle's jazz, at least as I'm reading it, has a powerful liberatory edge, some of the spoken-word monologues presented during his performances (and the fact that they *are* presented in performance is key here, I think) run the very real risk of reinforcing structures of oppression and dominance. Gayle's music and pronouncements—or, rather, the complex ways in which they intersect—indeed seem to me to offer a direct invitation to confront ethical questions in music seriously and rigorously. The ethical challenges faced by listeners of Gayle's performances and recordings come to a focus in questions about intent and reception, about value and judgment, and about forms of responsibility (for listeners, for music programmers, for record producers). Gayle's music—a version of free jazz that recalls both Albert Ayler and the later John Coltrane—is musically extremely radical. It is characterized, in the words of one critic, by "piercing cries, gut-centred bellows, and melody-shredding phraseology" (Mandel, "Freedom Cry," 13). True, such departures from the musical norm needn't always be transformative in positive political ways, in ways, that is, that necessarily reduce the effects of hierarchies in the production and valuation of knowledge. Yet, as the previous chapters have suggested, the historical and cultural specificities that have given rise to many of jazz's most powerful dissonances have certainly invited us to link free jazz with an oppositional politics. So, if Taylor and Attali are correct in seeing musical innovation as facilitating the transformation of dominant structures of understanding, then Gayle ought, politically, and perhaps by extension, ethically, to be an exemplary model for those of us who seek alternatives to the current distribution of power. Furthermore, Gayle's very position outside a particular stream of commerce—the fact that he has, literally, lived on the streets of New York, that he will perform for hours in the subway and make only three dollars (Mandel, "Freedom Cry," 14) because he sees that "unprofitable form of self-enterprise as 'the only honest alternative' for a black musician opposed to the almost exclusively white ownership of jazz venues" (Davis, *Bebop,* 145)—ought also to affirm his politics, especially if we agree (as I do) with theologian Gregory Baum when he tells us that "to arrive at an honest evaluation of our society, we must first listen to the people who suffer injustice, we must look at history from below" (55).

Yet the emancipatory politics implied by that history, by that struggle for access to representation, and indeed by Gayle's brand of free jazz, cannot automatically in this case be equated with a salutary ethical stance. For if Gayle's music is radical, his pronouncements—especially during his onstage monologues—would appear to be politically reactionary. A self-professed Christian whose composition and recording titles (*Consecration*, *Spirits Before*, *Kingdom Come*, *Delivered*, "O Father," "Rise Up," "Redemption," "Eden Lost") point to his religious and spiritual leanings, Gayle has been known to offend his audiences—many of whom (like me) deeply admire his music—with long onstage monologues that deploy a particular rhetoric of Christianity to denounce homosexuality and abortion as sinful. One might, here, be inclined to argue that Gayle's nonreferential music should be kept separate from his personal views, but the song titles should, I think, lead us to see Gayle's music and his religious philosophizing as part of a continuum, as should the fact that his diatribes against homosexuality and abortion occur with musical accompaniment during his public performances.

Here, then, we have the case of a contemporary leading-edge jazz artist whose uncompromising music seems, whatever his intentions, at ethical odds with the reactionary politics expressed in his onstage monologues. The dilemma, perhaps, is a familiar one; as Cornel West writes: "All evaluation—including a delight in Eliot's poetry despite his reactionary politics, or a love of Zora Neale Hurston's novels despite her Republican party affiliations—is inseparable from, though not identical or reducible to, social structural analyses, moral and political judgments and the workings of a curious critical consciousness" (*Keeping Faith,* 24). Booth's assertion that "ethical quarrels always take place against a backdrop of agreement" (422) is also germane here. In raising doctrinal questions about the work of Rabelais, Booth suggests that "[w]e can quarrel with Rabelais's sexism only because we do not quarrel with him or among ourselves about his being worth a quarrel. . . . We would not read him at all, or talk about him, if he had not embodied a far larger collection of acceptable fixed norms than the set of those we might question" (422). Charles Gayle too, I want to suggest, is worth an ethical quarrel precisely because there is much about him that is admirable. In many ways, for example, his position outside commerce makes him emblematic of the potential for music to resist hegemonic social relations and the dominant workings of the culture industry. Combined with a music that is similarly "outside"—what Gayle himself calls "the self-expressive, sort of *out*, make-up-your-own-rules kind of thing" (quoted in Mandel, "Freedom Cry," 14)—his refusal to be co-opted by the culture industry suggests that Gayle might well exemplify what Attali, in his schematic history of the relationship between music and political economy, calls the stage of Composition, the stage at which people will make their own music rather than allow it to be shaped and influenced by the industry. Composition, says Attali, "is a foreshadowing of structural mutations, and farther down the road of the emergence of a radically new meaning of labor, as well as new relations among people and between men [*sic*] and commodities" (135). As Fredric Jameson writes in his foreword to Attali's book, "The argument of *Noise* is that music . . . has precisely this annuciatory vocation; and that the music of today stands . . . as a promise of a new, liberating mode of production" (xi). Indeed, in his chapter on the stage of Composition, Attali cites free jazz (mentioning in particular Archie Shepp, Bill Dixon and the Jazz Composers Guild, the Association for the Advancement of Creative Musicians, and the Jazz Composer's Orchestra), suggesting that these artists and self-managed collectives were engaged in the gradual "production of a new music outside of the industry" (138).

Even if, as we saw in chapter 1, free jazz might be read as a modernist movement away from representationalism, the efforts of many of its practitioners to "[become] more independent of capital" (Attali, 138) and to take control over the production and distribution of their music suggest that it remains deeply political. Alfred Willener, moreover, suggests in his book on May 1968 in France that free jazz offers an instructive analogy for understanding both the revolutionary activities of the participants in the May strike and the more general implications of cultural politicization. To what extent can we locate this kind of progressive politics in the texts (recordings, performances, pronouncements) of Charles Gayle?

"Perhaps better than any living musician," says Francis Davis in his liner notes to Gayle's *Consecration* CD, "Gayle epitomizes the difference between jazz as a way of making a living and jazz as a way—music isn't simply what he does, but who he is, and he might prefer us to believe that music is all that he is; that everything else about him, including the first fifty or so years of his life is of little importance to anyone, especially himself." Davis continues: "His stance is that of A Man Alone, someone utterly without aspiration, regret, or other emotional baggage, cut-off not just from the rest of the jazz world (especially its business arm), but from everyone." Gayle's remark that such cuttings-off may be "the only honest alternative" for black musicians wanting to resist being co-opted by the white cultural mainstream suggests, again, that here is an artist who, like Sun Ra, has a strong sense of social purpose. As Robin Balliger writes in her essay "Sounds of Resistance," "For the African diaspora and other groups oppressed by colonialism and repressive regimes, cultural expressions of music and dance have been a source of strength and identity formation critical to liberation struggles" (20). And if, as R. Radhakrishnan puts it, "'postcoloniality' as a field could well be the arena where inequalities, imbalances, and asymmetries could historicize themselves 'relationally,' an arena where dominant historiographies could be made accountable to the ethicopolitical authority of emerging histories" (171), then how are we to assess Charles Gayle's "ethicopolitical authority," his eligibility for the kinds of oppositional postcolonial analysis Radhakrishnan has in mind, when his public pronouncements work to reinforce dominant, naturalized, and media-sanctioned assumptions about, for example, homosexuality as sinful and unnatural?

The ethical problem posed by Gayle is, indeed, very tricky. Why, after all, should I assume that there must be some kind of reconciliation between what musicians play and what they say? There are certainly several examples of jazz artists who make beautiful music, but who still say and do what might be seen as horrible things. What distinguishes Gayle from most of these others is that he says deplorable things *in performance*: Gayle makes his comments about the sinfulness of homosexuality while he is playing wonderful music. I acknowledge that a fuller study of the complexities at work here ought properly to be deferred to a biographer, and that this is the chapter in which, perhaps, I most regret not having interviewed the artist whose work is under consideration. I'm not, though, writing Gayle's biography, and while it is with much critical trepidation that I approach the ethical dilemma that his art presents, the urgency of the performances themselves is such that Gayle himself likely wouldn't want the issues at stake to be ignored. Gayle's own reticence to talk much about his background, his insistence (in interviews) that his music *is* who he is, suggests, perhaps, that he might well want us to see his performances as constituting his biography. While there's a growing body of work (reviews, interviews) focused on Gayle, critics have generally stayed clear of broaching the ethical issues raised by his performances.[1] For many reasons, I too am reluctant: because I admire his music, because I know that in recent years he has abandoned the monologues (though I don't know why),[2] and because I need to know more about his background. But I would also feel remiss if I chose to ignore something as outspoken, challenging, and dramatic as Gayle's spoken-word material, especially, again, since it is presented in the context of his public performances.

Throughout the book, I've asked whether we can (or should) attach a direct meaning (or a politics) to particular styles of music. Now, as I've already implied, the kind of free jazz Gayle performs has an illustrious history, and there is, in both the statements and sentiments of some of its well-known practitioners in the '60s (most notably "New Thing" proponents Archie Shepp and Max Roach) and some prominent critics (Amiri Baraka, A. B. Spellman, and Frank Kofsky) the basis for an evolving discourse that sees the music as being linked to a progressive politics. The music, these artists and critics have reminded us, emerged in the context of black nationalism, the decolonization of the Third World, and the radicalization of civil rights movements. Its dissonances, "harsh" tones, and "wrong" notes, when read in relation to these broader movements, offer significant critiques of white hegemony, innovative African-American alternatives to European standards of judgment and propriety. Also important, as Gayle's timbral extremes exemplify, is the music's emancipation from the staves, the fact that it so often resists being codified by Western systems of notation.

My argument that the value of music comes from imposed judgments about how these outlawed musical techniques get taken up in particular historical contexts by subordinated social groups needs, however, to acknowledge just how complicated these contexts can be. Moreover, it needs to acknowledge how, without knowledge of a particular musician's politics or worldviews, it's possible for the listener to assign a political meaning to the music that may be at odds with that musician's intent. The paradox here is that while Gayle plays a music whose dissonant sounds I have learned to value for their transgressive political potential, they fail to be used in the service of the kind of antioppressive political work I want to endorse. In contrast, as the consideration of gender in jazz in chapter 5 would suggest, many women performers who have historically and institutionally been discouraged from producing these dissonant sounds have nonetheless been engaged in a profound political struggle—even if that struggle cannot be articulated so clearly in the music.

We've seen, then, how the connections between dissonant musics and oppositional politics are not always readily sustainable. In Kofsky's *Black Nationalism*, too, there's an implicit sense that a figure such as John Coltrane doesn't quite fit the political structure that the author wants to impose on the music. The present chapter on Charles Gayle forces me to confront a related set of issues around the complexities and contradictions of free jazz's social moorings and commitments, and to open up broader questions about how best to understand the ideological workings of jazz's musical properties. For Gayle's music, as Francis Davis points out in his *Consecration* liner notes, is indeed "the stuff of paradox." Davis continues: "As Coltrane and Albert Ayler did, [Gayle] regards music as spiritual in nature and seems fully at peace with himself only when playing it. Yet free jazz—Gayle's chosen style, if a label has to be fixed to it—is both visceral and abstract, and this combination puts the question of the meaning of such music up for grabs."

There is, perhaps, a tendency for postmodern critics to see such abstractness and open-endedness as preferable to routine forms of (musical or literary) closure. Linda Hutcheon, for example, writing about postmodern fiction, suggests that "[t]here has been a general (and perhaps healthy) turning from the expectation of sure and single meaning to a recognition of the value of difference and multiplicity" (*Canadian Postmodern*, 23). Booth, in discussing the relationship between ethics and literary form, interrogates the prevailing critical assumption that "techniques or styles or plot forms that 'close' questions are always inferior, the very mark of the non-literary or non-aesthetic or didactic. In contrast, narratives that raise questions that are open-ended and leave the reader unresolved—and thus presumably unable to remain passive in facing either life or literature—are in general superior" (61). I must confess to having labored under such an assumption for most of this book. Open-endedness, after all, has always been an important part of the African-American jazz tradition, improvisatory interventions a key focus for artists seeking alternative models of expression: Duke Ellington, Amiri Baraka, and others have explicitly theorized jazz in just such terms. What's of interest in Gayle's case is how the multiple voices at work in any of his group recordings or performances (think, for example, of the intricate dynamics of interaction, confrontation, and polyphony on "O Father," the lively pattern of call and response between drums and horn from the opening notes of "Justified"—both on *Consecration*) seem at odds with Gayle's tendency toward monologue.

In chapter 1, I implied that Ornette Coleman's atonality was aesthetically superior to the diatonic and closed forms of more traditional jazz, that the poetics of the open (to return to Umberto Eco's formulation) was somehow more interesting, more valuable, than the poetics of the closed. Closure, both in literary manifestations such as the heaven-on-earth endings of realist novels by Charles Dickens or Jane Austen and in the "return to the tonic" structure of diatonic music, is, I argued, an ideological convention, a way of reinforcing the status quo, or, in Barbara Hernnstein Smith's terms, "a modification of structure that makes *stasis*, or the absence of further continuation, the most probable succeeding event" (34). What postmodernism has helped to do is to promote a questioning of closed systems of thinking, to foster an "urge to trouble, to question, to make both problematic and provisional any . . . desire for order or truth through the powers of the human imagination" (Hutcheon, *Canadian Postmodern,* 2). For oppositional critics, the insights of postmodernism have clearly been instrumental in exposing the ideological basis of positions and values which we have tended to naturalize, take for granted, or accept as truth.

Yet the "make-up-your-own-rules kind of thing" that characterizes the openness, the unaccountability, of Gayle's brand of free jazz, I'm suggesting, offers something of a peculiar problem. While both postmodern theory and theories of black cultural expression might encourage us to see the openness of such music as healthy and valuable, to see the unparalleled intensity of Gayle's saxophone shrieks, shouts, and hollers as posing an important challenge to normative models of musical expression, what happens when our response to that music is complicated by Gayle's own spoken-word insistence that he is, as he implies in his monologues, preaching the truth? How, that is, are we to understand open form music in the context of an artist who, by his own admission, is preaching not multiple truths, but rather a single truth? Moreover, how do we understand the openness of such music when our ethics tells us that we must counter Gayle's single truth with our own requisite moral choices and decisions, with our own need to reassert normative claims? Are there times, that is, when, even in the face of our leanings toward open-endedness, we need to insist on closure?

Consider, for example, the following excerpt from Gayle's spoken-word monologue "Eden Lost" from his solo recording *Unto I AM*:

> You want to fornicate
> You don't want to marry
> You want the men to lust for the men and the women to lust after the women
> That's called an abomination
> No matter what your government, what your mother, and what your father say
> It's called an abomination
> You say I want to find my own way, I want to do what I want to do
> No matter what
> 'Coz you say I'm good, and, oh, I'm just a little bad
> Christ said, "There's no way that is not righteous

I'm the way to the truth and the light
Ain't nobody comes to the Father but by me."
Oh, you can deny that . . . but that's out of ignorance.

Gayle, "Eden Lost"

Before I go any further, I need to acknowledge that this is my own transcription. In imposing a particular kind of written structure on this oral performance, I'm admittedly running the risk of predetermining how Gayle's text might be read. Furthermore, to the extent that such monologues draw powerfully on the expressive cultural forms and significations of the black sermonic tradition, a fuller account of "Eden Lost" would need to take into account the specificities of the performance context. In his study of the performed African-American sermon, *I Got the Word in Me and I Can Sing It, You Know*, Gerald Davis explains that the "African-American sermon and the sermon environment are rich and complex events. A complete analysis of the African-American sermon in performance must capture visual elements, trace foot patterns and arm gestures, as well as record the words and analyze the structures of the genre" (11). Obviously, the recorded version of the monologue (and my transcription of it) leaves few openings for such detailed analysis of performative context. What I can say about the piece is that it features Gayle on piano, complementing (and sometimes punctuating) his spoken words with thunderous outbursts of tonal clusters, and, on occasion, with more searching and introspective atonal explorations. In the textual fragment I've transcribed, there's also something to be said about the structural patterns in use: the interplay between a vernacular voice and a formal one, the shift from the second person ("You want to fornicate") to a more conclusive and declarative poetics of pronouncement ("That's called an abomination"), the balance between concrete wordly examples and generalized religious principles. Such shifts, Davis points out, are characteristic of the narrative structure of many African-American sermons in performance (4).

The link between Gayle's music and the black sermonic tradition opens up issues relevant to our consideration of jazz and struggles for access to self-representation. Dolan Hubbard, in *The Sermon and the African American Literary Tradition*, makes the point that as a form of black American expressive culture, the sermon has played a vital role in enabling both the preacher and the people "to articulate the self" (5). Given that, historically, the Bible was often the first text that many blacks were (illicitly) taught to read, that it became a kind of compendium of many issues related to their social suffering, it may well be that Gayle's involvement with African-American Christianity is a reflection of black people's subjugation and their consequent struggle for self-definition.

In drawing on the black sermonic tradition, Gayle's performances, in the words of Toronto-based jazz critic Matt Galloway, "often seem more like fiery revival meetings than your average gale-force free-jazz blowout." Galloway also points out that "Gayle's explosive playing is tempered with equally incendiary testifying on matters of race, religion, and abortion." When asked about these matters, Gayle himself has explained: "The thing is, I don't want to be so arty that I have to separate my forms of expression as a human being. Instrumental music's just not enough for me, so I do a little talking as well. It's just who I am, and I've always felt that if you're paying money to see Charles Gayle, that's who you'll see" (quoted in Galloway). This "little talking," this insistence on an expression of identity—"it's just who I am"—has, as Gayle himself admits, led to some problems: "It's cost me a lot. People have stopped speaking to me, crowds have left, the phone has stopped ringing for a while. It's strange, because you'd think the people coming to see me would be up for a challenge. But the moment you give them something different, it throws them" (quoted in Galloway).

While Gayle is, I think, right to assume that his audiences are likely to be "up for a challenge," he seems unable to understand why many of his otherwise open-minded listeners are so quick to condemn him for his onstage monologues. Also of interest here is the fact that he is critical of those who "want to find [their] own way," those who, for example, through their sexual orientation, follow alternative models of self-expression and identity formation, all the while that he reclaims the right to his own, often highly controversial expressions of identity. He asserts that right, as we've seen, both through a music that he himself characterizes as a "self-expressive, sort of *out*, make-up-your-own-rules kind of thing" and through an insistence that everything he says and does, no matter how offensive and derogatory, is "just who I am." For Gayle, I suspect, there would be no contradiction here: his rights *are* right, or so his comments and monologues would seem to imply, because they are rooted in the teachings of a particular kind of Christianity.

History, of course, provides no shortage of examples where intolerable statements are expressed and deplorable political actions carried out in the name of some moral good (such as religion, the nation, the state). These examples may, in some measure, have accounted for the tendency, even among the more politically oriented and socially engaged of contemporary theorists, to see ethics not as a viable and indeed urgent model of inquiry, but rather as part of the dominant ideology. Fredric Jameson, for example, suggests by way of Nietzsche that "ethics itself . . . is the ideological vehicle and the legitimation of concrete structures of power and domination" (*Political,* 114). Similarly, Geoffrey Galt Harpham tells us, in his entry on ethics in the second edition of Frank Lentricchia's and Thomas McLaughlin's *Critical Terms for Literary Study*, that "virtually all the leading voices of the Theoretical Era . . . organized their critiques of humanism as *exposés* of ethics, revelations of the transgressive, rebellious, or subversive energies that ethics had effectively masked and suppressed" (388; emphasis added).

Yet the very appearance of Harpham's entry in Lentricchia's and McLaughlin's book—a text that's widely used to teach critical theory and practice to undergraduates—clearly signals a renewed interest in ethics on the part of contemporary theorists. In part, I suspect, this renewed interest has much to do with a growing dissatisfaction with postmodernism, with an evolving recognition that, as Seyla Benhabib puts it in *Situating the Self: Gender, Community, and Postmodernism in Contemporary Ethics,* while "[p]ostmodernism, in its infinitely skeptical and subversive attitude toward normative claims, institutional justice and political struggles, is certainly refreshing . . . it is also debilitating" (15). In an era dominated by relativist assumptions, Gayle, somewhat similarly, may be pressing for a new religious forum for teaching and preaching: in his case, through music.

His example is instructive not only because it encourages us to make judgments and to announce our normative commitments, but also because it may, indeed, sharpen our understanding of the way in which those judgments and commitments are grounded in complex patterns of social and historical relevance. Let me try to be more precise about what I have in mind here. If, regardless of our appreciation of Gayle's music, we side with the audience members who storm out when Gayle launches into his spoken-word attacks on homosexuality and gay rights (or with the music programmers who decide *not* to hire Gayle), if, contrary to the decision of the Bollingen Prize committee to honor Ezra Pound's work on the basis of "some central stylistic quality that redeems all doctrinal faults" (Booth, 381), we continue to be vigilant in our assessment of "doctrinal faults" in Gayle's texts, then we need some way to account for these choices. For our decision about Gayle's ethics, as we have seen, necessarily has to be made in the context of intersecting historical struggles for social justice, legitimacy, identity formation, and access to representation.

Much of the argument I've been presenting in this chapter—in fact, in this book—is, if perhaps in somewhat different terms, articulated by Satya Mohanty in the concluding chapter of *Literary Theory and the Claims of History*. Mohanty writes:

> If our views about identities are partly explanations of the world in which we live and these explanations are based on the knowledge we gather from our social activities, then the claim that oppressed social groups have a special kind of knowledge about the world as it affects them is hardly a mysterious one . . . it is an empirical claim, tied to a wider (empirical and theoretical) account of the society in which these groups live. (234-5)

Now our understanding of Gayle's identity, we've noted, is predicated not only on the densely patterned and historically rooted structures of intelligibility evident in his music, but also on other forms of mooring such as race, class, and religion. These various moorings, however, are not coextensive; the ethicopolitical authority and "special kind of knowledge" that we may, for instance, be willing to grant Gayle on the basis of his race and class taxonomies are not, in this case, readily compatible with his religious perspective. Furthermore, Christianity's attitude toward homosexuality is, we perhaps ought to add, more complicated than Gayle acknowledges in his public pronouncements. As Wilfrid Koponen notes in *Embracing a Gay Identity*, "Christian churches are not monolithic in their condemnation of homosexuality, nor has Christianity been homophobic throughout its history. Much recent scholarship on the Bible, as well as on ancient apocryphal Christian manuscripts and church history, has challenged traditional homophobic interpretation of scripture and homophobic claims about the Christian tradition" (84). Beside such scholarship, Gayle's take on Christianity appears to be bereft of historical depth and complexity, his assertion that justifications for gay rights are made "out of ignorance" itself an ineffective justification for imposing his own codes of sexual ethics, his own personal preferences, on others.

We can now perhaps see a little more clearly how the patterns of social and historical relevance I spoke of earlier should lead us, in this particular case, to grant what Mohanty calls "epistemic privilege" to one oppressed social group (gays and lesbians) rather than to others. We can also see how, in Radhakrishnan's words, "[a]mong the many selves that constitute one's identity, there exists a relationship of unevenness and asymmetry" (161), a relationship that, in fact, has forced cultural theorists to recognize the abiding need for what Stuart Hall and others have called principles and methodologies of articulation. As Slack and Whitt put it, "Recognizing that cultural studies cannot adequately ground its interventionist strategy by appealing to a *single* principle (class, gender, race), cultural theorists [began] to shift their concern to the articulating principles that *connect* gender, race, and class, principles in which relations of subordination and domination are entailed" (579). Catherine Hall, in a discussion which, like Slack's and Whitt's essay, appears in the Routledge *Cultural Studies* reader, makes a similar point, one that, given its relevance to the problem at hand, seems worth quoting at some length:

> I don't think that we have, as yet, a theory as to the articulation of race, class, and gender and the ways in which these articulations might generally operate. The terms are often produced in a litany, to prove political correctness, but that does not necessarily mean that the forms of analysis which follow are really shaped by the grasp of the workings of each axis of power in relation to the others. Indeed, it is extremely difficult to do such work because the level of analysis is necessarily extremely complex with many variables at play at any one time. Case studies, therefore, whether historical or contemporary, which carefully trace the contradictory ways in which these articulations take place both in historically specific moments and over time, seem to me to be very important. (270–71)

Mohanty too, in his salutary attempt to rehabilitate models of realism, objectivity, and universalism, asks us to think rigorously about the connections among various principles governing the formation of identities: "How do we determine that one social identity is more legitimate than another? How do we justify one 'strategy' over another? Is such justification purely a matter of pragmatic calculation, or does it obey some epistemic constraints as well? Does what we know about the world . . . have any bearing on our understanding of this justification?" (232). His answer to these questions, we are told, involves "emphasizing the continuity of accounts of cultural identity with accounts of the social justification of knowledge, especially the knowledge involved in our ethical and political claims and commitments" (232).

What happens, we need to ask, when, under certain conditions, these accounts are seen to clash, when, as in Gayle's case, accounts of the social justification of knowledge are used to belittle or dismiss accounts of the struggle to define sexual orientation as a basis for one's social and political identity? What does it mean to dismiss accounts of that struggle in an era in which, as Dennis Altman puts it, "[t]he greatest single victory of the gay movement . . . has been to shift the debate from behavior to identity, thus forcing opponents into a position where they can be seen as attacking the civil rights of homosexual citizens rather than attacking specific and (as they see it) antisocial behavior" (9)? Altman, writing about the United States, points out that "[i]n a country where people identify themselves by reference to ethnicity and religion, it is not surprising that homosexuals have increasingly come to see themselves as another ethnic group and to claim recognition on the basis of this analogy" (viii). Denial of such recognition, of such struggle for legitimacy and identity formation, I'm suggesting, needs to be seen as a denial of human rights.

Gayle, we've seen, refuses to grant that sense of worth to gays and lesbians; he insists that homosexuality is a moral "abomination" because, according to his reading of Christianity, it disrupts the natural social order. Something more, I think, needs to be said about the urgency with which the specifics of our particular cultural moment compel us to take issue with him on these matters. As recently as 1992, for example, a measure was added to the ballot of the U.S. presidential election proposing to "write into the Oregon constitution a moral condemnation of homosexuality." As J. Richard Middleton and Brian Walsh point out in *Truth Is Stranger Than It Used to Be: Biblical Faith in a Postmodern Age*, "The campaigns for and against this measure were characterized by bitterness, fear, hatred, violence and even murder" (198). What are we to make of the fact that a blatant violation of human rights can be legitimized through such a powerful institutional context? And what does such a measure mean—and what might be its consequences—when, as Eve Kosofsky Sedgwick tells us, "[t]here is reason to believe that gay-bashing is the most common and most rapidly increasing among what are becoming legally known as bias-related or hate-related crimes in the United States"? For Sedgwick, "[t]here is no question that the threat of this violent, degrading, and often fatal extrajudicial sanction works even more powerfully than, and in intimately enforcing concert with, more respectably institutionalized sanctions against gay choice, expression, and being" (18). Such intolerable social injustices—especially in light of the institutional formations of hegemony—can be overcome, it seems to me, only through tough coalitional struggles for public legitimacy.

In the context of the urgent need for such struggles, the example of Charles Gayle points tellingly to the fact that neither jazz (no matter how much it stands outside the culture industry) nor race can, by themselves (or even in partnership), provide an effective guarantee of a progressive cultural practice and politics. Stuart Hall, taking up a similar issue in a different context, puts it thus:

> We should put this as plainly as possible. Films are not necessarily good because black people make them. They are not necessarily "right on" by virtue of the fact that they deal with the black experience. Once you enter the politics of the end of the essential black subject you are plunged headlong into the maelstrom of a continuously contingent, unguaranteed, political argument and debate: a critical politics, a politics of criticism. You can no longer conduct black politics through the strategy of a simple set of reversals, putting in the place of the bad old essential white subject, the new essentially good black subject. ("New Ethnicities," 443–44)

Hall's critique of the essential black subject is germane here. Also at stake is the loss of an essentialized identity politics, a politics that, for much of this book, I have tended to associate with jazz. In the face of such a loss, how then, to quote Hall once again, can we conceive of a politics "which works with and through difference, which is able to build those forms of solidarity and identification which make common struggle and resistance possible but without suppressing the real heterogeneity of interests and identities" (444)? Charles Gayle's art, as we've seen, forces us to reckon with the difficulty of conceptualizing the logic and the efficacy of such a coalitional politics. Yet as Hall (rightly, I think) tells us, that difficulty "does not absolve us of the task of developing such a politics" (444).

I suggested earlier that such a politics involves a struggle on the part of oppositional discourses for public legitimacy. At a time when inequality and injustice are, in ways that I've only just touched on here, institutionally sanctioned and perpetuated, it seems imperative that we find ways to broaden what Nancy Fraser aptly calls "the universe of legitimate public contestation" (22). Now, jazz, as I've implied throughout, and as I'll suggest more fully in the book's concluding chapter, undoubtedly has a role to play in fostering such a broadening, in promoting purposeful oppositional interventions in the public sphere. After all, despite its private fields of signification, its intensely personal meanings for both musicians and audiences, jazz remains a public activity. Consider, for instance, Ingrid Monson's remarks:

> When a musician successfully reaches a discerning audience, moves its members to applaud or shout praises, raises the energy to dramatic proportions, and leaves a sonorous memory that lingers long after, he or she has moved beyond technical competence, beyond the chord changes, and into the realm of "saying something." Since saying something . . . requires soloists who can play, accompanists who can respond, and audiences who can hear within the context of the richly textured aural legacy of jazz and African American music, this verbal aesthetic image underscores the collaborative and communicative quality of improvisation. (*Saying Something,* 1–2)

Somewhat similarly, Edward Said reminds us that although music is "an art whose existence is premised undeniably on individual performance, reception, or production," it, "like literature, is practiced in a social and cultural setting" (*Musical Elaborations,* xiv). The interpretive problems (is musical meaning best judged as a function of intent or effect?) that necessarily accompany such a collaborative communicative setting clearly need to be taken into account when we enter into an ethical criticism of music. To borrow Mohanty's words, we "need to pay attention to the way . . . social locations facilitate or inhibit knowledge by predisposing us to register and interpret information in certain ways" (234). While Mohanty, in this passage, is speaking of the situatedness of the reader or critic, and how that situatedness (or social location) plays a role in our understanding of the epistemic privilege we grant to the experience of victims of oppression, his comments, I think, have some bearing on our assessment of Charles Gayle's texts (and on how our own commitments may predispose us to particular kinds of assessment). More generally, his comments point to the need to understand any such assessment in the context of our analysis of music's public function.

In gesturing towards some sense of that function, Said points out that "it is both interesting and novel to note that there have been consistent transgressions by music into adjoining domains—the family, school, class and sexual relations, nationalism, and even large public issues" (*Musical Elaborations,* 56). Given his claims for the public function of music and, of course, his pioneering forms of oppositional cultural and literary criticism, it's interesting to note that Said has little interest in jazz, that there are only a few incidental references to jazz in his book on music. Nevertheless, some of what he says about Western classical music would certainly seem to apply here. Indeed, in a chapter which considers the relation between Wagner's music and anti-Semitism, Said probes the very "question of whether moral and political affiliation or guilt in the world of everyday life can have a serious bearing upon the quality and interpretation of works of mind, works that are principally aesthetic and intellectual" (36). Said's answer, in part, involves recognizing that music's "way of inhabiting the social landscape varies so much as to affect compositional and formal styles with a force as yet largely uninventoried in cultural studies now" (70). Of particular interest to him is music's "nomadic ability to attach itself to, and become part of, social formations, to vary its articulations and rhetoric depending on the occasion as well as the audience, plus the power and the gender situations in which it takes place" (70).

Jazz, given its emphasis on improvisation, might be said to provide, at least in some measure, an exemplary instance of this nomadic quality. But what's at stake in jazz's nomadicism, what is up for grabs, is precisely its ethicopolitical authority, its status as a music of protest, as an oppositional form of discourse. In an era of widespread inequality, privation, and injustice, an era when subjugated knowledges struggle for public legitimacy only to be met with various forms of institutional disparagement and intolerance, music can carry an impressive (and, if Attali is correct, even an annuciatory) public force. What, then, does it mean for Charles Gayle to link free jazz (a music historically associated with an oppositional politics) with a public denunciation of gay rights and reproductive rights? I've suggested throughout that the historical and cultural force of jazz resides not only in its interventions into ongoing debates about the political function of music, but also in the rich and ever-changing interpretive frameworks it has sought to establish for articulating the terms of its own self-representation. Those ever-changing frameworks, as we see especially clearly in the case of Charles Gayle, complicate our understanding of jazz's oppositional character.

Yet something more, I think, needs to be said here, for, as I've indicated already, Gayle's music does not, in itself, sit comfortably next to his homophobic politics. Gayle himself would likely disagree with any suggestion that there's a tension between his art and his politics; instead, as the comments I quoted from him earlier would imply, he sees both as fundamentally tied to his own identity, and would undoubtedly argue that there are strong filaments of continuity between a music that's deeply rooted in a tradition which includes, for example spirituals and gospels—indeed a music that he refuses to call avant-garde—and a political worldview predicated on the teachings of black Christianity. We find ourselves here once again broaching the question of whether meaning is best understood as a function of intent or effect. To rework and reverse the passage I quoted earlier from Monson, when a musician fails in his or her attempt to reach a discerning audience and causes its members to feel offended, to be hurt, how do we assess meaning, especially when, by the musician's own account, the performance has been successful? Do we arrive at judgment on the basis of the artist or of the offended audience? And what if only half of the audience is offended, and the other half is moved to applaud or shout praises?

In 1994, I considered booking Gayle to play at the first Guelph Jazz Festival. Though I'd read some reviews of his work, my main exposure to Gayle at that point was through some of his recordings. I found (and still find) his saxophone playing on those recordings to be extraordinarily powerful (and sometimes, even with its hard-edged quality and its intense use of high-register sonorities, to be profoundly beautiful, sometimes even lyrical). Like other festival organizers, I was initially quite keen to present Gayle's music to our community, though I knew that we would need to think hard about how to market what some would see as challenging music (this was, after all, our first year of operation). After a number of us heard him perform in Toronto, we decided, in the end, not to hire him because of the troubling nature of his monologues. At that show, Gayle (as on the *Unto I AM* recording) performed a spoken-word piano piece that used Christian rhetoric to make public pronouncements against homosexuality and abortion. While we were all in awe of his music, we were taken aback by his monologues. I remember looking around me at others in the audience who seemed similarly unprepared for what they were hearing. On the way back to Guelph after the concert (and, in fact, for many weeks after), we continued to discuss Gayle's Toronto performance, trying to think through whether or not to feature him at our festival. If we decided against booking Gayle, would our decision not to book him itself be an act of suppression comparable to Gayle's own suppression, in those monologues, of the voice of gays and lesbians? What ethical obligation did we (do we) have to our audiences? What if people walked out? What if they were hurt by Gayle's words? How might Gayle's monologues have an impact on the festival's future relations with the community? Would there be a second festival or would patrons and sponsors simply refuse to renew their support in light of what would undoubtedly be a hugely controversial event? After much debate and extensive consultation with others (both in our community and in jazz circles elsewhere), we decided to take an ethical stand: we couldn't, despite our attachment to Gayle's music, authorize public performances that constituted an overt disparagement of human rights. Just as I believe that Pound ought not to have received the Bollingen Prize—because the stylistic complexities of his *Cantos* do *not* redeem or make permissible anti-Semitic statements—our exclusion of Gayle from the festival forced us to confront the fact that aesthetically engaging (and often intensely beautiful) music can express underlying values that are contrary to what we, as listeners, think they ought to be. In this case, neither the formidable power of the music nor the emergent social locations out of which that music emerged would enable us to sanction the explicit homophobia in Gayle's performances.

Gayle's texts (his recordings, performances, and pronouncements), I've been suggesting, provide a highly resonant point of entry into an ethical criticism of music precisely because they force us to confront head-on these sorts of difficult questions about the complex ways in which we negotiate musical meaning. What makes these questions so particularly difficult to answer in the case of Charles Gayle is, of course, the music. Whatever his intent, the music, in its unrelenting free-form intensity, abandon, and power, and with its driving emphasis on overtones, microtones,and timbral innovation, represents a radical retreat from customary sources of musical meaning. Indeed, what I admire in Gayle's music is similar to what (as I've suggested in my introduction) I value in the music of many of the performers discussed in this book: a liberating ability to engage in a kind of conceptual block-busting, a spirit of innovation that's capable of shaking us out of our settled habits of response and judgment. In an era when the idiom of tenor saxophone playing has become increasingly laden with clichés, there is something genuinely refreshing and compelling about Gayle's musical unpredictability, about his continuing efforts to discover new sonic possibilities. Listen, for example, to Gayle's FMP recording *Touchin' on Trane*. This is, to my mind, communal music making of the highest possible order. Here, as the outing's title would suggest, Gayle evokes Coltrane in ways that are obliquely, yet respectfully, mindful of tradition. But he's also characteristically forward-looking as he slices through snatches of melody with the frenzied lyricism of his otherworldly upper-register tenor playing. His widely varying timbres and non-tempered sounds—sounds that, for a variety of historical and institutional reasons, have, as I've suggested, held salient oppositional values for African-American musicians and their listeners—are a perfect match for the remarkably involving performances by his musical colleagues here: the formidable textural inventiveness and extended techniques of bassist William Parker and the liberating rhythmic drive of Coltrane's *Interstellar Space* partner Rashied Ali, a drummer well known for having revolutionized our understanding of the possibilities of musical timekeeping. In *Touchin' on Trane*, I hear a trenchant critique of the stability of normative models of expression.

There is also an integrity to Gayle's art, a heartfelt spiritual intensity to everything he plays, a sense, whether he's working in free contexts (as he is most often), or whether (as on his 1997 *Delivered* recording) he's interpreting black spirituals, that he's pouring his soul into every single note. This is, in short, monumentally eloquent music, music that, as Gayle's groundings in the signifying practices emerging out of the black church might suggest, calls out to be read in the context of the affirmative powers of the black sermon. In Dolan Hubbard's words, "the black sermon is a testament to black people's powers of conception, a suggestion that their abilities to create, grasp, and use symbols are just as valid as those who oppress and would deny them their humanity" (145). Furthermore, as practitioners of free jazz ranging from John Coltrane and Albert Ayler to members of the Association for the Advancement of Creative Musicians have all amply illustrated, the rejection of received harmonic and tonal practices was often made in the name not only of ideological freedom but also, precisely, of spiritual fulfillment (Radano, *New Musical Figurations,* 108). By contrast, as Roscoe Mitchell once suggested, "Cats that play bop are more [often] concerned with things like chords and changes rather than spirits" (quoted in Radano, *New Musical Figurations,* 104). Pressed into service, even if only implicitly, is an illustrious history that locates a spiritual basis in the theory and cultural practice of innovative black free jazz artists. Jostling against Gayle's own forms of reinforcement of social authority and dominant structures of understanding, then, are the sounding strategies (to use Houston Baker's helpful phrase) of emergent histories, the elaboration of alternative affiliations and social energies.

Even as these alternatives are heard for the challenges they imply to dominant social arrangements, epistemic privilege has to reside elsewhere, largely, as I've been suggesting, because music's complex and multiple ways of inhabiting the social landscape necessarily complicate our understanding of any determinate ethicopolitical allegiances. The point of "strategic opposition to reigning truths and norms," after all, as Jim Merod so eloquently argues in what is surely the most compelling treatment to date of jazz's relation to contemporary critical theory, "is to prepare for both individual and collective assertions of noncompliance with coercions that allow domination to exist with guiltless, sometimes invisible abandon" ("Resistance," 188). Moreover, the refusal to grant epistemic privilege to Gayle, despite his embeddedness in various histories from below, needs to be understood in the context of our urgent need to generate what Cornel West has called "the transgendered, transracial, transsexual orientation of social motion, social momentum, social movement" ("A Matter," 19). West is forthright in arguing that we need to be vigilant in finding ways to create infrastructures for the transmission of oppositional identities that would cut across race, class, gender, and sexuality. And "when you don't have institutions and infrastructures that can sustain the transmitting of values, or the constitution of subcultures over time and space," he explains, "the best you can do is try to initiate momentum and possible movement. And we do that first by stressing a moral discourse that makes linkages and connections" (23). It's here, precisely, I would argue, that Gayle fails the test, for what we discover when we consider the points of intersection between his music, his life, and his pronouncements is an impediment to such social movement, to such a moral discourse.

For West, asking the fundamental question, "What is the moral content of your identity?" involves "raising the question of how radically democratic you are when you talk about defining your identity, especially in relation to [the] maldistribution of resources" (17). And as Mohanty writes:

> Whether we inherit an identity—masculinity, being black—or we actively choose one on the basis of our radical political predilections—radical lesbianism, black nationalism, socialism—our identities are ways of making sense of our experiences. Identities are theoretical constructs that enable us to read the world in specific ways. It is in this sense that they are valuable, and their epistemic status should be taken very seriously. In them, and through them, we learn to define and reshape our values and commitments, we give texture and form to our collective futures. Both the essentialism of identity politics and the skepticism of the postmodernist position seriously underread the real epistemic and political complexities of our social and cultural identities. (216)

As a test case for thinking through the possibilities of an ethics of jazz criticism, Charles Gayle forces us to confront those epistemic and political complexities, just as the pressing questions opened up by his oeuvre point both to the loss of an essentialized understanding of politicized identities and to the unsustainability of postmodernism's skepticism of normative claims and moral judgments.

It's the music, however, that I seem to be revisiting over and over again, as if, even in the very structure of this chapter, I remain unsatisfied with my ethical indictment of Gayle; it's the music, after all, which, as I said earlier, makes Gayle worth a quarrel. Perhaps I still need some way to account for the fact that, despite my unease with Gayle's sexuality politics, I will continue to purchase his recordings. In taking seriously my public responsibilities as a music programmer, however, I'll know to be on my guard, for the dissonances that resound in Gayle's music, I'm forced to confess, remain insufficient for discerning and articulating the ethical character and "moral content" of either Gayle's or jazz's complex investments in variously politicized identities. I may, after all, have been wrong, then, in chapter 1, for here is a case where the "poetics of the open" seems less abiding than the need for an ethics premised on social justice, human solidarity, and normative commitments to various forms of closure.

Notes

1. One notable exception can be found on a website devoted specifically to Gayle's views on abortion. The site seems to have been inspired by a Gayle performance in Seattle and includes responses from various listeners. We are told by the creators of the site that "Charles Gayle makes music with passion and delivers polarizing opinion with an equal degree of passion. In this live show, recorded in Seattle on 2.16.96, the audience got a lot of both. The music was well-received. His views on abortion and how he chose to present them were not. The conviction in his beliefs were [sic] clearly recognized" (http://www.sonarchy.org/audio/archives/gayle_abort.aiff).

2. While I have not seen Gayle perform since 1994, those who have had the opportunity to see Gayle in concert more recently would, quite rightly, point to the ways in which his use of performance codes associated with mime further complicates our assessment of his art. If Gayle has, indeed, been forced into silence by audiences and festival organiz-

ers (like me) who are troubled by his on-stage monologues, he now appears to have responded to his critics by remaking himself into what one advance reviewer of this book described as "a figure of pathos who has been deprived of a voice." Complete with black hat, tattered tails, white face paint, and a red nose (see, for example, the inside tray photo on his *Delivered* CD or the front cover image on his most recent recording, *Ancient of Days*), Gayle has taken to representing himself as what that same reviewer called "an impoverished but sensitive soul [who has been] shut out of society," as a kind of "sad clown," with the white paint below his eyes looking rather like tears.

Conclusion

Alternative Public Spheres

I do not think there are final and definite answers to any of the really important questions in human life; there are only useful and useless answers—answers, that is, that lead in the direction of enrichment of experience or of its impoverishment.

Christopher Small, *Musicking: The Meanings of Performance and Listening,* 17

It's true that I have difficulty concluding my books. Despite what I just said about my ethical commitment to forms of closure, I'm always uneasy about ending on the wrong note. No, perhaps I'd better rephrase that: what troubles me is the possibility that I might end too resolutely on the *right* note, that is, by adhering to expected cadences or by fulfilling familiar patterns of harmony, coherence, and judgment. That's not to say I'm against endings that struggle to take stands on issues, to provide purposeful illustrations of principles, or to offer blueprints for the achievement of social justice. On the contrary, as I hope both the last chapter and, more generally, the book itself have made clear, these are, to my mind, precisely the kinds of struggles that need to animate our critical work. And if the study of jazz, as I've argued, can reinvigorate our understanding of the social function of art and of culture's role in the process of unsettling historically and institutionally determined habits of privilege and privation, then what's at stake in our understanding and assessment of the music, I would suggest, is nothing less than the struggle to reconstruct public life.

Listening to (or performing) jazz is clearly not a simple substitute for ethically responsible work of public concern; nevertheless, my contention is that the music needs to be understood in relation to the cultural and institutional practices that promote both action and reflection in the public arena, its oppositional aspirations reconfigured as part of a broader critical model of public discourse. The music's very embeddedness in the structures of critical public debate is, indeed, one of the things that makes it so difficult for me to conclude this study. Just as jazz itself, with its blue notes, altered harmonies, irregular rhythms, nontempered sounds, polyrhythms, and scat vocals, has generated a multiplicity of cultural practices that accent dissonance and variance rather than fixity, stability, or stasis (recall Mackey's argument), and just as, to quote once again from George Lipsitz, the driving force behind the music has always been "relentless innovation" rather than "static tradition" (178), so too is there a spirit of open-endedness that tends to inform the workings of the public sphere. As Nancy Fraser notes, the very concept of a public "emphasizes discursive interaction that is in principle unbounded and open-ended, and this in turn implies a plurality of perspectives" (31).

For Fraser, that plurality gets played out in the "parallel discursive arenas where members of subordinated social groups invent and circulate counterdiscourses, so as to formulate oppositional interpretations of their identities, interests, and needs" (14). In the last chapter, I touched on some of the complexities that arise from a consideration of the unbounded and heterogeneous nature of those identities, interests, and needs. There, I suggested that the difficult case of Charles Gayle, a black free jazz saxophonist who for many years was a homeless person on the streets of New York, points compellingly to the fact that "people participate in more than one public" (Fraser, 19). Gayle's case tellingly illustrates the extent to which the subject positions characterizing the lived realities of even a single individual are so complex and so diverse that any attempt at articulating a collective political valence becomes reductive and misleading. On a broader scale, one of the questions that needs to be posed is what this heterogeneity might mean for coalitions of oppressed social groups struggling to make oppositional public interventions.

My interest in thinking about jazz in the context of debates that have emerged around notions of the public sphere is, in part, a function of my attempt in this book to argue for a "fit" between my academic scholarship and my involvement in organizing a community jazz festival. The festival itself, as I've implied throughout, offers a site for the articulation of alternative models of performance, identity formation, and knowledge production. And in wrestling with the complex connections between artistic practices, institutional politics, audience-building strategies, community involvement, and economic effects, I, like other festival organizers, have been forced to confront direct questions about the ways in which our social and institutional positioning can and does inform the production and the reception of knowledge about the music. In planning, programming, organizing, and publicizing a jazz festival, we have, in short, been engaged in acts of meaning-making: in constructing narratives, histories, identities, and epistemologies that—sometimes modestly, sometimes profoundly—shape the way in which the music gets understood, listened to, and talked about. If it has been one of the tasks of this book to consider jazz in the context of the complex processes through which members of subordinated social groups struggle for access to self-representation and identity formation, then surely it behooves me to attend to the social and political consequences of my own representational acts as a festival programmer. In this sense, it's my involvement not only with the music and the players, but also with the institutions through which jazz gets produced, performed, promoted, and listened to that's of interest.

Let me try to give a rough example of the kinds of things I'm thinking about here. The nature of the music I tend to program is such that many of the artists who've been featured at the festival have been excluded from institutionalized narratives and mainstream histories of the music. Bassist William Parker, for example, a giant on the New York free jazz scene and an artist who, in smaller, independent jazz publications such as *Cadence* and *Coda* magazines, often gets heralded as one of the most influential musicians of our generation, doesn't even merit his own entry in the most recent edition of the otherwise monumental *Penguin Guide to Jazz*. While my decision to feature artists like Parker at the festival may not always consciously stem from a desire to redress such oversights, I've certainly become acutely aware of how various kinds of artistic and material considerations—whom to program, in what context, with what kind of publicity, for what ticket prices—can, again, sometimes subtly, sometimes powerfully, work to counter (or to reinforce) dominant public perceptions of jazz. By having William Parker perform in the sanctuary of a historic church rather than in a dingy bar or even in a modern performing arts center, we're sending particular kinds of messages about the meaning, value, and dignity of the music, as well as, implicitly, about its historical and social worth.

Somewhat similarly, as Mark Anthony Neal notes in *What the Music Said: Black Popular Music and Black Public Culture,* several of the free jazz players who emerged in tandem with the black nationalist movement in the '60s "effectively countered critical renderings which often reduced jazz as the music of brothels, drug addicts, and a socially deviant subculture" (32). Because such attempts to overturn instilled perceptions about jazz have frequently taken the form of recordings and performances that, to borrow again from Neal, were and still are "[c]erebrally challenging to both musicians and audiences" (32), these artists' attempts to offer counterhegemonic representations of their lives and their art are often articulated at the expense of core audiences. All the while that artists such as Sun Ra, Muhal Richard Abrams, the Art Ensemble of Chicago, Bill Dixon, and others have been engaged in efforts to seize control over the means of production, and thus to construct alternative public spheres that seek to correct the dominant historical record, they have often been performing the kind of "out" jazz that runs the risk of limiting their exposure to wider audiences. Indeed, the struggles that these artists have faced in trying to establish alternative institutions and communication networks (AACM, Saturn Records, Jazz Composers Guild, and so forth) seem very much in keeping with what Fraser identifies as the dual character of subaltern counterpublics. She writes:

> On the one hand, they function as spaces of withdrawal and regroupement; on the other hand, they also function as bases and training grounds for agitational activities directed toward wider publics. It is precisely in the dialectic between these two functions that their emancipatory potential resides. This dialectic enables subaltern counterpublics partially to offset, although not wholly to eradicate, the unjust participatory privileges enjoyed by members of dominant social groups in stratified societies. (15)

What interests me, then, is the efficacy of jazz—and especially of more innovative, more "cerebrally challenging" forms of jazz—as a vehicle for facilitating alternative social formations. How, that is, do we make sense of the tension between an involvement with innovative modes of musical expression that may appeal only to limited numbers of the general public and the oft-stated purpose of wanting to construct alternative public spheres, of wanting the music to intervene in dominant social relations? How do artists such as the Art Ensemble of Chicago, Sun Ra, and others remain true to the specificities of their own innovative aesthetics while also performing a more collective and widespread political function? Robert O'Meally suggests that "[f]or all its supposed abstruseness, jazz is an insistently democratic music, one that aims to sound like citizens in a barbershop or grocery line, talking stuff, trading lines" (*Jazz Cadence,* 117–18). I'd like to agree with this. But the question we need to ask is about whether that democratic potential has something to do with the music itself or whether it is better understood as a function of the material conditions that shape performance and listening situations at particular moments in history.

The essays collected in the "Black Public Sphere" special issue of the journal *Public Culture*, while only sometimes touching on matters of music, certainly push us to theorize public programs of action, debate, and criticism in relation to material practices and struggles for institutional authority. Michael Dawson, for example, tells us that "[t]hroughout Black history, a multiplicity of Black institutions have formed the material basis for a subaltern counterpublic. An independent Black press, the production and circulation of socially and politically sharp popular Black music and the Black church have provided institutional bases for the Black counterpublic since the Civil War" (206). Dawson's reference to black popular music, we should note, is here expressly framed in the context of the music's production and distribution, that is, not only in terms of its social meanings, but also in terms of how those meanings are negotiated through complex material processes. For Dawson, the black public sphere is best understood as "a set of institutions, communication networks and practices which facilitate debate of causes and remedies to the current combination of political setbacks and economic devastation facing major segments of the Black community, and which facilitate the creation of oppositional formations and sites" (197). Many of the artists I've been considering in this book turn explicitly to alternative institution-building strategies in an effort to facilitate such oppositional formations and to become active subjects of their own histories.

Elsewhere in the book I've quoted from thinkers as diverse as

Asian-American baritone saxophonist Fred Wei-han Ho, Algerian liberation theorist Frantz Fanon, and Canadian philosopher Charles Taylor, all of whom have pointed to the ways in which aggrieved populations suffer from having their histories and identities defined and (mis)represented by dominant social orders. To what extent, I've been asking throughout, might jazz offer an opportunity for recasting those identities and histories, and thus of diminishing the sense of misrecognition fostered through representations in the official public sphere? To what extent ought jazz to be heard in the context of the black public sphere's critique of dominant social and cultural institutions? And, more generally, to what extent should jazz be theorized in relation to the kinds of revisionist historiography which "records that members of subordinated social groups—women, workers, peoples of color, and gays and lesbians—have repeatedly found it advantageous to constitute alternative publics" (Fraser, 14)?

We've seen how musicians' cooperatives such as the Chicago-based AACM, self-managed record companies and music distribution networks such as Sun Ra's Saturn Records and John Zorn's Tzadik imprint, independent music festivals (Bill Dixon's October Revolution, Max Roach's Alternative Newport, and, more locally, The Guelph Jazz Festival), and, in some instances, jazz autobiography have all, at least in part, emerged in response to exclusions and misrepresentations in dominant public institutions. Archie Shepp has been forthright in his insistence on the need to see the problem in racial terms, famously pronouncing that "jazz is the product of the whites—the ofays—too often my enemy. It is the progeny of the blacks—my kinsmen. By this I mean: you [white producers and recording executives] own the music, and we [black musicians] make it. By definition, then, you own the people who make the music" (11). Others such as Melba Liston and Pauline Oliveros have encouraged us to take issue with mainstream histories and representations of the music by paying particular attention to gendered exclusions and gender-related practices of exploitation. Their counternarratives invite us to enlarge our base of valued knowledges by recognizing the role that women have played in the history and development of what is traditionally institutionalized as a male-dominated realm. Now, with an increasing number of women entering into the music industry (as performers and composers, but also as promoters, producers, and managers) and with the continuing growth of black-owned record labels and independent artist-run organizations, the terms of the debate appear to be changing somewhat: instead of focusing primarily on the need for access to self-representation and for control over the means of production, current theoretical and political debates will likely see critics staking claims over whether such institutional changes have actually transformed subordinated social groups into areas favored by social patronage or privilege. What also remains to be seen is whether (and to what extent) changes in institutional structures will result in concomitant shifts in ideology, and how those shifts might get reflected in musical practice. Has the fact that black jazz players now have greater control over the production and distribution of their music changed public assumptions about the music, and its relation to social realities? Has the entry of more women into the music industry meant a change in the nature of the music these women are performing?

In this book, I've attempted a critical inventory of the changing interpretive and institutional frameworks that jazz musicians have sought to establish for articulating the terms of their own cultural histories and social identities. Those diverse frameworks, which I have here read in the context of parallel debates and developments in contemporary cultural theory—specifically, debates in (and critical intersections between) theories of formalism, New Historicism, autobiography, postcolonialism, feminism, popular culture, and ethics—have called attention to the difficulty, if not the impossibility, of reducing jazz to fixed doctrines or political positions. Jazz is not, in and of itself, oppositional or emancipatory. Those sorts of meanings depend on and are determined by a complex set of historical, material, and social factors: where and when the music is performed and produced, under what conditions, for whom, in whose interests, and so forth. As much as it may be that I want to align myself with forms of cultural practice that use dissonance to disrupt the workings of hegemonic social orders, that use sonic innovation as a model for oppositional interventions in the public sphere, the very heterogeneity of the music and the rich and unbounded nature of the debates that it sparks will continue to give me pause. But then, one of the great lessons of contemporary cultural theory has to do with the way in which it has liberated us from having to respond to particular texts and life situations in a given, predigested manner, with its insistence that we subject to rigorous and ongoing scrutiny the assumptions that shape our relationship to the world around us. And as the epigraph from Christopher Small implies, theory has also taught us that the most pressing questions in human life often have no "final" or "definite" answers, only, in the best instances, "useful" ones. Jazz, too, has always been about different ways of knowing (and thinking about) the world, about using contingency, variance, improvisation, and risk as models for critical (and social) practice. Perhaps the difficulties I'm having concluding this book are a testament to the challenge that jazz poses to the fixed and deadening certainties of dominant models of history making and knowledge production. Perhaps ending on the wrong note is, after all, the most "useful" way I could have chosen to conclude this book.

Works Cited

Achebe, Chinua. *Morning Yet on Creation Day*. London: Heinemann, 1975.

Adorno, Theodor W. Reviews of *American Jazz Music*, by Wilder Hobson, and *Jazz: Hot and Hybrid*, by Winthrop Sargeant. *Studies in Philosophy and Social Science* 9.1 (1941): 167–78.

——. "On Popular Music." *Studies in Philosophy and Social Science* 9.1 (1941): 17–48.

——. *Introduction to the Sociology of Music*. Trans. E. B. Ashton. New York: Seabury, 1976.

——. *Philosophy of Modern Music*. Trans. Anne G. Mitchell and Wesley V. Blomster. New York: Continuum, 1985.

——. "Perennial Fashion—Jazz." In *Critical Theory and Society: A Reader*, ed. Stephen Eric Bronner and Douglas MacKay Kellner, trans. Samuel and Shierry Weber. New York: Routledge, 1989, 199–209.

Adorno, Theodor, and Max Horkheimer. *Dialectic of Enlightenment*. Trans. John Cumming. New York: Herder and Herder, 1972.

Altman, Dennis. *The Homosexualization of America: The Americanization of the Homosexual*. New York: St. Martin's, 1982.

Andrews, William. *To Tell a Free Story: The First Century of Afro-American Autobiography, 1760–1865*. Chicago: U of Illinois P, 1988.

——. "Toward a Poetics of Afro-American Autobiography." In *Afro-American Literary Study in the 1990s*, ed. Houston A. Baker Jr. and

Patricia Redmond. Chicago: U of Chicago P, 1989. 78–91.

Asante, Molefi Kete, and Abu S. Abarry. "African Sources: An Introduction." In *African Intellectual Heritage: A Book of Sources*, ed. Molefi Kete Asante and Abu S. Abarry. Philadelphia: Temple UP, 1996, 1–7.

Attali, Jacques. *Noise: The Political Economy of Music*. Trans. Brian Massumi. Minneapolis: U of Minnesota P, 1996.

Baker, Houston A., Jr. *Modernism and the Harlem Renaissance*. Chicago: U of Chicago P, 1987.

Baldwin, James. *The Devil Finds Work: An Essay*. New York: Dell, 1990.

Bali, Paul. "Drums, Drums, and More Drums at This Year's Guelph Jazz Festival." *The Ontarion* [U of Guelph], September 10, 1996, 20.

Balliger, Robin. "Sounds of Resistance." In *Sounding Off! Music as Subversion/Resistance/Revolution*, ed. Ron Sakolsky and Fred Wei-han Ho. Brooklyn: Autonomedia, 1995, 13–26.

Baraka, Amiri (formerly LeRoi Jones). *Black Music*. New York: Apollo, 1968.

———. *Dutchman*. London: Faber & Faber, 1983.

Baum, Gregory. *Compassion and Solidarity: The Church for Others*. Toronto: CBC Enterprises, 1987.

Baxter, Nicky. "Jazzman Charles Gayle Dispenses with Such Conventional Notions as Harmony and Melody in His Pursuit of Pure Sound." Online. (http://www.metroactive.com/papers/metro/02.22.96/gayle-9608.html): August 13, 1999.

Bayles, Martha. *Hole in Our Soul: The Loss of Beauty and Meaning in American Popular Music*. New York: Free Press, 1994.

Benhabib, Seyla. *Situating the Self: Gender, Community and Postmodernism in Contemporary Ethics*. New York: Routledge, 1992.

Bennett, Tony. "Introduction: Popular Culture and 'the Turn to Gramsci.'" In *Popular Culture and Social Relations*, ed. Tony Bennett, Colin Mercer, and Janet Woollacott. Milton Keynes: Open UP, 1986, xi–xix.

———. "The Politics of 'The Popular' and Popular Culture." In *Popular Culture and Social Relations*, ed. Tony Bennett, Colin Mercer, and Janet Woollacott. Milton Keynes: Open UP, 1986, 6–21.

Berendt, Joachim E. *The Jazz Book: From Ragtime to Fusion and Beyond*. Trans. H. and B. Bredigkeit. Westport, CT: Lawrence Hill and Company, 1982.

Berliner, Paul F. *Thinking in Jazz: The Infinite Art of Improvisation*. Chicago: U of Chicago P, 1994.

Bernal, Martin. *Black Athena: The Afroasiatic Roots of Classical Civilization*. New Brunswick, NJ: Rutgers UP, 1987.

Blumenfeld, Larry. "Joseph Jarman's Biggest Leap." *Jazziz: Art for Your Ears* 15.11 (November 1998): 54.

Booth, Wayne C. *The Company We Keep: An Ethics of Fiction*. Berkeley: U of California P, 1988.

Brantlinger, Patrick. *Crusoe's Footprints: Cultural Studies in Britain and America*. New York: Routledge, 1990.

Brathwaite, Kamau. "Jazz and the West Indian Novel." *Roots*. Ann Arbor: University of Michigan Press, 1993, 55–110.

Brown, Lloyd L. "Preface." *Here I Stand*. By Paul Robeson. Boston: Beacon Press, 1971, ix–xx.

Brydon, Diana. "Response to Hart." *Arachne* 1.1 (1994): 100–12.

Bürger, Peter. *Theory of the Avant-Garde*. Trans. Michael Shaw. Minneapolis: U of Minnesota P, 1984.

Butler, Judith. "Performative Acts and Gender Constitution: An Essay in Phenomenology and Feminist Theory." In *Performing Feminisms: Feminist Critical Theory and Theatre*, ed. Sue-Ellen Case. Baltimore: Johns Hopkins UP, 1990, 270–82.

Cabral, Amilcar. "National Liberation and Culture." In *Colonial Discourse and Post-Colonial Theory: A Reader*, ed. Patrick Williams and Laura Chrisman. New York: Columbia UP, 1994, 53–65.

Campbell, Robert L. *The Earthly Recordings of Sun Ra: A Discography*. Redwood, NY: Cadence, 1994.

——. "From Sonny Blount to Sun Ra: The Birmingham and Chicago Years." Online. From a talk presented at Alabama Jazz Hall of Fame. March 26, 1995. (http://dpo.uab.edu/~moudry/camp1.htm): May 24, 1999.

Carlson, Marvin. *Performance: A Critical Introduction*. London: Routledge, 1996.

Carmichael, Thomas. "Beneath the Underdog: Charles Mingus, Representation, and Jazz Autobiography." *Canadian Review of American Studies* 25.3 (1995): 29–40.

"A Charles Gayle Abortion Statement." Online. (http://www.sonarchy.org/audio/archives/gayle_abort.html): August 13, 1999.

Chase, Mildred Portney. *Improvisation: Music from the Inside Out*. Berkeley, CA: Creative Arts Book Company, 1988.

Chow, Rey. *Ethics after Idealism: Theory-Culture-Ethnicity-Reading*. Bloomington: Indiana UP, 1998.

Citron, Marcia J. "Feminist Approaches to Musicology." In *Cecilia Reclaimed: Feminist Perspectives on Gender and Music*, ed. Susan C. Cook and Judy S. Tsou. Chicago: U of Illinois P, 1994, 15–34.

Clifford, James. *The Predicament of Culture*. Cambridge, MA: Harvard UP, 1988.

Coleman, Ornette. Liner notes. *Change of the Century*. By Ornette Coleman. Atlantic, 1959.

——. "Harmolodic = Highest Instinct: Something to Think About." In *Free Spirits: Annals of the Insurgent Imagination*, ed. Paul Buhle, et al. San Francisco: City Lights Books, 1982, 117–20.

Collier, James Lincoln. *Duke Ellington*. New York: Oxford UP, 1987.

——. "Local Jazz." In *Reading Jazz: A Gathering of Autobiography, Reportage, and Criticism from 1919 to Now*, ed. Robert Gottlieb. New York: Pantheon, 1996, 997–1005.

Comaroff, Jean. *Body of Power, Spirit of Resistance: The Culture and History of a South African People*. Chicago: U of Chicago P, 1985.

Connor, Steven. *Postmodernist Culture: An Introduction to Theories of the Contemporary*. 2nd ed. Oxford: Blackwell, 1989.

Cook, Richard, and Brian Morton. *The Penguin Guide to Jazz on CD: The Comprehensive Critical Guide to Recorded Jazz—From Its Beginnings until the Present*. 4th ed. London: Penguin, 1998.

Cooke, Deryck. *Language of Music*. London: Oxford UP, 1960.

Corbett, John. *Extended Play: Sounding Off from John Cage to Dr. Funkenstein*. Durham, NC: Duke UP, 1994.

Cutler, Chris. *File under Popular: Theoretical and Critical Writings on Music*. London: November Books, 1985.

Dahl, Linda. *Stormy Weather: The Music and Lives of a Century of Jazzwomen*. London: Quartet Books, 1984.

David, Ron. *Jazz for Beginners*. New York: Writers and Readers Publishing Inc., 1995.

Davis, Angela Y. "Black Nationalism: The Sixties and the Nineties." In *Black Popular Culture: A Project by Michele Wallace*, ed. Gina Dent. New York: The New Press, 1983, 317–24.

——. *Blues Legacies and Black Feminism*. New York: Pantheon, 1998.

Davis, Charles T., and Henry Louis Gates, Jr. "Introduction: The Language of Slavery." In *The Slave's Narrative*, ed. Charles T. Davis and Henry Louis Gates, Jr. Oxford: Oxford UP, 1985, xi–xxxiv.

Davis, Francis. *In the Moment*. New York: Oxford UP, 1986.

——. "Hottentot Potentate." *Outcats: Jazz Composers, Instrumentalists, and Singers*. New York: Oxford UP, 1990, 24–27.

——. Liner notes. *Consecration*. By Charles Gayle. Black Saint, 1993.

——. *Bebop and Nothingness: Jazz and Pop at the End of the Century*. New York: Schirmer Books, 1996.

Davis, Gerald L. *I Got the Word in Me and I Can Sing It, You Know*. Philadelphia: U of Pennsylvania P, 1985.

Dawson, Michael C. "A Black Counterpublic?: Economic Earthquakes, Racial Agenda(s) and Black Politics." *Public Culture* 17.1 (1994): 195–224.

Deleuze, Gilles, and Félix Guattari. *Anti-Oedipus: Capitalism and Schizophrenia*. Trans. Robert Hurley, Helen R. Lane, and Mark Seem. New York: Viking, 1977.

Dening, Greg. *Performances*. Chicago: U of Chicago P, 1996.

Derrida, Jacques. "The Purveyor of Truth." *Yale French Studies* 52 (1975): 31–114.

DeVeaux, Scott. "Constructing the Jazz Tradition: Jazz Historiography." *Black American Literature Forum* 25 (fall 1991): 525–60.

——. *The Birth of Bebop: A Social and Musical History*. Berkeley: U of California P, 1997.

Dyer, Richard. *Heavenly Bodies: Film Stars and Society*. New York: St. Martin's, 1986.

Eco, Umberto. "The Poetics of the Open Work." *The Role of the Reader: Explorations in the Semiotics of Texts*. Bloomington: Indiana UP, 1979, 47–66.

Ellington, Duke. *Music Is My Mistress*. New York: Da Capo, 1976.

——. "The Race for Space." In *The Duke Ellington Reader*, ed. Mark Tucker. New York: Oxford UP, 1993, 293–96.

Ellington, Mercer, with Stanley Dance. *Duke Ellington in Person: An Intimate Memoir*. 1978: rpt., New York: Da Capo, 1979.

Elworth, Steven B. "Jazz in Crisis, 1948–1958: Ideology and Representation." In *Jazz among the Discourses*, ed. Krin Gabbard. Durham, NC: Duke UP, 1995, 57–75.

Fanon, Frantz. *The Wretched of the Earth*. Trans. Constance Farrington. New York: Grove Press, 1963.

Finkelstein, Sidney. *Jazz: A People's Music*. New York: Da Capo, 1975.

Fischer, Michael. "Ethnicity and the Postmodern Arts of Memory." In *Writing Culture: The Poetics and Politics of Ethnography*, ed. James Clifford and George E. Marcus. Berkeley: U of California P, 1986, 194–233.

Fiske, John. *Reading the Popular*. London: Routledge, 1989.

——. "Popular Culture." In *Critical Terms for Literary Study*, 2nd ed., ed. Frank Lentricchia and Thomas McLaughlin. Chicago: U of Chicago P, 1995, 321–35.

Floyd, Samuel A., Jr. *The Power of Black Music: Interpreting History from Africa to the United States*. New York: Oxford UP, 1995.

Folkenflik, Robert. "Introduction: The Institution of Autobiography." In *The Culture of Autobiography*, ed. Robert Folkenflik. Stanford, CA: Stanford UP, 1993, 1–20.

Ford, Alun. *Anthony Braxton: Creative Music Continuums*. Exeter: Stride Publications, 1997.

Ford, Theodore P. *God Wills the Negro: An Anthropological and Geographical Restoration of the History of the American Negro People, Being in Part a Theological Interpretation of Egyptian and Ethiopian Backgrounds*. Chicago: The Geographical Institute Press, 1939.

Fraser, Nancy. "Rethinking the Public Sphere: A Contribution to the Critique of Actually Existing Democracy." In *The Phantom Public Sphere*, ed. Bruce Robbins. Minneapolis: U of Minnesota P, 1993, 1–32.

Gabbard, Krin. "Introduction: Writing the Other History." In *Representing Jazz*, ed. Krin Gabbard. Durham: Duke UP, 1995, 1–8.

——. "Signifyin(g) the Phallus: *Mo' Better Blues* and Representations of the Jazz Trumpet." In *Representing Jazz*, ed. Krin Gabbard. Durham, NC: Duke UP, 1995, 104–30.

——. *Jammin' at the Margins: Jazz and the American Cinema*. Chicago: U of Chicago P, 1996.

Gaiter, Colette. "SPACE|R A C E." Online. *Bad Subjects: Political Education for Everyday Life* 33 (September 1997). (http://english-www.hss.cmu.edu/bs/33/gaiter.html): May 24, 1999.

Galloway, Matt. "Charles Gayle Preaches Free-Jazz Gospel." *Now* (August 21–27, 1997): 58.

Garofalo, Reebee. "Black Popular Music: Crossing Over or Going Under?" In *Rock and Popular Music: Politics, Policies, Institutions*, ed. Tony Bennett, Simon Frith, Lawrence Grossberg, John Shepherd, and Graeme Turner. London: Routledge, 1993, 231–48.

——. "Culture versus Commerce: The Marketing of Black Popular Music." *Public Culture* 17.1 (1994): 275–88.

Gates, Henry Louis, Jr. "Preface." In *The Slave's Narrative*, ed. Charles T. Davis and Henry Louis Gates, Jr. Oxford: Oxford UP, 1985 v–vii.

——. "Introduction: On Bearing Witness." In *Bearing Witness: Selections from African-American Autobiography of the Twentieth Century*, ed. Henry Louis Gates, Jr. New York: Pantheon, 1991, 3–9.

Gendron, Bernard. "Theodor Adorno Meets the Cadillacs." In *Studies in Entertainment: Critical Approaches to Mass Culture*, ed. Tania Modleski. Bloomington: Indiana UP, 1986, 18–38.

Gennari, John. "Jazz Criticism: Its Development and Ideologies." *Black American Literature Forum* 25 (fall 1991): 449–523.

George, Don. *Sweet Man: The Real Duke Ellington*. New York: G.P. Putnam's Sons, 1981.

Gill, John. *Queer Noises*. Minneapolis: U of Minnesota P, 1995.

Gourse, Leslie. *Madame Jazz: Contemporary Women Instrumentalists*. New York: Oxford UP, 1995.

Gracyk, Theodore. *Rhythm and Noise: An Aesthetics of Rock*. Durham, NC: Duke UP. 1996.

Green, John. "Interview: Lester Bowie, Don Moye. Two Spirited Forces behind the Art Ensemble of Chicago." *Be-Bop and Beyond* (January/February 1984): 16–23.

Grindley, Mark. *Jazz Styles: History and*

Analysis. Englewood Cliffs, NJ: Prentice Hall, 1985.

Gruneau, Richard. "Introduction: Notes on Popular Cultures and Political Practices." In *Popular Cultures and Political Practices*, ed. Richard Gruneau. Toronto: Garamond, 1988, 11–32.

The Guelph Jazz Festival. Mission Statement. 1994.

Gusdorf, Georges. "Conditions and Limits of Autobiography." In *Autobiography: Essays Theoretical and Critical*, ed. James Olney, trans. James Olney. Princeton, NJ: Princeton UP, 1980, 28–48.

Hadlock, Richard. *Jazz Masters of the Twenties*. New York: Da Capo, 1986.

Hall, Catherine. "Missionary Stories: Gender and Ethnicity in England in the 1830s and 1840s." In *Cultural Studies*, ed. Lawrence Grossberg, Cary Nelson, and Paula Treichler. New York: Routledge, 1992, 240–76.

Hall, Stuart. "Ethnicity: Identity and Difference." *Radical America* 23.4 (1989): 9–20.

——. "New Ethnicities." In *Stuart Hall: Critical Dialogues in Cultural Studies*, ed. David Morley and Kuan-Hsing Chen. London: Routledge, 1996, 441–49.

——. "What Is This 'Black' in Black Popular Culture?" In *Stuart Hall: Critical Dialogues in Cultural Studies*, ed. David Morley and Kuan-Hsing Chen. London: Routledge, 1996, 465–75.

Hall, Stuart, and Paddy Whannel. *The Popular Arts*. New York: Pantheon, 1965.

Hansen, Mariam. "Introduction to Adorno, 'Transparencies on Film' (1966)." *New German Critique* 24–25 (fall-winter 1981–82): 186–98.

Harlos, Christopher. "Jazz Autobiography: Theory, Practice, Politics." In *Representing Jazz*, ed. Krin Gabbard. Durham, NC: Duke UP, 1995, 131–66.

Harlow, Barbara. *Resistance Literature*. New York: Methuen, 1987.

Harpham, Geoffrey Galt. "Ethics." In *Critical Terms for Literary Study*, 2nd ed, ed. Frank Lentricchia and Thomas McLaughlin. Chicago: U of Chicago P, 1995, 387–405.

Hawkes, Terence. *That Shakespeherian Rag: Essays on a Critical Process*. London: Methuen, 1986.

Heble, Ajay. "The Poetics of Jazz: From Symbolic to Semiotic." *Textual Practice* 2.1 (1988): 51–68.

——. *The Tumble of Reason: Alice Munro's Discourse of Absence*. Toronto: U of Toronto P, 1994.

Hentoff, Nat. "The Duke." *Down Beat* 24 (January 9, 1957): 20.

Ho, Fred Wei-han. "'Jazz,' Kreolization and Revolutionary Music for the 21st Century." In *Sounding Off! Music as Subversion/Resistance/Revolution*, ed. Ron Sakolsky and Fred Wei-han Ho. Brooklyn: Autonomedia, 1995, 133–43.

Hobsbawm, Eric. *The Jazz Scene*. New York: Pantheon, 1993.

Holiday, Billie, with William Dufty. *Lady Sings the Blues*. 1956. Harmondsworth, UK: Penguin, 1992.

hooks, bell. *Talking Back: Thinking Feminist, Thinking Black*. Toronto: Between the Lines, 1988.

Hubbard, Dolan. *The Sermon and the African American Literary Tradition*. Columbia: U of Missouri P, 1994.

Hutcheon, Linda. *The Canadian Postmodern: A Study of Contemporary English-Canadian Fiction*. Toronto: Oxford UP, 1988.

——. *The Politics of Postmodernism*. New York: Routledge, 1989.

Iyer, Vijay. "Steve Coleman, M-Base, and Music Collectivism." Online. 1996. (http://cnmat.berkeley.edu/

~vijay/mbase2.html): May 19, 1999.

Jafa, Arthur. "69." In *Black Popular Culture: A Project by Michele Wallace*, ed. Gina Dent. New York: The New Press, 1983, 249–54.

Jakobson, Roman. "Concluding Statement: Linguistics and Poetics." In *Style in Language*, ed. Thomas A. Sebeok. Cambridge, MA: MIT Press, 1960, 386–95.

James, George G. M. *Stolen Legacy: Greek Philosophy Is Stolen Egyptian Philosophy*. 1954. Trenton, NJ: Africa World P, 1992.

Jameson, Fredric. *The Political Unconscious: Narrative as a Socially Symbolic Act*. Ithaca, NY: Cornell UP, 1981.

——. "Foreword." In *Noise: The Political Economy of Music*, by Jacques Attali. Minneapolis: U of Minnesota P, 1985, vii–xiv.

Jost, Ekkehard. *Free Jazz*. New York: Da Capo, 1981.

Kaplan, Fred. "Horn of Plenty." *The New Yorker* (June 14, 1999): 84–90.

Keil, Charles. "Participatory Discrepancies and the Power of Music." *Cultural Anthropology* 2.3 (1986): 275–83.

——. "The Theory of Participatory Discrepancies: A Progress Report." *Ethnomusicology: Journal of the Society for Ethnomusicology* 39.1 (1995): 1–20.

Kellner, Douglas. *Media Culture: Cultural Studies, Identity and Politics between the Modern and the Postmodern*. London: Routledge, 1995.

Kenney, William Howland. *Chicago Jazz: A Cultural History 1904–1930*. New York: Oxford UP, 1993.

Kerman, Joseph. *Contemplating Musicology*. Cambridge, MA: Harvard UP, 1985.

Kofsky, Frank. *Black Nationalism and the Revolution in Music*. New York: Pathfinder Press, 1972.

Koponen, Wilfrid R. *Embracing a Gay Identity: Gay Novels as Guides*. Westport, CT: Bergin and Garvey, 1993.

Kristeva, Julia. *Desire in Language: A Semiotic Approach to Literature and Art*. Trans. Thomas Gora, Alice Jardine, and Leon S. Roudiez. New York: Columbia UP, 1980.

La Capra, Dominick. *Rethinking Intellectual History: Texts, Contexts, Language*. Ithaca, NY: Cornell UP, 1983.

Lacan, Jacques. *Écrits: A Selection*. Trans. Alan Sheridan. New York: Norton, 1977.

Leavis, F. R., and Denys Thompson. *Culture and Environment*. 1933. London: Chatto and Windus, 1960.

Lejeune, Phillipe. *On Autobiography*, ed. John Eakin. Trans. Katherine Leary. Minneapolis: University of Minnesota Press, 1989.

Leppert, Richard, and Susan McClary. "Introduction." In *Music and Society: The Politics of Composition, Performance and Reception*, ed. Richard Leppert and Susan McClary. Cambridge: Cambridge UP, 1987, xi–xix.

Lewis, Alan. "The Social Interpretation of Modern Jazz." In *Lost in Music: Culture, Style and the Musical Event*, ed. Avron Levine White. London: Routledge & Kegan Paul, 1987, 33–55.

Lewis, George E. "Improvised Music after 1950: Afrological and Eurological Perspectives." *Black Music Research Journal* 16 (spring 1996): 91–122.

Lipsitz, George. *Dangerous Crossroads: Popular Music, Postmodernism and the Poetics of Place*. London: Verso, 1997.

Litweiler, John. *The Freedom Principle: Jazz after 1958*. New York: Da Capo, 1984.

Lock, Graham. *Forces in Motion: The*

Music and Thoughts of Anthony Braxton. New York: Da Capo, 1988.
——. *Chasing the Vibration: Meetings with Creative Musicians*. Devon: Stride Publications, 1994.
Loesser, Arthur. *Men, Women, and Pianos: A Social History*. New York: Simon and Schuster, 1954.
Mackey, Nathaniel. *Discrepant Engagement: Dissonance, Cross-Culturality, and Experimental Writing*. Cambridge: Cambridge UP, 1993.
Mandel, Howard. "It *Can* Be Done. Why Aren't More Doing It?" *Ear: A Magazine of New Music* 15 (February 1991): 40–41, 43.
——. "Freedom Cry." *The Wire* 121 (March 1994): 12–14.
——. "Sheltering." *Jazziz: Art For Your Ears* 15.11 (November 1998): 56–58.
Marek, George. "From the Dive to the Dean: Jazz Becomes Respectable." *Good Housekeeping* 142 (June 1956): 120, 122, 124.
McClary, Susan. *Feminine Endings*. Minneapolis: U of Minnesota P, 1991.
Mercer, Kobena. "Welcome to the Jungle: Identity and Diversity in Postmodern Politics." *Welcome to the Jungle: New Positions in Black Cultural Studies*. New York: Routledge, 1994, 259–85.
Merod, Jim. "Resistance to Theory: The Contradictions of Post-Cold War Criticism (with an Interlude on the Politics of Jazz)." In *Critical Theory and Performance*, ed. Janelle C. Reinelt and Joseph R. Roach. Ann Arbor: U of Michigan P, 1992, 179–95.
——. "Jazz as a Cultural Archive." *boundary 2* 22 (summer 1995): 1–18.
Middlebrook, Diane Wood. *Suits Me: The Double Life of Billy Tipton*. Boston: Houghton Mifflin Company, 1998.
Middleton, J. Richard, and Brian J. Walsh. *Truth Is Stranger Than It Used to Be: Biblical Faith in a Postmodern Age*. Downers Grove, IL: InterVarsity Press, 1995.
Miller, Mark. "Good Beat at Tiny Perfect Festival." *Globe and Mail*, September 9, 1996: C4.
——. "Guelph Features All That Jazz." *Globe and Mail*, September 8, 1997: C4.
Mingus, Charles. *Beneath the Underdog: His World as Composed by Mingus*. 1971. New York: Vintage, 1991.
Mohanty, Satya P. *Literary Theory and the Claims of History: Postmodernism, Objectivity, Multicultural Politics*. Ithaca, NY: Cornell UP, 1997.
Monson, Ingrid. "The Problem with White Hipness: Race, Gender, and Cultural Conceptions in Jazz Historical Discourse." *Journal of the American Musicological Society* XLVIII (fall 1995): 396–422.
——. *Saying Something: Jazz Improvisation and Interaction*. Chicago: U of Chicago P, 1996.
Montrose, Louis A. "Professing the Renaissance: The Poetics and Politics of Culture." In *The New Historicism*, ed. H. Aram Veeser. New York: Routledge, 1989, 15–36.
Murray, Albert. *Stomping the Blues*. New York: Da Capo, 1989.
Nachmanovitch, Stephen. *Free Play: Improvisation in Life and Art*. New York: J.P. Tarcher/Putnam, 1990.
Nandy, Ashis. "Shamans, Savages, and the Wilderness: On the Audibility of Dissent and the Future of Civilizations." *Alternatives* 14 (1989): 263–78.
Neal, Mark Anthony. *What the Music Said: Black Popular Music and Black Public Culture*. New York: Routledge, 1999.
Neuman, Shirley. "'An Appearance Walking in a Forest the Sexes Burn':

Autobiography and the Construction of the Feminine Body." In *Autobiography and Postmodernism*, ed. Kathleen Ashley, Leigh Gilmore, and Gerald Peters. Amherst: U of Massachusetts P, 1994, 293–315.

Nielsen, Aldon Lynn. *Black Chant: Languages of African American Postmodernism*. Cambridge: Cambridge UP, 1997.

Nunn, Tom. *Wisdom of the Impulse: On the Nature of Musical Free Improvisation*. San Francisco: self-published, 1998.

Oliveros, Pauline. *Software for People: Collected Writings 1963–80*. Gwyndale, Baltimore: Smith Publications, 1984.

O'Meally, Robert. *Lady Day: The Many Faces of Billie Holiday*. New York: Arcade Publishers, 1993.

——, ed. *The Jazz Cadence of American Culture*. New York: Columbia UP, 1998.

Ondaatje, Michael. *Coming through Slaughter*. 1976. Toronto: General, 1982.

Palmer, Don. "About Time." *Jazziz: Art for Your Ears* 15.11 (1998): 49–53.

Palmer, Robert. "*Beauty Is a Rare Thing*: The Ornette Coleman Quartet's Complete Atlantic Recordings." Booklet. *Beauty Is a Rare Thing: The Complete Atlantic Recordings*. By Ornette Coleman. Atlantic, 1993.

Peretti, Burton W. *The Creation of Jazz: Music, Race, and Culture in Urban America*. Urbana: U of Illinois P, 1992.

——. "Plantation Cafés: Jazz, Postcolonial Theory, and Modernism." In *Postcolonial Discourse and Changing Cultural Contexts: Theory and Criticism*, ed. Gita Rajan and Radhika Mohanram. Westport, CT: Greenwood, 1995, 89–99.

Plato. *Republic*. Trans. Paul Shorey. London: Loeb Classical Library, 1930.

Pleasants, Henry. *Serious Music—And All That Jazz! An Adventure in Music Criticism*. London: Victor Gollancz, 1969.

Pratt, Ray. *Rhythm and Resistance: The Political Uses of American Popular Music*. 1990. Washington: Smithsonian Institution P, 1994.

Priestly, Brian. *Mingus: A Critical Biography*. London: Quartet Books, 1982.

Ra, Sun. Liner notes. *Sun Song*. By Sun Ra. LP. Transition, 1956.

——. Liner notes. *Pictures of Infinity*. By Sun Ra. Black Lion, 1967.

Radano, Ronald. "Jazzin' the Classics: The AACM's Challenge to Mainstream Aesthetics." *Black Music Research Journal* 12.1 (1992): 79–95.

——. *New Musical Figurations: Anthony Braxton's Cultural Critique*. Chicago: U of Chicago P, 1993.

Radhakrishnan, R. *Diasporic Mediations: Between Home and Location*. Minneapolis: U of Minnesota P, 1996.

Rampersad, Arnold. "Biography, Autobiography, and Afro-American Culture." *Yale Review* 73 (1983): 1–16.

Raschka, Chris. *Mysterious Thelonious*. New York: Orchard Books, 1997.

Read, Alan. *Theatre and Everyday Life: An Ethics of Performance*. London: Routledge, 1993.

Rieger, Eva. "'Dolce semplice'? On the Changing Role of Women in Music." In *Feminist Aesthetics*, ed. Gisela Ecker, trans. Harriet Anderson. Boston: Beacon, 1986, 135–49.

Robeson, Paul. *Here I Stand*. Boston: Beacon, 1971.

Rockwell, John. *All American Music: Composition in the Late Twentieth Century*. New York: Alfred A. Knopf, 1983.

Rosenwald, George, and Richard Ochberg. *Storied Lives: The Cultural Politics of Self-Understanding*. New Haven, CT: Yale UP, 1992.

Rusch, Robert D. *Jazztalk: The Cadence Interviews: Ten Jazz Masters Speak Candidly about Their Lives and Music*. Secaucus, NJ: Lyle Stuart, 1984, 61–72.

Said, Edward W. *Musical Elaborations*. New York: Columbia UP, 1991.

——. *Culture and Imperialism*. New York: Alfred A. Knopf, 1993.

——. *Out of Place: A Memoir*. New York: Alfred A. Knopf, 1999.

Sargeant, Winthrop. *Jazz: Hot and Hybrid*. New York: Da Capo Press, 1975.

Saussure, Ferdinand de. *Course in General Linguistics*. Trans. Wade Baskin. New York: McGraw-Hill, 1966.

Schuller, Gunther. "Ornette!" Liner notes. *Ornette!* By Ornette Coleman. Atlantic, 1962.

——. *The Swing Era: The Development of Jazz, 1930–1945*. Vol. 2 of *The History of Jazz*. New York: Oxford UP, 1989.

Scott, James, and Benedict J. Tria Kerkvliet. *Everyday Forms of Peasant Resistance in South-East Asia*. London: Frank Cass, 1986.

Sedgwick, Eve Kosofsky. *Epistemology of the Closet*. Berkeley: U of California P, 1990.

Sharp, Elliott. "Interview with Elliott Sharp." May 8, 1998. Online. (http://www.algonet.se/~repple/esharp/slovene1.htm): July 15, 1999.

Shepherd, John. "Value and Power in Music: An English Canadian Perspective." In *Relocating Cultural Studies: Developments in Theory and Research*, ed. Valda Blundell, John Shepherd, and Ian Taylor. London: Routledge, 1993, 171–206.

Shepp, Archie. "An Artist Speaks Bluntly." *Down Beat* 32 (December 16, 1965): 11, 42.

Slack, Jennifer Daryl, and Laurie Anne Whitt. "Ethics and Cultural Studies." In *Cultural Studies*, ed. Lawrence Grossberg, Cary Nelson, and Paula Treichler. New York: Routledge, 1992, 571–92.

Small, Christopher. *Musicking: The Meanings of Performance and Listening*. Hanover, NH: Wesleyan UP, 1998.

Smith, Barbara Herrnstein. *Poetic Closure: A Study of How Poems End*. Chicago: U of Chicago P, 1968.

Smith, Hazel, and Roger Dean. *On Improvisation, Hypermedia, and the Arts Since 1945*. Amsterdam: Harwood, 1997.

Spellman, A. B. *Four Lives in the Bebop Business*. New York: Pantheon, 1966.

Stuckenschmidt, H. H. *Twentieth Century Music*. Trans. Richard Deveson. Toronto: McGraw-Hill, 1969.

Swindells, Julia. "Introduction." In *The Uses of Autobiography*, ed. Julia Swindells. London: Taylor and Francis, 1995, 1–12.

Szwed, John. Liner notes. *Soundtrack to the Film* Space Is the Place. By Sun Ra. Evidence, 1972.

——. *Space is the Place: The Lives and Times of Sun Ra*. New York: Pantheon, 1997.

Taylor, Charles. "The Politics of Recognition." In *Multiculturalism: Examining the Politics of Recognition*, ed. Amy Gutmann. Princeton, NJ: Princeton UP, 1994, 25–73.

Taylor, Timothy D. *Global Pop: World Music, World Markets*. New York: Routledge, 1997.

Terdiman, Richard. *Discourse/Counter-Discourse: The Theory and Practice of Symbolic Resistance in Nineteenth-Century France*. Ithaca, NY: Cornell UP, 1985.

Tester, Keith. *Media, Culture and Morality*. London: Routledge, 1994.

Tuan, Yi-Fu. *Space and Place*. Minneapolis: U of Minnesota P, 1981.

Tucker, Mark, ed. *The Duke Ellington Reader*. New York: Oxford UP, 1993.

Ulanov, Barry. *Duke Ellington*. New York: Da Capo, 1972.

von Braun, Werner. "The First Man on the Moon." *Encyclopedia Americana*. 1988 ed.

Wallace, Michele. "Variations on Negation and the Heresy of Black Feminist Creativity." In *Reading Black, Reading Feminist: A Critical Anthology*, ed. Henry Louis Gates, Jr. New York: Meridian, 1990, 52–67.

Waterman, Christopher. Review of "Theory of Participatory Discrepancies," by Charles Keil. *Ethnomusicology: Journal of the Society for Ethnomusicology*. 39.1 (1995): 92–94.

Weinstein, Norman C. *Night in Tunisia: Imaginings of Africa in Jazz*. New York: Limelight, 1992.

Werner, Craig Hanson. *Playing the Changes: From Afro-Modernism to the Jazz Impulse*. Urbana: U of Illinois P, 1994.

West, Cornel. *Keeping Faith: Philosophy and Race in America*. New York: Routledge, 1993.

——. "A Matter of Life and Death." In *The Identity in Question*, ed. John Rajchman. New York: Routledge, 1995, 15–31.

White, Hayden. *The Content of the Form: Narrative Discourse and Historical Representation*. Baltimore, MD: Johns Hopkins UP, 1987.

Willener, Alfred. *The Action-Image of Society: On Cultural Politicization*. Trans. A. M. Sheridan Smith. London: Tavistock, 1970.

Williams, K. Leander. "Tenor Madness: David S. Ware—Charles Gayle." *Down Beat* 62.1 (1995): 34–37.

Williams, Martin. *The Jazz Tradition*. 2nd rev. ed. Oxford: Oxford UP, 1993.

Williams, Mary Lou. "How This Concert Came About." Liner notes. *Embraced*. By Mary Lou Williams and Cecil Taylor. Pablo, 1995.

Wilmer, Valerie. *As Serious as Your Life: The Story of the New Jazz*. New York: Quartet Books, 1977.

Witkin, Robert W. *Adorno on Music*. London: Routledge, 1998.

Wolff, Christian. "On Political Texts and New Music." In *Contiguous Lines: Issues and Ideas in the Music of the '60's and '70's*, ed. Thomas DeLio. Lanham, MD: University Press of America, 1985, 193–211.

X, Malcolm, with Alex Haley. *The Autobiography of Malcolm X*. New York: Grove Press, 1965.

Zorn, John. Liner notes. *Spillane/Two-Lane Highway/Forbidden Fruit*. By John Zorn. Elektra Nonesuch, 1987.

——. Tzadik Web Site. Online. (http://www.tzadik.com/): August 13, 1999.

Sound and Video Recordings Consulted

Armstrong, Louis. *The Genius of Louis Armstrong, Vol. 1: 1923–1933*. LP. Columbia, n.d.

——. *Louis Armstrong's Greatest Hits*. LP. Columbia, n.d.

Art Ensemble of Chicago. *Full Force*. LP. ECM, 1980.

——. *Urban Bushmen*. LP. ECM, 1982.

——. *Coming Home Jamaica*. Atlantic, 1998.

Art Ensemble of Soweto (Art Ensemble of Chicago with Amabutho). *America–South Africa*. DIW, 1991.

Ayler, Albert. *Live in Greenwich Village: The Complete Impulse Recordings*. GRP, 1998.

Bunnett, Jane, and Don Pullen. *New York Duets*. Music and Arts, 1989.

Coleman, Ornette. *Change of the Century*. LP. Atlantic, 1959.

——. *The Shape of Jazz to Come*. LP. Atlantic, 1959.

——. *Tomorrow Is the Question*. LP. Contemporary Records, 1959.

——. *Free Jazz*. LP. Atlantic, 1960.

——. *Beauty Is a Rare Thing: The Complete Atlantic Recordings*. Atlantic, 1993.

Coltrane, John. *Live at the Village Vanguard Again!* LP. Impulse! 1967.

——. *Interstellar Space*. Impulse! 1991.

——. *Live in Japan*. Impulse! 1991.

——. *The Major Works of John Coltrane*. Impulse! 1992.

——. *My Favorite Things*. LP. Atlantic, n.d.

Ellington, Duke. *Black, Brown and Beige*. RCA Bluebird, 1988.

Gayle, Charles. *Consecration*. Black Saint, 1993.

——. *Touchin' on Trane*. FMP, 1993.

——. *Unto I AM*. Victo, 1994.
——. *Delivered*. 2.13.61 Records, 1997.
——. *Ancient of Days*. Knitting Factory Records, 1999.
Hemingway, Gerry. *The Marmalade King*. hat Art, 1995.
——. *Acoustic Solo Works*. Random Acoustics, 1996.
Ibarra, Susie. *Radiance*. Hopscotch Records, 1999.
McPhee, Joe. *Legend Street One*. CIMP, 1996.
Melford, Myra. *Even the Sounds Shine*. hat Art, 1995.
——. *The Same River, Twice*. Gramavision, 1996.
Monk, Thelonious. *The Complete Blue Note Recordings of Thelonious Monk*. Mosaic, 1983.
——. *The Complete Black Lion and Vogue Recordings of Thelonious Monk*. Mosaic, 1985.
Nichols, Herbie. *The Complete Blue Note Recordings*. Blue Note, 1997.
Oliveros, Pauline. *The Roots of the Moment*. hat Art, 1987.
Parker, Charlie. *The Very Best of Bird*. LP. Warner Bros., 1977.
Parker, William, and In Order to Survive. *The Peach Orchard*. AUM Fidelity, 1998.
Parker, William, and The Little Huey Creative Music Orchestra. *Sunrise in the Tone World*. AUM Fidelity, 1997.
Ra, Sun. *Super Sonic Jazz*. LP. Saturn, 1956.
——. *Outer Spaceways Incorporated*. LP. Saturn, 1966–67.
——. *Pictures of Infinity*. LP. Black Lion, 1967.
——. *Sunrise in Different Dimensions*. LP. hat Art, 1980.
——. "When Spaceships Appear." Untitled. LP. Saturn, 1985.
——. *Jazz in Silhouette*. Evidence, 1991.
——. *Fate in a Pleasant Mood/When Sun Comes Out*. Evidence, 1993.
——. *Sun Song*. Delmark, 1990.
Sanders, Pharoah. *Black Unity*. Impulse! 1997.
Space Is the Place. Dir. John Coney. Perf. Sun Ra and his Arkestra. Rhapsody Films, 1974.
Taylor, Cecil. *For Olim*. Soul Note, 1987.
——. *Dark to Themselves*. Enja, 1990.
——. *Looking (Berlin Version)*. FMP, 1991.
——. *Air above Mountains*. Enja, 1992.
Williams, Mary Lou. *Zodiac Suite*. Smithsonian Folkways, 1995.
Williams, Mary Lou, and Cecil Taylor. *Embraced*. Pablo, 1995.
Zorn, John. *Spillane/Two-Lane Highway/Forbidden Fruit*. Elektra Nonesuch, 1987.
——. *Spy Vs Spy*. Elektra Musician, 1989.
——. *Naked City*. Elektra Nonesuch, 1989.
——. *Cobra*. hat Art, 1994.
——. *Masada: Tet*. DIW, 1998.

Index

Abrams, Muhal Richard 66, 67, 70, 175, 187, 233; "Conversation with the Three of Me" 97
Achebe, Chinua 139n
Adorno, Theodor 18, 25–26, 36, 45, 83, 84, 167–70, 172–8, 184, 187, 188, 189, 193, 195, 196, 197, 198n
Ali, Rashied 224
Alpert, Herb 121
Alternative Newport Festival 129, 235
Altman, Dennis 217
Amabutho Male Chorus 73
Andrews, William 89, 109, 112, 115; "free storytelling" 110
Apollo 11 134
Armstrong, Louis ix, 22, 32, 34–9, 41, 51, 53, 54, 55, 56; "Mahogony Hall Stomp" 34; "Savoy Blues" 34
Art Ensemble of Chicago 13, 61, 68–88, 90, 123, 129, 202, 233; *Coming Home Jamaica* 82, 85–7; *Full Force* 72; "Grape Escape" 82; little instruments 74, 78; "Lotta Colada" 82; "Malachi" 82; "Old Time Southside Street Dance" 72–3; "Strawberry Mango" 82; "Theme from Sco" 74; "U.S. of A.—U. of S.A." 71, 73, 78–9; *Urban Bushmen* 74, 88n
Asante, Molefi, and Abu Abarry 124
Association for the Advancement of Creative Musicians (AACM) 23, 27, 61, 64–70, 74–5, 81, 82, 84, 85, 87, 119, 127, 129, 170, 201, 205, 225, 233, 235
atonality 13, 22, 29, 30, 35, 48, 50–2, 53, 55–7, 147, 167, 175, 209, 211
Attali, Jacques 1, 170, 192, 195–6, 198n, 200–1, 202, 204–5, 221
Austen, Jane 209
Ayler, Albert 202, 208, 225

Bach, J.S. 177
Bailey, Derek 183
Baker, Houston 83, 115, 225
Baldwin, James 94
Bali, Paul 189
Balliett, Whitney 149
Balliger, Robin 205–6
Baraka, Amiri (LeRoi Jones) 35, 36, 37, 40, 50, 133, 207, 209; *Dutchman* 40–7, 62n

Baron, Joey 182
Barthes, Roland 95
Basie, Count 123
Baum, Gregory 203
Baxter, Nicky 199
Bayles, Martha 57, 59
bebop 35, 37–40, 44, 49, 51, 59, 123, 126, 151, 156, 172, 175, 177, 225
Benhabib, Seyla 213–14
Bennett, Tony 169, 186
Berendt, Joachim 64, 66, 123
Berg, Alban 176
Berio, Luciano 49
Berliner, Paul 3, 90, 91
Bernal, Martin 138n
Berne, Tim 182
big bands 126, 128, 139n
Blackman, Cindy 149, 162
Blassingame, John 89
Bloom, Jane Ira 162
Blumenfeld, Larry 88n
Bolden, Buddy 97
Bollingen Prize 199, 214, 223
Booth, Wayne 26, 199, 200, 204, 208–9, 214
Bowie, Lester 68, 69, 71–2, 81, 82
Brahms, Johannes 173
Brantlinger, Patrick 11, 12, 71, 127
Brathwaite, Kamau 27, 119
Braxton, Anthony 10, 39, 67, 81, 117, 121–2, 175, 189
Brown, Lloyd 116n
Brydon, Diana 137
Bunnett, Jane 163, 187
Bürger, Peter 58
Butler, Judith 144, 149, 156–7

Cabral, Amilcar 24, 118, 122
Campbell, Robert 123, 124, 126, 135, 138n, 139n
Cardew, Cornelius 75
Carlson, Marvin 77
Carmichael, Thomas 103–4
Carter, Betty 120
Carter, John 70
Chase, Mildred Portney 95
Chernoff, John Miller 91
Chicago 10, 23, 27, 63–4, 66–7, 71, 73, 74, 81, 124, 132, 139n, 235
Chow, Rey 21
chromaticism 37–40, 44, 48
Citron, Marcia 148
Cixous, Hélène 147
Clark, Sonny 182
Cleage, Pearl 143
Clément, Catherine 147
Clifford, James 77
Clooney, Rosemary 146
Coleman, Janet 102
Coleman, Ornette ix, 9, 21, 22, 48–60, 64, 75, 171, 176, 180, 182, 209; "Bird Food" 51; "Blues Connotation" 51; *Change of the Century* 52; *Free Jazz* 48–9, 52, 56, 59; harmolodic theory 54; "The Legend of Bebop" 51; "Monk and the Nun" 51; *The Shape of Jazz to Come* 59; *Tomorrow is the Question* 59; "When Will the Blues Leave" 51
Collier, James Lincoln 114, 192
Coltrane, John 31, 70, 121, 152, 176, 208, 224, 225; "My Favorite Things" 31; *Interstellar Space* 224
Columbus, Christopher 135
Comaroff, Jean 122
Coney, John 131
Connor, Steven 197
Cooke, Deryck 32
cool jazz 177
Corbett, John 24, 66, 130, 131, 132, 202
Crouch, Stanley 82, 165n
cultural studies 2, 8, 65, 91, 215, 221
Cutler, Chris 88n, 121

Dahl, Linda 150, 152–3, 154–5, 163, 164
Dance, Stanley 114
Davis, Angela 104–5, 168–9
Davis, Anthony 175
Davis, Charles 90, 91, 97
Davis, Francis 59, 128, 182, 183, 184, 203, 205, 208
Davis, Gerald 211
Davis, Miles 34, 143–4
Dawson, Michael 234
deconstruction 61
Deleuze, Gilles, and Félix Guattari 36
Dening, Greg 76
Derrida, Jacques 51, 61, 95
DeVeaux, Scott 10, 11, 37, 60
diatonicism 13, 29, 30, 31–5, 37–8, 40, 48, 50, 53, 55, 57, 147, 173, 209
Dickens, Charles 33, 209
Diddley, Bo 82
Diop, Cheikh Anta 124
dissonance x, 4, 9, 20, 21, 22, 23, 25, 28, 31, 51, 53, 55, 76, 83, 99, 111, 113, 133, 144, 145, 146, 147, 170–72,

174, 177–8, 183, 185, 186, 187, 196, 198n, 200, 202, 207, 208, 227, 230, 237; *see also* free jazz
Dixieland 13, 35, 63
Dixon, Bill 119, 133, 205, 233, 235
Dixon, Willie 82
Douglas, Dave 181–2, 197
Dresser, Mark 182, 187
Drinkard, Carl 107
DuBois, W.E.B. 116n
Dufty, William 106, 107
DuMaurier Downtown Jazz Festival in Toronto 189
Dyer, Richard 93

Eco, Umberto 49, 51, 209
Eliot, T.S. 204
Ellington, Duke 20, 21, 116n, 117, 123, 127, 154, 174–5, 177, 209; *Black, Brown and Beige* 116n, 174; *Music Is My Mistress* 23, 96, 110–16; "The Race for Space" 139n
Ellington, Mercer 111
Elworth, Steven 58
ethics x, 18, 26, 30, 58, 59, 60–1, 66, 75, 78, 80–1, 88, 171, 199–227, 230, 236

Fanon, Frantz 122, 123, 126, 235
Favors, Malachi 68, 72, 82
Feldman, Mark 187
Finkelstein, Sidney 188
Fischer, Michael 98
Fiske, John 168, 169, 190
Floyd, Samuel 78–9
Folkenflik, Robert 23, 97
Ford, Alun 66
Ford, Theodor P. 124
formalism 13, 14, 15, 23, 31, 38, 40, 55, 64, 65, 72, 79, 236
Foucault, Michel 95
Frankfurt School 168, 195
Fraser, Nancy 27, 219, 230–31, 233
free jazz x, 21, 48, 49, 52, 54, 56, 57, 59, 60, 64, 75, 123, 126, 132, 133, 147, 171, 172, 182, 183, 201, 202, 203, 205, 207, 208, 209, 221, 224, 225, 231, 232; *see also* dissonance
Frisell, Bill 182
Frith, Fred 182

Gabbard, Krin 13, 17, 18, 23, 90, 96, 149, 175–6
Gaiter, Colette 135, 139n
Galloway, Matt 212
Garofalo, Reebee 85, 87
Garvey, Marcus 131
Gates, Henry Louis 23, 78, 89–90, 91, 96–7
Gayle, Charles 6, 26, 199, 201–15, 217–27, 227n, 228n, 231; *Ancient of Days* 228n; *Consecration* 203, 205, 209; *Delivered* 203, 224, 228n; "Eden Lost" 203, 210–11; "Justified" 209; "O Father" 203, 209; "Redemption" 203; "Rise Up" 203';*Touchin' on Trane* 224; *Unto I AM* 210, 222
Gendron, Bernard 177
Gennari, John 8, 14, 17, 21
George, Don 111–12
Gill, John 135, 165n
Gillespie, Dizzy 19, 37, 151, 152–3, 154
Gilmore, John 126
Gilroy, Paul 169
Glass, Philip 182
Goodman, Benny 38, 126, 139n
Gourse, Leslie 163, 164
Gracyk, Theodore 173, 177
Gramsci, Antonio 169
Grateful Dead 82, 183
Great Black Music 67, 68, 71, 84, 87
Green, John 67, 68
Grindley, Mark 72
Gruneau, Richard 168
Guelph Jazz Festival 2, 3, 4, 6, 17, 24, 25, 86, 158–65, 186–97, 222–3, 231, 235
Gusdorf, Georges 92

Hadlock, Richard 126
Hall, Catherine 216
Hall, Stuart 12, 65–6, 79, 95, 169, 215, 218–19; and Paddy Whannel 188, 192, 196
Hansen, Mariam 177
Harlem Renaissance 115
Harlos, Christopher 23, 90–1, 97, 102, 143
Harlow, Barbara 122
Harpham, Geoffrey Galt 213
Hawkes, Terence 79–80
Hemingway, Gerry 187, 189, 191, 195
Henderson, Fletcher 123, 126–8, 138n-139n
Ho, Fred Wei-han 15, 27, 70, 235
Hobsbawm, Eric 16, 17, 18, 19, 21, 188
Hobson, Wilder 36

Holiday, Billie 19, 17, 141; *Lady Sings the Blues* 23, 96, 104–10, 112, 113, 114
hooks, bell 122, 130
Horkheimer, Max 168
Horn, Shirley 146
Houston, Whitney 82
Hubbard, Dolan 212, 225
Hughes, Langston 110
Hurston, Zora Neale 204
Hutcheon, Linda 74–5, 208, 209

Ibarra, Susie 149, 162, 187
Ibrahim, Abdullah 70
identity x, 11–12, 13, 15, 20, 21, 23, 24, 25, 27, 29, 30, 59, 65–6, 67, 70, 71, 77, 78, 80, 87, 90, 91–116, 125, 130, 141, 145, 155, 156, 200, 201, 206, 212–13, 214–15, 216–19, 221, 226, 227, 230–31, 235
improvisation 13, 20, 23, 24, 26, 34, 35, 37, 38, 48–9, 52, 59, 66, 68, 73, 75, 77, 80, 91–8, 99–110, 112–16, 130, 132, 141, 157, 168, 172, 175, 196, 200, 209, 219, 221, 237
International Festival de Musique Actuelle in Victoriaville, Quebec 183
Iyer, Vijay 129

Jackson, John Shenoy 67
Jackson, Michael 82
Jafa, Arthur 125
Jakobson, Roman 33, 42
James, George G.M. 123, 138n
Jameson, Fredric 204–5, 213
Jarman, Joseph 66, 68, 71, 72, 88n
Jarrett, Keith 175
Jazz Composer's Orchestra 205
Jazz Composers Guild 133, 205, 233
Jensen, Ingrid 162
Jerde, Curtis D. 150
Jost, Ekkehard 133, 139n
Joyce, James 49, 55, 147

Kansas City 10
Kaplan, Fred 179, 180
Keil, Charles 101, 102; *see also* participatory discrepancies
Kellner, Douglas 169
Kenney, William Howland 88n
Kerman, Joseph 13–14, 18
Kerouac, Jack 170
King, Nel 100, 101, 102, 103
klezmer 180, 183

Kofsky, Frank 60, 85, 119, 129, 130, 207, 208
Koponen, William 215
Krall, Diana 146, 163
Kristeva, Julia 53–4, 55, 57, 147

Lacan, Jacques 36, 42, 55
LaCapra, Dominick 73
Leandre, Joelle 162
Leavis, F.R. 187, 196; and Denys Thompson 168
Lee, Peggy 163
Lee, Pui Ming 163, 187
Lejeune, Phillipe 99
Lentricchia, Frank, and Thomas McLaughlin 213
Leppert, Richard 13, 18
Lerner, Marilyn 163
Lewis, Alan 60
Lewis, George 20, 28, 39, 84, 175, 183
Lipsitz, George 8, 58, 169–70, 185–86, 197, 230
Liston, Melba 19, 152–4, 157, 159, 163, 235
Litweiler, John 118
Lock, Graham 16, 67, 68, 119–120, 124
Loesser, Arthur 148, 149–50

Mackey, Nathaniel 2, 4, 30, 65, 94, 97, 104, 230
Mandel, Howard 66, 81, 202, 203, 204
Marsalis, Wynton 6, 8, 83, 84, 184
McClary, Susan 13, 18, 54, 60, 142, 144–6, 147, 148, 149
McNeilly, Kevin 184
McPhee, Joe 187
Melford, Myra 163, 187
Mengelberg, Misha 187
Mercer, Kobena 11, 12
Merod, Jim 3, 4, 12, 16, 17, 18, 90, 122, 170, 225
Middlebrook, Dianne Wood 156
Middleton, J. Richard, and Brian Walsh 217
Miller, Glenn 38
Miller, Mark 187, 194–5
Mingus, Celia 102
Mingus, Charles 143, 176; Debut Records 129; *Beneath the Underdog* 23, 96, 97–104, 105–6, 109, 110, 111, 112, 113, 114
Mingus, Sue 102
Mitchell, Roscoe 68, 72, 87, 146, 225

modernism 13, 30 35, 56, 57, 58, 59, 61, 75, 171, 205; black discursive modernism 115
Mohanty, Satya 214–15, 216, 219, 226
Monk, Thelonious ix, 38, 51, 154
Monson, Ingrid 2, 7–8, 90, 91, 143, 151–2, 156, 219, 222
Montrose, Louis 18
Mott, David 187
Moye, Don 67, 68, 72, 82
Muhammad, Elijah 63
Munro, Alice 1, 2, 3
Murray, Albert 61n
Murray, David 82, 183
Myers, Amina Claudine 163, 187

Nachmanovich, Stephen 93, 94–5, 96
Nandy, Ashis 15
Navarro, Fats 100–1
Neal, Mark Anthony 113, 115, 232–3
Neuman, Shirley 96
New Criticism 14
New Historicism 18, 80, 236
New Orleans 10, 13, 35, 64, 150
New Thing 53, 57, 133, 207
Nicols, Maggie 175
Nielsen, Aldon 72
Nietzsche, Friedrich 213
Nixon, Richard 113, 134
Nono, Luigi 75
Nunn, Tom 93

O'Meally, Robert 106, 107, 108, 234
Obenga, Theophile 124
October Revolution in Jazz (1964) 133, 235
"Ol' Man River" 93
Oliveros, Pauline 2, 3, 157–9, 162, 163, 175, 187, 235
Olney, James 92
Ondaatje, Michael 107, 108, 109

Palmer, Don 76, 84
Palmer, Robert 57–8
Parker, Charlie 34, 37–40, 44–5, 47, 48, 49, 51, 55–6, 61n, 154; "Ornithology" 37
Parker, William 146, 187, 224, 232
Parks, Carol 81
Parks, Rosa 131
participatory discrepancies 101, 145
Patrick, Pat 119
Penguin Guide to Jazz 182, 183, 232
Perelman, Ivo 187
Peretti, Burton 15, 119, 150–1, 153
Plato 201
Pleasants, Henry 60
Poitier, Sidney 16
Pollack, Jackson 59
popular culture 18, 25–6, 105, 107, 144, 167–97, 236
postcolonial theory 3, 13, 15, 16, 119, 122, 123, 124–5, 134, 137, 206, 236
postmodernism 2, 11, 13, 61, 74–5, 80, 200, 208–10, 213–14, 226–7
Pound, Ezra 199, 200, 214
Pratt, Ray 122, 128, 144, 154, 160
Prévost, Eddie 92–3
Priestly, Brian 102
Public Enemy 177

Ra, Sun 13, 24, 27, 70, 85, 117–39, 170, 171, 176, 201, 202, 205, 233; "Big John's Special" 126, 127; "Enlightenment" 121, 127; "Light from a Hidden Sun" 126; "Outer Spaceways Incorporated" 117; *Pictures of Infinity* 118; "Rocket Number Nine" 134; "Saturn" 134; Saturn Records 27, 125, 129, 139n, 233, 235; "Saturn Rings" 134; "Space is the Place" (composition) 120; *Space is the Place* (film) 120, 131, 134, 135; "Strange Mathematic Rhythmic Equations" 127; *Sun Song* 117–18; *Sunrise in Different Dimensions* 125–6; *Super-Sonic Jazz* 137; "We Travel the Spaceways" 134; "When Spaceships Appear" 125
Rabelais 204
Radano, Ronald 10, 67, 70, 74, 75, 81, 225
Radhakrishnan, R. 122, 206, 215
Radical Jewish Culture 181
ragtime 13, 35
Rampersad, Arnold 109–10
Raschka, Chris ix
Read, Alan 88n
Reich, Steve 182
responsibility 26, 60, 66, 202
Rieger, Eva 153
Roach, Max 119, 129, 170, 171, 207, 235
Robeson, Paul 19, 93–4, 101, 116, 116n; *Here I Stand* 116n
Rockwell, John 66, 182
Rollins, Sonny 70

Rosenwald, George, and Richard Ochberg 92, 107–8
Rothenberg, Ned 187
Rout, Leslie B. 138n
Rusch, Robert 120, 128

Said, Edward 3–4, 13, 18, 61, 64, 65, 118, 122, 219–21
Sargeant, Winthrop 34, 36
Saussure, Ferdinand de 22, 39–40, 48, 51
Schoenberg, Arnold 176, 177
Scholem, Gershom 180–81
Schonberg, Harold 164
Schuller, Gunther ix, 14, 19, 34, 56, 57, 58, 90
Scott, James 122
Sedgwick, Eve Kosofsky 217–18
Shapiro, Nat 154
Sharp, Elliott 181
Shepherd, John 11
Shepp, Archie 60, 119, 133, 170, 171, 176, 205, 207, 235
Siddall, Gillian 6, 24
Slack, Jennifer Daryl, and Laurie Anne Whitt 215–16
slave narratives 89–90, 97, 112
Small, Christopher 229, 237
Smith, Barbara Herrnstein 33, 209
Smith, Bessie 44, 45, 127
Smith, Hazel, and Roger Dean 95–6, 102
Snow, Michael 187
Spellman, A.B. 207
Stockhausen, Karlheinz 49
Stravinsky, Igor 38
Stuckenschmidt, H.H. 32, 33
Subaltern Studies collective 122
Swindells, Julia 97
swing 31, 34, 37, 123, 124, 126, 127, 128, 138n, 177
Szwed, John 118, 119, 120, 129, 130, 131–2, 133, 134, 135–6, 139n

Tapscott, Horace 69, 129
Taylor, Cecil x, 48, 49, 52, 53, 133, 146, 147, 154, 155, 165n, 201, 202
Taylor, Charles 95, 235
Taylor, Timothy 157
Terdiman, Richard 122
Tester, Keith 167
Third Stream 58
Tipton, Billy 155–7, 159
Tuan, Yi-Fu 117
Tucker, Mark 174
Tyson, Cicely 143

Ulanov, Barry 20, 154
Underground Railroad 131

value 26, 27–8, 78, 112, 171, 200, 202, 207–8, 232
van Vechten, Carl 109–10
Vaughn, Sam 112

Wagner, Richard 220
Wallace, Michele 141
Ware, David S. 201
Waterman, Christopher 101
Webern, Anton 176
Weinstein, Norman 70
Werner, Craig Hanson 97, 103
West, Cornel 15, 128, 130, 204, 225–6
Weston, Randy 2, 3, 70, 163
White, Hayden 161
Wilkerson, Edward 66
Willener, Alfred 201, 205
Williams, Cootie 34
Williams, K. Leander 202
Williams, Martin 15
Williams, Mary Lou 154–5, 157, 159
Williams, William Carlos 50
Wilmer, Valerie 50, 51, 74, 119
Wilson, Gerald 152
Witkin, Robert 172, 176
Wolff, Christian 75
women in jazz 6–7, 24–5, 141–65, 171, 208, 235–6

X, Malcolm 63, 76

Young, Karen 163

Zorn, John 25, 178–86, 187, 195, 197; Masada 179–80; Naked City 179; Tzadik 179, 181, 185, 235